Mass Media
and
Social Change

Mass Media and Social Change

Major Suresh Goel (Retd)

MD PUBLICATIONS PVT LTD
NEW DELHI
www.mdppl.com

Published by :

MD Publications Pvt Ltd
"MD House", 11, Darya Ganj,
New Delhi-110 002
Phone : +91-11-41563325 (Customer Service)
+91-11-41562846 (Editorial)
E-mail (orders) : order@mdppl.com
Website : www.mdppl.com

ISBN : 978-81-7533-210-2

Published and Printed by Mr. Pranav Gupta on behalf of **MD Publications Pvt Ltd** at Printext, New Delhi.

PREFACE

Mass media plays a crucial role in forming and reflecting opinion. Media connects the world to individuals and reproduces the self-image of society. With the media on generating information from a network of relations and influences and with the individual interpretations and evaluations of the information provided, as well as generating information outside of media contexts. The consequences and ramifications of the mass media relate not merely to the way newsworthy events are perceived but also to a multitude of cultural influences that operate through the media.

The media has a strong social and cultural impact upon society. This is predicated upon its ability to reach a wide audience which often sends a strong and influential message. It is through the persuasiveness of media such as television, radio and print media that reach the target audience. These have been influential media as they have been largely responsible in structuring people's daily lives and routines.

Because of its immense ability to provide access to information, the mass media can play a crucial role in promoting reproductive health and social changes affecting gender, reproduction, and sexuality. An especially powerful aspect of the mass media is its ability to create visual imagery, either directly or, in the case of radio, through projections made as a result of messages heard. In the developing world, mass media communication provides a link to the global village and can play a culturally interactive role.

Social movements that are long lived and effectively institutionalised within society, tend not to challenge the status quo directly, and so consequently are less dependent on media coverage for their survival. However, media coverage may be crucial for other, less well known social movements often transitional and adversarial nature tends to weaken their ability to secure public legitimacy. Their outsider status - that is, their marginalisation from central political decision-making processes - along with their often resource-poor nature, means that traditional avenues of publicity are not easily accessible which forces them to rely on alternative methods to obtain media access. Traditionally, this involves some form of public spectacle - like a protest - to attract media attention.

I am very grateful to Mr. Pranav Gupta, Director, MD Publications Pvt Ltd, New Delhi, for his cooperation and support for this book.

Major Suresh Goel (Retd)

CONTENTS

1

Introduction

Social movements come and go, represent all manner of political beliefs, and aim to achieve their political objectives by influencing a particular target group's opinion. Some groups reach out directly to just a few key decision makers or constituencies, while others act more indirectly by broadcasting their message to as wide an audience as possible. Writing in 1993, William Gamson and Gadi Wolfsfeld suggested that social movements rely on the media for three main services,

- Mobilisation of political support,
- Legitimisation (or validation) in the mainstreams discourse, and
- To broaden the scope of conflicts. Consequently, the quality and nature of the media coverage that social movements obtain, strongly influences how they are perceived in the public eye – to the extent that good or bad coverage can help to make or break a social movement.

Social movements that are long lived and effectively institutionalised within society, tend not to challenge the status quo directly, and so consequently are less dependent on media coverage for their survival. However, media coverage may be crucial for other, less well known social movements whose often transitional and adversarial nature tends to weaken their ability to secure public legitimacy. Their outsider status – that is, their marginalisation from central political decision-making processes – along with their often resource-poor nature, means that traditional avenues of publicity are not easily accessible which forces them to rely on alternative methods to obtain media access. Traditionally, this involves some form of public spectacle – like a protest – to attract media attention.

Typical protest actions include sit-ins, pickets, street theatre, strikes, rallies, mass demonstrations and their more recent relative, reclaim the street parties. These activities have become accepted as mechanisms by which social problems are communicated in the public sphere, alongside public opinion polls and elections and they act as vital means by which citizens can signal their discontent. Consequently, the way that such protest activities are reported in the media is fundamental to the effectiveness of the feedback loop between the public and their politicians.

Unlike other 'legitimate' social groups, like the police and mainstream politicians, most social movements are not the focus of regular news beats. This means that unless social movements stage big public events, they struggle to get their message heard, as "the vast majority of demonstrations are ignored by the mainstream media"– particularly small demonstrations. Governments are often openly critical of social movements that undermine their authority, but perhaps what is more damaging is the subtle nature of the mass media's marginalisation of the activities of many social movements. Linda Kensicki highlighted some of these consequences:

"There are repeated cases of slanting, trivialisation, and outright omission of those who deviate from the norms of an elite media and form a political movement to combat injustice. Negative media frames have been discovered in the anti-nuclear movement, the women's movement, and the gay and lesbian movement, and the National Environ-mental Policy Act faced a media blackout." Joseph Chan and Chin-Chuan Lee first described the "protest paradigm" in 1984 to illustrate how the mass media tended to focus on limited features of social protests to portray protestors as the 'other'.

Characteristics of this reporting paradigm, which work

to separate protestors (them) from non-protesting audiences (us, or at least some of us) include a reliance on official sources to frame the event, a focus on police confrontation, and an analysis of the protestors activities (and appearances) rather than their objectives. This somewhat internalised selection process serves to filter which protests are reported, and which are ignored.

Reporting within this paradigm typically gives the impression that protests "'erupt out of nowhere' and are 'irrational' manifestations of self-interest by sectional interest groups operating without concern for, and at the expense of, the 'organic whole' – the national interest." Understanding the relationship between social movements and the media's coverage of their actions is crucial, especially if this increasingly important political resource is to be utilised effectively for progressive social change. This aims to analyse this pivotal relationship from two directions.

Firstly, it will examine incidents where the media facilitates social change via protest actions within democratic countries, which will be followed by an examination of the media's role in catalysing major social change, that is, revolutions in authoritarian nations.

Secondly, this will chart the ways in which the media (in democratic countries) can act to undermine social movements in the public sphere. Finally, this will attempt to understand why social movement protest coverage is so variable and conclude by making recommendations for how progressive organisations may best address their relationships with the media.

MEDIA 'SUPPORTED' SOCIAL MOVEMENT

Gaining positive media coverage is crucial for many social movements, as the way they are portrayed in the mass media can have important implications for their ability to mobilise citizens to participate in their protests. Indeed in 1987, social movement researchers Bert Klandermans and Dirk Oegema found that only 5% of the people who agreed with the objectives of a peace protest were motivated enough to participate in the subsequent protest. Despite such evident barriers to participation, in Belgium on 20 October 1996, a brand new social movement (formed in the wake of the controversy surrounding the arrest of murderer Marc Dutroux) mobilised the White March.

What made this event remarkable was that the White March involved around 300,000 citizens and was Belgium's largest ever demonstration. Stefaan Walgrave and Jan Manssens studied the media coverage of this mobilisation and concluded that, contrary to most social movement research, it was the media itself that made the White March successful. In fact, they described how the media "undertook large-scale and unconcealed motivational framing efforts" to actively break down barriers to participation.

Similarly in Australia, the media took on an advocacy role for a protest in Australia when Howard Sattler, the host of a popular Australian talkback radio program, stirred up racist sentiments amongst his listeners, when a young indigenous boy was involved in a fatal hit and run car incident in 1991. Sattler heavily promoted a "Rally for Justice" amidst the ensuing "public hysteria" – generated for the most part from his radio show – which drew thirty thousand angry protestors on to the streets. Worryingly, the rally succeeded in pressuring the Australian government to "introduc[e] poorly framed, racist legislation which contravene[d] the Convention on Human Rights, the Convention on the Rights of the Child, the International Convention on Civil and Political Rights and possibly the *Racial Discrimination Act (1975)*".

One US group that seem to have their protest coverage (positively) amplified in the mass media is the Promise Keepers, "an evangelical men's organization with an anti-feminist and anti-gay theology". Dane Claussen analysed their coverage in US newspapers – from 1991 (their founding year) through to April 1996 – and concluded that it was "overwhelmingly positive". In fact, one of their protests in

Washington DC received "more than three times the coverage" the television networks devoted to a women's march held the day before, which was more than double its size.

Another example of contrasting media coverage can be seen in the reporting of the protests surrounding the US-led invasion of Iraq (in 2003). Catherine Luther and Mark Miller analysed pro-war and anti-war coverage in eight US newspapers and showed how reporters were more likely to use delegitimation cues when referring to anti-war protestors, while using legitimation cues to refer to pro-war campaigners. Recent anti-war protests held in the US (in September 2005) were downplayed by the media, when between 100,000 and 300,000 people marched through Washington DC.

There were however, a few hundred pro-war protestors and the Washington Post amazingly managed to produce a headline that reported: "Smaller but spirited crowd protests antiwar march; more than 200 say they represent majority." Clear Channel, the US media conglomerate took this one step further in the lead-up to the war in Iraq by "sponsoring and supporting" a number of pro-war rallies through its radio stations. The various examples of media-supported protests examined here, raise concerns over the role of the media in democracies. Yet even more startling questions arise in the following section, which demonstrates how the media can in some circumstances actually work to support social movements to overthrow governments.

Media-Facilitated Revolutions

Since the recent revolution in Serbia, which ousted President Slobodan Milosevic in 2000, a series of 'coloured revolutions' have swept across Eastern Europe. These were the Rose revolution in Georgia (2003), the Orange revolution in Ukraine (2005) and the Tulip revolution in Kyrgyzstan (2005). In each case, after stolen elections, the media played an important role in catalysing public participation in mass protests, which led to success of each of the revolutions. This section will outline, the integral role the independent media played in each of these four revolutions.

To many political commentators and media scholars, it was clear that the independent media in Serbia "facilitated the regime change and paved the way for democracy". Names of independent media broadcasters (particularly, *Radio B 92*) were even "[c]hanted as slogans during the numerous street protests" during the 1990s, becoming "symbols of resistance" for democracy. In this case, the Serbian independent media fulfilled an overtly political function and were highly involved in coordinating and organizing protests throughout the decade prior to the revolution (in 2000). These activities made the independent media particularly prone to pressure from government censors, especially after 1998 when Milosevic's government cracked down on their efforts to undermine his authority.

However, Western countries had significant interests in toppling Milosevic's regime, so they stepped in to support Serbia's opposition groups and the independent media. Thus, external financial and diplomatic assistance from foreign countries, particularly from the United States, played a vital role in protecting and amplifying the voice of the independent media. Assistance for the creation of the Asocijacija Nezavisnih Elektronskih Medija (Association of Independent Electronic Media) which was formed in 1993, turned out to be crucial for the survival of the Serbian independent electronic media after 1998, as the international support it received helped protect many broadcasters from state repression. External funding for media development was not insignificant and during the early 1990s the international community provided between US$7-10 million to the former Yugoslavia for this goal, while after 1995 the US gave a further US$23 million and the European Union augmented this with another 17 million Euros.

As in Serbia, Georgia's independent media played an important role in challenging legitimacy of their authoritarian government led by President Eduard Shevardnadze. Consequently, this meant that the independent media was often viewed by Shevardnadze as an enemy of the state. So in October 2001, Shevardnadze tried to "shut down Georgia's most popular independent TV station *Rustavi* 2". This prompted *Rustavi* 2 and other media outlets to draw widespread public attention to the governments heavy handed attempt at censorship, which "led to three days of non-stop protest demonstrations" against the actions of the government. These protests were so successful in mobilising popular support that they led to the resignation of several ministers, and enabled *Rustavi* 2 to continue broadcasting without further state interference.

This turned out to be a critical win for the opposition parties. This is because when Shevardnadze attempted to steal the elections in November 2003, *Rustavi* 2 acted as a vital part of the opposition's propaganda machinery, providing "almost non-stop" protest coverage and "inform[ing] Georgians about upcoming demonstrations and actions". These protests were part of the Rose Revolution, which led to the ousting of Shevardnadze, and the election (in January 2004) of the opposition's leader, Mikhail Saakashvili. During the protests Saakashvili was aware of *Rustavi* 2 significance and "called on [his] supporters to protect Rustavi-2's headquarters".

As the International Institute for Democracy and Electoral Assistance recognised: "The development of independent media is often considered to be the single greatest achievement of Georgia's democratic transition." Thus foreign assistance was arguably the key to the success of the independent media and of the Rose revolution, with opposition organisations receiving significant financial assistance from international democracy promoting bodies. In addition, Shevardnadze was placed under significant diplomatic pressure from the US government and the World Bank and International Monetary Fund to leave the opposition organisations alone. It is interesting to note that the independent media that helped oust Shevardnadze, have now replaced their adversarial relationship with the government with a symbiotic one: "For instance, before the new elections on March 28, 2004, major TV stations announced the shut down of all political talk-shows and debates" and the abolishment of public debate of the elections.

The focal point for Ukraine's Orange revolution was the December 2004 elections, in which authoritarian President Leonid Kuchma was accused of tampering with the electoral processes for his preferred candidate Viktor Yanukovich. Again the independent media played an important part in the success of the revolution. Indeed, prior to the revolution in July 2003, Andrii Shevchenko, the first president of the Independent Journalists Trade Union, argued that the "media is the thread which can be used to unravel the power of the establishment". Coincidentally, around this time in mid-2003, two small media companies were able to secure a broadcast license for what was to be the opposition's first TV station – *Channel 5*. Up until this point, Kuchma and his supporters had maintained control of "all the mainstream media outlets in the county", which had enabled them to sustain an effective "information blockade" against the opposition leader Viktor Yushchenko.

A top Ukrainian television critic, explained how this information blockade was also used to denigrate opposition-led protests following the contested parliamentary elections in September 2002: "Initially the large protests in Kiev were not reported at all on national television, then the number of protesters who turned up was dramatically under-reported, and later the situation was misrepresented by showing images of street people and drunks when reporting on the protests". Kuchma's government had always tolerated some degree of dissent within society, but just before the 2004 elections they clamped down on *Channel 5* by freezing their bank accounts and attempting to revoke their broadcasting license. However, *Channel 5* still remained on air, so their staff launched a hunger strike on 25 October 2004 that was broadcast until the government stopped harassing them on 2 November 2004.

Channel 5 went on to play an important mobilising role during the revolution, providing information on where protests were taking place: they even had a participatory presence at the opposition rallies themselves on large TV screens which broadcasted Yushchenko's speeches and provided news and music to the protestors in the streets. The situation in previous elections had been very different, as in September 2002, the Kuchma's government only allowed TV stations to broadcast once the regime was in "full control of all the news rooms". While Marta Dyczok suggests that this difference might be partly explained by presences of the large international media contingent covering the 2004 elections, it also seems likely that other more direct external assistance may have had a hand in explaining Kuchma's comparably tolerant attitude towards dissent. This is because over the previous two years Ukrainian opposition groups had received around US$65 million from US democracy promoting organisations.

Kyrgyzstan's Tulip revolution - which resulted in the ousting of President Askar Akayev - occurred in March 2005, following the disputed parliamentary elections. US democracy promoters (amongst others) were again working behind the scenes, providing US$26.5 million to various 'independent' groups between 2003 and 2004. That said, it appears that the US was not always interested in ousting Akayev, as for most of the 15 years he was in power the US maintained fairly positive relations with Kyrgyzstan. Such congenial relations were disrupted by 2003, a change which may be partly explained by Akayev's greater diplomatic engagement with Russia.

During his long reign in power, Akayev had not any qualms with closing down opposition newspapers that threatened his authority, so in May 2003 he forced an important opposition newspaper, *Moya Stolitsa*, out of business with a libel suit. Just one month later though, the indignant editor of *Moya Stolitsa* created a new opposition newspaper, called *Moya Stolitsa-Novosti* (*MSN*) which obtained funding from the US-based neoconservative organisation, Freedom House. In November 2003, the US then also funded the creation of a new independent printing press, on which *MSM* and other opposition papers were produced.

The Kyrgyz regime was demonstrably worried by *MSN's* adversarial coverage and at one point they cut off the electricity supply to the newspaper's offices: however, "pressure from foreign governments" came quickly which subsequently "forced" the Kyrgyz administration to stop harassing the 'independent' media. In this case, as in the lead-up to the other revolutions, the foreign diplomatic and financial support for *MSN* (and the opposition media) was vital, as *MSN* has been credited as being "a major, transformative force", "fanning the fires of dissent" and printing the locations of opposition demonstrations, facilitating the Tulip revolution that drove Akayev out of the country. As the revolutionary examples in this section have demonstrated, the media has a powerful role in both generating and harnessing public sentiment around specific issues. It then seems logical to conclude that if the media can rig the rules of the media game to create winners, it can certainly select losers.

UNDERMINING SOCIL MOVEMENTS AND DEMOCRACY

One of the first comprehensive studies on the communicative aspects of a protest (completed in 1970) investigated the press and television coverage of a mass demonstration held against the Vietnam War, in London (UK) on 27 October 1968. The demonstration in question involved approximately 60,000 protesters, most of whom marched peacefully through the streets of London (with an insignificant number of protestors involved in violent actions). Yet despite the overwhelmingly peaceful nature of the march, the media concentrated most of its coverage on the issue of violence – where even "[r]eporting of the peaceful main march suggested disorder and quasi-violence".

Since then, many researchers have followed up on this investigation, examining how the interplay between social movements and the media. A notable study is Todd Gitlin's (1980) *The Whole World Is Watching*, which illustrated how the mass media worked to undermine the objectives of both the Students for a Democratic Society and the anti-war movement. More recently, Christopher Martin has updated the longstanding thesis that has demonstrated the media's hostility towards the labour movement in his excellent book *Framed! Labor and the Corporate Media*.

One characteristic that strongly influences a social

movement's media treatment are the degree to which they are perceived to be 'extreme' (that is, challenging the status quo) and 'militant' (in their tactics); whereby, the more extreme and militant a group, the more critical the media coverage. Critical coverage is also sometimes complemented by another delegitimising strategy, which involves downplaying the size of a protest. Prominent examples include: the British May Day protests in both 1973 and in 2001, the biggest ever British anti-war march, Washington DC's biggest ever protest, protests opposing the bombing of Yugoslavia in 1999, and protests opposing the North American Free Trade Agreement in Seattle. Research in the US has shown that protests or social movements that challenge the legitimacy of the governments foreign policies, are less likely to be covered by the mass media or more likely to be heavily "denigrated and delegitimized".

Laura Ashley and Beth Olson studied how women's movements were represented in the *New York Times, Time* and *Newsweek* from 1986 to 1996, and concluded that one of the "most astounding" results of their research was that the "women's movement was rarely covered". This is important, because as James Hertog and Douglas McLeod's work demonstrated, depending on the version of protest coverage audiences watched, people showed big differences in opinion on the way they viewed both the issues raised and the protestors themselves. Other research has shown how media coverage of protests can act to increase public hostility towards the protestors' cause. These findings have particularly important implications for social movements because, if a single report can determine how sympathetic the public is to their goals, consistently antagonistic media treatment is likely to have very negative repercussions regarding public support of protests themselves.

In 1998, John McCarthy and his colleagues compared the number and coverage of protests which took place in Washington DC in 1982 and 1991, and found that although there were 50% more protests in 1991, the number reported in the media (the *New York Times*, the *Washington Post, ABC, CBS,* and *NBC*) decreased by 16% (from 158 to 133). Critically, this reduction in protest coverage serves to increase competition between social movements to secure a piece of the valuable media pie. Rising financial pressure is then placed on smaller social movements unable to secure consistent positive media coverage, because donor organisations (especially corporate ones) may prefer to fund groups with better media profiles. Indeed, well-publicised media events – like the recent tsunami – can encourage donors to switch from funding smaller social movements towards larger more media-philic ones.

Critically in order to gain a ticket to this exclusive media club, an unwritten price must be paid; because as William Gamson points out "the media may offer occasional models of collective action that make a difference, but they are highly selective ones". Moreover as Todd Gitlin points out, for progressive reformist groups to maintain any semblance of positive media coverage, they have to partake in an ongoing fight to shape the daily news to prevent their messages being rendered unintelligible. These processes encourage social movements to water down their political demands – to make themselves appear less challenging to the status quo – which in turn leaves them more vulnerable to cooption by political and economic elites. Problematically even when progressive activist groups obtain positive media coverage supportive of some of their objectives, their longer-term ambitions may still be undermined – on this point, see Josh Greenberg and Graham Knight's work for a discussion of the US anti-sweatshop movements relations with the media.

The issues arising in this amply demonstrate the wide variety in the quality and quantity of the media's coverage of protests: but how might these differences be explained, and what are there consequences for progressive social change? Answering these questions is particularly important, as it is fundamental to the maintenance of democratic institutions that citizens are able to participate actively in the administration of their society to determine their collective objectives. On this point it is important to reflect upon the neoliberal environment in which the media currently operates (within Western democracies at least).

This is because neoliberal politics facilitates the rising power of (predominantly Western) global media conglomerates and serves to marginalise the majority of citizens from meaningful participation in media policy making. Consequently for any social movement to draw beneficial attention to its activities in the media the first barrier they must overcome are the structural constraints of this communicative medium itself. Despite the extremely negative picture painted in the previous section, there are still some winners in the 'media game'. So while losers, like the largest protest ever held in Washington, DC (the 2004 Women's March) received just a "handful of march-related stories over a few days" in the *New York Times* and the *Washington Post*; other protestors have their message amplified by the media, as the first two sections of this illustrated. Stefaan Walgrave and Jan Manssens suggest that the specific contextual factors that encouraged the media to support the White March protests in Belgium included,

- Clear opposition between the public and elites;
- A "highly emotional and symbolic issue that create[s] an atmosphere of consensus, emotion, and togetherness";
- Lack of a social movement - so that the media can appear objective and committed to the public good;
- A simple issue;
- A politically neutral, valence issue;
- A media environment that is "commercial and characterized by depoliticisation and de-ideologisation";
- Turbulent times during which the reporting should take place (that is, not under normal circumstances); and lastly
- A high degree of public trust in the media. Mobilising criteria like these are unlikely to be met by many social movements, and are even less likely to be fulfilled by any progressive movements.

However, whatever the ultimate reason, the media's differential treatment of protestors is unlikely to be conducive to supporting the diversity and longevity of social movements required to support democratic forms of governance. This appears especially true when genuine grassroots social movements find themselves competing alongside manufactured (media friendly) corporate social movements or astroturf groups, whose business driven interests are cleverly disguised from their participants and the public. All social movements and interest groups should be able to compete on equal grounds for media coverage, not just a select few that satisfy the media's news values – which usually act to "reinforce conventional opinions and established authority".

Although the discussion so far may help explain why certain protests are 'backed' by the media, it does not explain why the independent media has often been able to play such a crucial role in ousting governments during revolutions. Interestingly, similar forms of independent media exist in Western democracies, but there they have little influence on the public sphere and are unlikely to facilitate a popular revolution in the near future. In fact, the independent media in the West, like their counterparts in authoritarian regimes, have often been targets of secret state-led 'wars'. During the 1960s and 1970s, in America.

"This offensive included a variety of repressive actions, including: the monitoring of personal finances of underground journalists; arrests and assaults on staff members; government-inspired distribution hurdles for radical periodicals; loss of printing facilities; grand-jury subpoenas for editors and reporters; the release of 'disinformation' falsely attributed to underground media; publication of 'underground' papers secretly funded by the government; the bombing, burning, and ransacking of newspaper offices; and, possibly, the destruction of the transmitter of a listener-sponsored radio station."

So how are the independent media in authoritarian states able to successfully challenge the status quo, when, in even democratic countries, governments have succeeded in repressing and marginalising their voices so effectively? Part of the answer to this question, seems to lie in the support foreign governments provide to the independent media (and social movements) in authoritarian states, financially and diplomatically, through both supportive and coercive mechanisms. The National Endowment for Democracy (NED) is important in this regard, as they are the main US-based democracy promoting organisation, and they act as a key coordinating body for many of the world's democracy promoting organisations.

Since the late 1980s, Ellen Hume - who herself sits on the advisory council for the NED's Center on International Media Assistance - estimates that international democracy promoting organisations have spent anywhere up to US$1 billion promoting independent media overseas. Many scholars have questioned the benign rhetoric surrounding the intentions of these 'democracy promoters', and they have illustrated that democracy promoting initiatives are usually strongly tied to the donor countries' geo-strategic priorities, or more generically to the interests of transnational capitalism. Thus, in 1991, the NED's president noted that "[a] lot of what [the NED] do today was done covertly 25 years ago by the CIA".

William I. Robinson suggests it is more appropriate to refer to the activities of the democracy manipulating community as promoting polyarchy (that is, low-intensity democracy) and explains that: "The promotion of 'low-intensity democracy' is aimed not only at mitigating the social and political tensions produced by elite-based and undemocratic status quos, but also at suppressing popular and mass aspirations for more thoroughgoing democratisation of social life in the twenty-first century international order."

The implications of such revelations are huge for the promotion of independent media organisations overseas (a phenomenon dealt with in full by Barker, In Press, The National Endowment for Democracy and the promotion of 'democratic' media systems worldwide). However, rather than just focusing on revolutions supported by foreign so-called 'democracy promoters' (read: democracy manipulators), it is enlightening to examine a case of an unsuccessful revolution in which the independent media played a supportive role for the would-be-revolutionaries. In Azerbaijan, on 15 October 2003, the incumbent authoritarian President Heydar Aliyev was accused of stealing the election results when he handed over control of his regime to his son, Ilham Aliyev.

Thousands of citizens immediately took to the streets to protest the results, but unlike the other successful colour revolutions in Eastern Europe, these protests were violently broken up, with hundreds of protestors imprisoned and one killed. For the three weeks following the elections, Ilgar Khudiyev compared the media coverage of the protests between state and independent newspapers, and found that the independent media were supportive of the protestors. He also showed how the independent media, as in the colour revolutions, "cited the protestors more than official and authoritative sources" and quoted "those sources that strengthened the position of the protestors". However, although external democracy manipulating organisations provided financial support to the independent media in Azerbaijan, it seemed that without international diplomatic support (as well), the calls for a revolution fell on deaf ears. So the revolution failed, with the US government even congratulating Ilham on his election 'win'.

In part, the contradictory nature of the international democracy manipulating communities support for Azerbaijan's government may be explained by the favorable relations they maintain with the US and other transnational elites. A relationship that was further bolstered by their support for the 'War on Terrorism', and for American and British interests in the development of the geostrategically important Baku-Tiblisi-Ceyhan oil pipeline.

So while democracy manipulating groups are happy to support and defend independent media organisations overseas (within limits) as a means of promoting social change, they will only fully support regime change when they are certain that they can ensure a smooth transition to polyarchal political arrangements that will serve the interests of imperial transnational elites more effectively than the incumbent government.

So without apparent contradiction, while the US is openly supportive of Azerbaijan's authoritarian regime it also simultaneously supports the ousting of other less 'friendly' authoritarian governments in other countries (i.e. the colour revolutions). Not surprisingly the selective nature of the US's 'democracy promoting' policies are echoed in the American media, which effectively serves to manufacture public consent for elite interests.

So the US media provided strong support for the ousting of Milosevic while they 'ignored' other revolutions: for example, in 2000 Greg Palast demonstrated how the *Washington Post* dismissed one of the biggest international stories of the year – the people's revolution in Bolivia (which rejected the US corporate-led privatisation of their water supply) – which it covered, or rather marginalised, in the Style section "dangled from the bottom of a cute little story on the lifestyle of some local anti-WTO protesters."

It seems that in the minds of the democracy manipulators and the US media that the Bolivian citizens were supporting the wrong type of democracy, that is, popular democracy rather than polyarchy. A similar affront on popular democracy occurred in Venezuela, in April 2002, when President Hugo Chavez (who was democratically elected in 1998) was temporarily removed from power in coup. In a manner reminiscent of the colour revolutions in Eastern Europe, there was clear support for the ouster of Chavez by transnational elites. In fact, the group which led the coup against Chavez received financial support from the NED, while the coup itself also received widespread support from the local independent media and from "some sections of the international media".

Prior to the coup, the Venezuelan independent media – "which includes five out of the seven major TV networks and nine out of the 10 major daily papers" – had called for the ousting of Chavez, and made regular broadcasts encouraging people to participate in the coup.

That is, they were working in direct opposition to the will of the majority of the Venezuelan public who had shown their overwhelming support for Chavez in numerous democratic elections. In the days following the coup, the radio, television and press then ignored the massive protests calling for the return of Chavez, casting a veil of invisibility over the protestors presence on the streets: this was clearly evident to Chavez's supporters, who subsequently focused their countercoup campaign on the primary supporters of the coup, the media institutions.

However, even when the media gave in to the protestors' demands for media coverage, they depicted the pro-Chavez campaigners as "the mob", in stark contrast to their coverage of the protestors who led the coup, who were framed as "civil society". So as this example illustrates, the presence of a vigorous independent media system, free from government control or manipulation, does not necessarily facilitate democratic decision-making. Lastly, it is important to acknowledge that both internal and external efforts to undermine Chavez's government continue to this day, with the strong support of the US media and government.

The Eastern European case studies provided in this demonstrate how the development and selective support of independent media outlets may be used as one important part of an array of foreign policy tools that are used by neoliberal elites to promote polyarchy through the ouster of 'unfriendly' governments (be they authoritarian or democratic). In part this helps explain why progressive social movements challenging the status quo in Western democracies are so regularly denigrated, while those groups whose interests are more easily incorporated into, already aligned with, or of marginal importance to the policy frameworks of powerful political and economic elites are more readily supported by the media.

This occurs because the media in the West are powerful corporate actors themselves and are staunch defenders of the status quo, and their interests are one and the same as those of transnational capitalism. Consequently, it is readily apparent that Western media systems are not fulfilling their democratic role within Western societies, and are in fact acting instead in ways that work to undermine popularly understood conceptions of democracy. In the light of this information, social movement activists need to start seriously thinking about how they might improve the (often anti-democratic) mainstream media they are forced to operate within, as Robert McChesney notes:

"...regardless of what a progressive group's first issue of importance is, its second issue should be media and communication, because so long as the media are in corporate hands, the task of social change will be vastly more difficult, if not impossible, across the board."

In the US, media reform groups are already on the rise, but in other countries the signs of change are less promising. So now is the time for social movements from across the board to work together in solidarity, to support independent, or what might be more accurately termed autonomous media, so they may begin to focus their efforts on the urgent task of global media reform.

Two particularly strong reasons stand out for why activists should address the issue of media democratisation right now, and they are:

- A democratic media would let them get their unadulterated message out to the public "enabling the movement to have its own definition of the situation featured rather than marginalized", and
- It is "integral to any radically democratic politics... because media corporations are part of the system that critical social movements are challenging". Each group may opt for different tactics, but together they need to collaborate on a common project that serves to democratise the mainstream media. In fact, media reform

may be the one issue that can unite all progressive social movements in a "broadly resonant counter-hegemonic discourse" that may enable them to overcome their differences and allow them to begin to work together against the antidemocratic discourse of neoliberalism for a progressive and equitable new world order.

2

Mass Media

The mass media have an important role in modern democratic society as the main channel of communication. The population relies on the news media as the main source of information and the basis on which they form their opinions and voting decisions. According to cultural selection theory, any selection of messages in the mass media will thus have a profound effect on the entire society. This chapter investigates the selective forces that govern the mass media in a free and unregulated market, and explains how these selection mechanisms may lead to regalization and the concentration of economic power.

Competition has become increasingly keen in the area of the mass media as they keep fighting for the attention of the readers, listeners, and TV-viewers. The life and death of each newspaper and TV station is at stake here when the income from advertising and sponsoring is proportional to the number of readers or viewers. The printed media have problems competing with the electronic media as sources of news. In order to survive, they are increasingly turning to other strategies such as entertainment, titillation, scandal mongering, and spreading fear - and spending fewer resources on serious researching of news. This is not only about the survival of the fittest of the news media, it is also about cultural selection and political selection. The news media are the most important channels for the propagation of culture, ideas, and opinions. Most opinion formation takes place when people sit and watch news and debates on television. Analyzing the cultural selection in the electronic information society, we find that an important part of the selection lies in the choice between TV channels.

Millions of lazy viewers sit in their comfortable armchairs with remote controls in their hands zapping between action films, revivalist preachers, and commercials for a new fragrance, hardly realizing that by choosing which cultural and political influences they expose themselves to, they also chose the cultural and political evolution of their country. It is very important to analyze which selection criteria are in effect here.

The electronic media are first and foremost pacifying. It is a relaxation machine, and the viewer wants to be entertained. The faces on the screen are not chosen for their opinions but for their entertainment value. TV stations do not compete on ideologies but on sense impressions. An extreme example is music videos, satiated with fast changing sense impressions in sound as well as in pictures.

Media scientists have often discussed how much influence the media have on people's opinions. People tend to selectively read what they already agree with and to rationalize their preformed opinions in the face of contrary arguments. Experimental evidence seems to indicate that the mass media have little power to change people's opinions on issues for which they already have formed a strong opinion, but they have a profound influence when it comes to setting the agenda and priming people on new issues. The way an issue is framed determines how it is discussed, which causes a social problem is blamed on, and which of the possible remedies are entered into the discussion. The production of news often goes through several steps: informants and sources, press agents, reporters, news agencies, journalists, and editors. Many media are citing other media or opinion leaders so that the complete chain of information flow becomes quite long. Selection and distortion may take place at every link in this chain of information transmission. In the following will discuss the main selective forces that shape the production of news.

Sources

The sources of news may be public institutions, politicians, private companies, police, courts, interviewees, etc. These all have an interest in providing information that portray themselves in a positive light and withhold compromising information. There is a trade going on between source and journalist. For example, the media rely heavily on the police for news about crimes and often report positively about the police in exchange for this information. Sources that are unsatisfied with the way they are portrayed in a certain newspaper or TV channel may retaliate by withholding information in the future.

Journalists and Editors

Obviously, journalists may have political opinions that shape their selection and framing of news. They also have ethical principles about fairness and about reporting everything that is relevant, although they may depart from these principles when competition is fierce. Their selection of news is mostly based on the concept of newsworthiness, i.e. what they believe the audience finds interesting.

Audience

News media depend very much on their audience for economic reasons. They have to publish whatever makes people buy their newspapers, listen to their radio programs, or tune in to their TV shows and stay tuned through the commercial breaks. This is what newsworthiness really is about: catching the attention of the audience by presenting something spectacular, unusual, emotionally touching, and something that people can identify with. The concept of psychological buttons is really in place here. Topics like danger, food and sex make people pay attention. Keeping informed about dangers in the environment was of vital importance to our ancestors in primeval society, which is the reason why we have a surveillance instinct that make us hunger for news about possible dangers.

News about deviance, crime, and disaster are particularly salient. In fact, Ericson and coworkers found that stories about deviance and control constitute more than half of the news. The media have often been criticized for publishing too much bad news, but the fact is that the audience actually pay more attention to stories about crime and disaster than to good news. The bad news are not always very relevant. Horrific stories about some bizarre and morbid crime that has happened in a far away place may be more button pushing than reports about well known and trivial dangers like traffic accidents or unhealthy eating habits.

The average TV viewer may pay more attention to the story about a bizarre crime although (s)he is extremely unlikely to be affected by a similar crime, at the same time ignoring warnings about the immensely higher risks of traffic accidents or unhealthy life style. Another pervasive psychological factor in the preferences of the audience is personal identification. A story is much more touching if presented in terms of personalities than if presented as abstract principles. A political conflict is perceived as much more interesting if it is framed as a personal battle between politicians than if framed as a clash between ideologies, and a crime story is more touching if vulnerable victims voice their anger and grief.

Owners

The owners and shareholders of news media may have political opinions that shape their decisions, but with increasing professionalism they often prefer their media to be politically neutral in order to cover as large an audience as possible. The present trend of concentration of business ownership means that many media owners also own other enterprises unrelated to news production. They may prevent their media from being too critical towards other firms that they own or towards business in general. The demand for economic efficiency and short time schedules means that journalists often have to print the messages from their sources with little or no editing. The thoroughgoing investigative journalism takes place more in myth than in reality.

Advertisers

Newspapers get more than half of their revenues from advertisers, and most radio and TV stations get all their revenues from advertising and sponsoring. Obviously, the advertisers have a strong influence on news contents. Such an influence is usually considered unethical, but is nevertheless difficult to avoid. In order to attract advertisers, the media often generate a *"buying mood"* by discussing topics of relevance to the advertised products and avoiding any criticism of commercial products or of consumerism in general.

The influence of advertisers may be even more direct, although clandestine. Occasionally, advertisers have imposed economic sanctions against newspapers that have criticized their products. Discussions of the health hazards of smoking are almost absent from magazines that carry tobacco advertisements, although less important health hazards are covered extensively. The owners of tobacco factories can influence even magazines that do not allow tobacco advertisements because the same investors also own other companies that advertise in these magazines. Advertisers and sponsors are afraid of controversial programs unless this is exactly their niche. It is easy to observe that the more competition there is between the news media, the more entertaining and less serious becomes the news programs and political debates.

Economic Selection

Economic selection can override other factors like ideology because economic selection can kill the news-producing company. Imagine a town where there are two newspapers, *A* and *B*. *A* is a quality newspaper where ethical principles of fairness and relevance are held in high regard, while *B* is a popular newspaper indulging in sensationalism, titillating sex scandals, and slander. Journalists prefer to work for *A* because it endorses the principles that they consider the hallmark of their trade. Many consumers, however, buy *B* because its sensational front-pages catch their attention. The advertisers, too, place more money in *B* than in *A* because *B* extols their products while *A* often criticizes poor products and unfair business methods. Soon *A* gets economic problems that forces it to reduce its journalistic staff, reduce the number of pages, and raise the price of the paper. The lowered quality of *A* now makes more readers turn to *B*. The vicious circle keeps turning and the economy of *A* keeps spiraling down until its total demise.

This example is not pure fiction. It can be observed everywhere. This proves that the overall economic selection can override selection processes that take place at a lower level and force the news producers to compromise their ethical principles. A study of the selection of news in major American TV stations and newsmagazines in the 1970'es concludes that economic factors had little influence on the journalists in their selection of stories. This was in a period where the media enjoyed the benefit of a rapid economic growth. Apparently, the good economy permitted the media the luxury of setting idealistic principles higher than economic considerations. Gans supports his claim about the independence of journalists by citing the example of the *Saturday Evening Post*: even when this magazine was going under, the editors remained free from business-department intervention.

Unfamiliar with selection theory, Gans has overlooked the possibility that this newsmagazine may have gone under exactly because economic considerations were ignored. Anyway, the amount of sensationalism, scandals and titillation in the media is steadily increasing. The present trend is a *homogenization* of the news media: different media rely increasingly on the same sources, they may have the same owners, the same advertisers, and share the same market. The result is that the different news outlets often tell the same stories and in the same way, only blended with different kinds of entertainment. They avoid controversy and complicated background information and rely increasingly on the button pushing effect of sensationalism and personalizing.

CONSEQUENCES FOR THE QUALITY OF NEWS

A further consequence of the abovementioned homogenization of news is that it becomes more and more difficult for the audience to evaluate whether news stories are true or distorted, and whether important information has been left out. Truth and relevance are not strong factors in the news selection process. Journalists work under a tight time schedule and have little time to verify their stories. Therefore, obviously, they sometimes make errors. These errors are seldom corrected because retractions and disclaimers are unfit. The media tend to stick to the interpretive frame originally assigned to a story, even in the face of strong contrary evidence. Misquoted sources and others who may be dissatisfied with inaccurate media stories have only very ineffective means for influencing the media to correct their stories.

Political Consequences

Politicians are very dependent on the news media because people mainly base their voting decisions on the presentation of politicians in the media. The media appeal of a politician may be more important than his/her political skills, and consequently we are seeing more and more media people and actors going into politics. The politicians have to adapt their messages to the media. The political debate becomes superficial and toothless. Political candidates resort to short slogans and entertainment and avoid controversial subjects and complicated issues. Favorite issues are the most button-pushing ones like crime and sex, and indeed these issues are among the most salient topics on the agenda of election campaigns. The need for personalization has often caused the private lives of politicians to figure more prominently on the public agenda than debates over complicated social issues.

The news media focus very much on deviance and, discussions of deviance is the arena where rules and moral boundaries are negotiated. Stories of crime and deviance therefore have a very important effect on social and political change, and we have to look at the selection mechanisms governing stories of deviance in order to understand the effect they have on social change. As explained above, the news media focus very much on the unusual and bizarre, and on button pushing stories. Trivial crimes like shoplifting or speedy driving are not newsworthy and therefore seldom mentioned, even by the local media. But the rare, bizarre and spectacular crimes are given massive, lengthy, and often worldwide coverage. The amount of crime reported in the newsmedia is hardly related to actual crime rates. In areas where the crime rate is low, the media tend to report on less serious crimes or crimes that have taken place far away. In addition, the media may write about some unsolved crime that has happened long ago, or about people's fear of crimes that might happen in the future.

For example, the grotesque crimes committed by Jack the Ripper in London in 1888 are still remembered and talked about today, more than a hundred years later, while countless more simple crimes committed in the meantime have been totally forgotten. In fact, the story of Jack the Ripper has had a significant effect in shaping public conception of sex criminals. The result of this powerful selection of discourses is that the population gets a distorted conception of crime and dangers. Many women are afraid of sex monsters like Jack the Ripper lurking in the dark, although they are much more likely to be victimized by someone in their own circle of acquaintances.

In countries like USA, where economic competition between news media is fierce and there is little government regulation, the sensationalist focus on button pushing crimes in the news media have created a public sentiment that many commentators have characterized as *obsession with crime*. Often the focus on particular types of crime has taken the shape of moral panic. In this case politicians are forced to show their commitment to the cause and *"do something"*. Some politicians are emotionally affected by the moral panic and honestly want to combat the perceived evil. Others may realize that the situation is just a moral panic, but they are forced to react anyway. When an eager journalist asks a politician what he is going to do about some (perceived) menace, there is no way he can stand up and say: *"This is not a serious problem. There is no need to do more about it than we already do"*. He has no other option than to find some laws that can be strictened, well knowing that it is wrong to make hasty legislation in a highly emotional climate. The press has more power than the politicians in this situation.

The *framing* of crime stories in the media is just as important as the selection. Personal stories are more touching than abstract principles. Crime stories are therefore framed as individual personal stories rather than thematizised as general social problems. This framing affects the way people think about crimes and their causes. The main cause of crime is perceived to be moral defects in the individual and - in the case of reoffending - an ineffective penal system. Social and structural causes of crime are seldom discussed because they do not fit into this frame and because such discussions are less newsworthy and button pushing. This consequence of personalized framing is very important because it controls how crime-fighting resources are allocated. In USA, people's attitudes towards crime have become more punitive despite an increased liberalism in other matters, and this change of attitude cannot be adequately accounted for by increased crime rates or increased fear of crime. Budgets for law enforcement and prisons have grown exponentially since world war II and the incarceration rate has risen to extreme levels.

The crime rate has hardly been affected by this dramatic increase in crime-fighting efforts because the structural causes of crime have largely been ignored. In many cases, the money spent on law enforcement and prisons have been taken from social programs targeted at the social causes of crime. In conclusion, the selection and framing of crime news has caused an ever increasing allocation of resources to ineffective and perhaps even harmful measures and away from measures that target the criminogenic environment. Criminologists have often criticized this prioritizing, but their messages are not favored by the powerful selection mechanisms that control mass media.

Personalization

The fact that the political debate has become entertainment has had the consequence that attention is concentrated on the personality of the politician rather than his message. These tendencies are characteristic of the kind of society that sociologist Richard Sennett calls *the intimate society*. Humans have become isolated from one another due to urbanization and division of labor in modern society, and consequently they have created an illusion of fellowship by attributing to other people the same feelings as they have themselves in order to satisfy the frustrated need for intimacy. People do not talk to one another on the street, but nevertheless they feel that they have something in common. This feeling of a group identity or a collective personality is created by a common fantasy, not by common actions.

Society has become so impersonal, complex, and difficult to grasp, that it appears meaningless unless you interpret it as personal. People thereby become more interested in the personality of the politician than in his policy. The politician takes advantage of this situation and diverts attention away from controversial matters by exposing his private life and make people interested in his wife or his dog. Exposing the private personality of the politicians has become a hidden agenda in political life. Politicians began to compare their public performance with that of actors as early as the mid nineteenth century. The politician becomes a credible leader by simulating spontaneity and human feelings, but also self-control. People will rather be moved by a charismatic leader than take a stance for or against his policy, just like they go to a theater to be moved by the actors.

Sennett does not think that this situation is created by the electronic media, because the tendency to make public life personal began before these instruments were invented. They are just tools invented for covering a psychological need to retract from public life and feel more like a person. I do, nevertheless, believe that the sharpened competition between the mass media has contributed significantly to the transformation of political debate into a superficial play. Symptomatic of this situation is that politicians in their election campaigns sometimes concentrate on disclosing scandalous details about the private lives of their opponents, while the ideological messages are reduced to short clichés so general that nobody can disagree with them.

Democratic election thereby becomes a competition about who can present the most exemplary private life, and the politicians have to put a conservative family policy on their program. An obvious example is the USA. During the economic depression around 1980, the population felt a need for a confidence inspiring leader who could solve the complicated social problems that people could not themselves comprehend. It was no accident that it was a former actor and movie hero, Ronald Reagan, who was elected for US president at that time. The outcome of the election is determined more by acting talent than by political talent in such a situation.

Regalization

The fact that crime and disaster are favorite topics of the media has the effect that people overestimate the dangers in their environment. They come to perceive the world as more dangerous and evil than it really is and demand ever stricter measures to fight the deviance. This has a clear regalizing effect. The enemy may be internal to the society, but the perceived danger is a danger to society as a whole rather than to the individual, and therefore has a regalizing effect. The regalizing effect of the media's *"obsession with crime"* is not evenly distributed on all r/k indicators. In the period where competition between news media in the USA has been most fierce, i.e. after the second world war, tolerance for crime has decreased while tolerance in other matters have increased.

Peace and improved economy has a kalyptic effect that counte.balances the regal effect of the mass media so that the net effect is near zero. Old scapegoats have disappeared and new scapegoats have been constructed. The competition between newsmedia has a considerable effect as part of the cultural selection process, but it would be an exaggeration to regard this as an autonomous process able to push social evolution in any arbitrary direction. The producers, as well as the audience, have personal preferences which are highly influenced by the general social situation, and these personal preferences find expression in the selection of news. Jorgenson (1975) has shown that TV programs become more authoritarian in contents in times of economic crisis, which is in accordance with the psychological theories.

ADVERTISING AND SPONSORING

Where we live, the highly advertised soft drinks cost three times as much as similar unadvertised drinks. Nevertheless, most consumers drink the expensive advertised brands. The extra money goes into advertising. Obviously, advertising has a strong effect when it can make consumers prefer the most expensive product. Modern advertising relies more on psychology and button pushing than on providing factual information about price and quality. Many advertisements contain no information other than merely repeating a product name and associating it with attention-catching images and the portrayal of an attractive lifestyle. It thereby attempts to influence the audience to make less rational consumer choices than they otherwise would.

Advertising not only influences the consumers, but also the mass media. The media are not as autonomous as they purport to be, because most of their revenues come from advertisers, as mentioned above. Even state subsidized and license based news media are becoming increasingly dependent on advertisements and sponsoring. Advertise-ment-free state-subsidized TV stations are indirectly being influenced by sponsoring because the events they are reporting from are financed by sponsoring. In modern society today, almost all major cultural events depend on sponsor money. In big sports events, for example, the sponsors usually have the final say in every detail of the planning and staging of the event. Likewise, many films and other entertainment programs are influenced by sponsors having their products placed in the context of the film or show in exchange for their financial contribution.

It is therefore important to analyze which selection criteria are at work in the sponsoring of news media and cultural events. The answer is straightforward: maximizing the exposure of the sponsor's name in the media in a positive context. This, of course, means attracting the greatest possible audience. TV programs contain more and more entertainment and button pushing films, and still fewer debates over complicated or controversial issues. The boundaries between news, entertainment, and advertising become increasingly blurred. The political effects of advertising are mainly indirect. Commercial advertisers have no political agenda. They are very sensitive to political consumer choices and therefore reluctant to take any political stance. At most they might have a pseudo-agenda, i.e. a non-controversial political message that nobody can disagree with, such as environment protection, peace, or charity.

This is to make people believe that they are idealistic do-gooders advertising benefits big companies more than small ones. This means that big companies grow still bigger whereby economic power is being concentrated on only a few hands. With the economic power also follows political power through the sponsoring of election campaigns and professional lobbyists.

The Competition for Attention

Organizations, firms, politicians, and advocacy groups of all kinds are constantly engaged in a fierce battle to win the attention of the population. Mass media lure with sensations and scandals to make people buy their stories. Politicians expose their private lives and engage in humorous media stunts to win the public's attention and confidence. Advertisers use emotional and arousing images for capturing the consumers' attention and make them remember the name of their product. Advocacy groups use demonstrations and dramatic actions to make their cause interesting for the media to write about and thereby communicating their message to the public. Charity organizations use button-pushing images of starving children for soliciting donations. Religious groups campaign for winning new proselytes.

Government and official organizations campaign to inform the public about certain important topics. Terrorists even go as far as to commit the most shocking crimes just to make the news media write about them and their political cause, and the journalists obey.

Several sociologists have studied how different topics compete for the attention of the mass media in what has been called *the social problems marketplace* or the *public attention market*. The abilities of different campaigners to dramatize their cause has crucial importance for their success in getting access to the mass media and the public's attention. Who take the lead in this competition? Obviously the ones that are able to dramatize their cause in the most newsworthy and button-pushing way, rather than the ones that have the most important message to tell. Charity organizations, for example, may need to use more money for campaigning than for their charitable cause in order to survive in this darwinistic competition. The conclusion is that it is not always the most important topics that win in the competition for the attention of the media and the population.

Major Legal and Kalyptic Factors

As described elsewhere, a regal factor is a force that makes society more authoritarian and bellicose, while a kalyptic factor is a force that makes the culture more tolerant. The analysis must start with an identification of the most important selective factors:

- *War:* International war will be rare in the future because of the intervention of the international community and because the cost in terms of interrupting economic and technological connections between countries will be too high. Civil wars will still be common for more than half a century as part of the process of disintegrating regal blocks in the Arabian countries, China, and several other regions.

- ***Migration:*** Immigration from poor and regal regions is a major regalizing factor in Europe today, and will continue to be so for many decades to come.
- ***Media panic:*** Fierce economic competition forces mass media to focus on dangers, horrors, and other bad news. This is an important regalizing factor in the USA today, and this factor will gain increasing strength in Europe and everywhere else as economic liberalism generates a global market for news media based on free economic market forces. Eventually, the need for independent funding of news media will become so obvious that intervention and regulations have to be implemented. But until the major news media become effectively independent of irrelevant commercial interests, media competition will continue to be a very strong factor shaping the political and social climate.
- ***Terrorism:*** Terrorism and hostage taking is connected to media panic. The intense media focus on the suffering of hostages may force decision makers to give in to the demands of hijackers and terrorists, and thereby encouraging new terrorist acts. Media attention is increasingly being recognized as a precious and limited resource, and terrorism remains a very effective way of gaining publicity, though certainly not sympathy. Consequently, terrorism and hostage taking will be rampant until international conventions be implemented to restrict the media attention or new weapons be invented to effectively stop terrorists.
- ***Economic crisis:*** The economic system in the industrialized countries is based on growth. There is a limit to growth, and when this limit is reached we are likely to see a major economic crisis with a significant regalizing effect. Since there is plenty of room for growth in the developing countries as well as advances in information technology and biotechnology, it will probably last several centuries before we hit the roof.

- ***Ecological crisis:*** A complete exhaustion of World resources is so far ahead that there is time for implementing effective means of recycling resources of all kinds. But another hazard is more threatening. Genetically engineered organisms may spread in the wild and disrupt ecological balance. Such a disaster is very likely to happen sooner or later, but it is impossible to predict when. Mass media may exaggerate or depreciate the problem, but it is likely to have some regalizing effect anyway.

Political Development

Kalypticism culminated in the Western countries in the 1970's thanks to the absence of war and the end of colonialism and imperialism. These countries will remain fairly kalyptic but with some regal tendencies due to the abovementioned factors. The Arabian countries, which have been very regal, are undergoing a fast kalyptization thanks to international forces preventing war, and thanks to the general modernization. This will lead to serious riots and witch hunts in these countries during the next several decades, but eventually these countries will adapt to a modern lifestyle. The same will happen in several other regions, though in most places it will be less violent. India will be among the latest empires to disintegrate, because the arms race with Pakistan will keep it moderately regal for a couple of decades more.

China will undergo a development of 'glasnost' similar to the recent history of the Soviet Union. Parts of China will revolt and become independent states, as it usually happens with old empires. The economy of China will be much better than in the former Soviet Union, because China has had economic reforms before political and social reforms. For this reason, China and some of the seceded states will become an economic superpower. All in all, the World will be more peaceful in the new millennium. The many international wars that have plagued the millennium of the one thousands, will almost disappear in the two thousands. *There will be no third world war.* But *intra*national wars - riots and civil wars - will still be common for most of this century. And so will international terrorism. The World will become more homogeneous due to improved communication, and r/k differences as well as other cultural differences will be leveled out. The rate of population growth will go down due to kalyptization and less poverty, and before the year 2100 the World population will be decreasing and will continue to do so.

Religion

Religion will be less strict everywhere in the World because of kalyptization. The successes of science are making the religious world view less important. Religion will increasingly become a matter of personal taste, where people pick different ideas from different religions and put them together to make their own personal belief. The main function of religion will be as psychotherapy, and the boundaries between creed, alternative medicine, healing, astrology, and psychotherapy will be blurred.

MASS MEDIA AND THE PUBLIC AGENDA

The mass media will soon become the most important power governing the World. In the situation of competition on a free market, the media will focus more and more on pushing the most sensitive 'buttons' that appeal psychologically to the audience: food, sex, danger, and children. Media stories will focus on persons rather than abstract principles. Everybody will compete for exposure in the media, and politicians as well as everybody else with a message will do crazy stunts in order to attract media attention. The senselessness of this situation will only be understood by a minority of the population. Non-commercial internet sites and a few non-commercial TV-stations run by idealists will provide an alternative and more serious source of news to a small intellectual elite, while the majority try to relax in front of the commercial TV-stations that bombard them with sense impressions at a breathtaking speed, where the boundaries between advertisements, political propaganda, entertainment, news, and information become increasingly blurred.

There will be a movement for making news media independent of commercial interests and this idea will cause major conflicts. The media profit from exposing new dangers and dramatizing the emotions of sufferers of all kinds. This tendency will soon escalate into absurdity due to the fierce economic competition between media. Highest on the social agenda will range all kinds of dangers, diseases, food poisoning, injustice, poverty, famine, natural disasters, and all kinds of crime, including sex crimes, corruption, random violence, child abuse, elder abuse, organized crime, and terrorism.

In the face of a highly emotional media campaign against any kind of evil, the politicians have no choice but to grant more money to the cause in question and propose new legislation. Prioritizing public budgets simply doesn't fit into this emotional agenda. The result will be more prisons, bigger hospitals, more spending on traffic safety and all other kinds of safety, more restrictions and control of food quality, more policemen, psychologists, physicians, lawyers, etc. etc. - And of course this will inevitably lead to ever higher taxes.

Stricter safety measures will be seen everywhere in society: Dangerous sports will be banned and replaced by simulations; there will be severe restrictions on tobacco and alcohol; transportation will be automatic and independent of human drivers; and there will be synthetic foods because the quality of natural foods is difficult to control and because the natural production of food may cause animal suffering. The fast kalypticizing of the more regal countries of the World is likely to lead to counter reactions in the form of witch hunts and moral panics. Possible scapegoats are, as usual, ethnic, religious, political, and sexual deviants. However, human rights rhetoric and exposing the suffering of the scapegoats will give witch hunters a hard time finding a scapegoat that everybody can agree to hate. Consequently, new imaginary or non-human boogeys will be invented, possibly science-fiction inspired such as aliens, genetically engineered monsters, or robots with artificial intelligence.

3

Media and its Influence

In psychology, communication theory and sociology, media influence or media effects refers to the theories about the ways the mass media affect how their audiences think and behave. The media has become a strong barrier of communication between families and the outside world. The shift of media and media industry over the past few years into new forms, such as DVD and the internet, right changes the modalities available for audiences to consume and receive media. The change has caused some media theorists to call into question the influence that the media has over attitudes and beliefs. Urbanization, industrialization and life is good modernization created by social conditions in which the mass media has developed. The bulk of the content of that mass media has created is not designed to challenge or modify the social and political structure of a nation, either in or out of the juda in a one party state or in a democratic society.

Mass media plays a crucial role in forming and reflecting public opinion, media connects the world to individuals and reproduce the self-image of society. Critiques in the early-to-mid twentieth century suggested that media weaken or delimit the individual's capacity to act autonomously - sometimes being ascribed an influence reminiscent of the telescreens of the dystopian novel *1984*. Mid twentieth-century empirical studies, however, suggested more limited effects of the media. Current scholarship presents a more complex interaction between the media and society, with the media on generating information from a network of relations and influences and with the individual interpretations and evaluations of the information provided, as well as generating information outside of media contexts. The consequences and ramifications of the mass media relate not merely to the way newsworthy events are perceived (and which are reported at all), but also to a multitude of cultural influences that operate through the media. The media has a strong social and cultural impact upon society. This is predicated upon its ability to reach a wide audience which often sends a strong and influential message. Marshall McLuhan uses the term "the medium is the message" as a means of explaining how the distribution of the message can often be more important than the message itself.

It is through the persuasiveness of media such as television, radio and print media that reach the target audience. These have been influential media as they have been largely responsible in structuring people's daily lives and routines. Television broadcasting has a large amount of control in influencing the content that society watches and the times in which they are viewed. This is a distinguishing feature of traditional media and although they are by no means redundant, the development of the internet has challenged the traditional participation habits involved in media such as television. The internet has lifted some of the restrictions placed on society by allowing for diversification of political opinions, social and cultural differences and heightened level of consumer participation. There have been suggestions that allowing consumers to produce information through the internet will lead to a bombardment of too much information. It can however allow society a medium for expressing opinions and moving away from the political restrictions placed on society.

Primary, Secondary and Tertiary Involvement

It has been suggested that the extent to which an audience engages with a media text can be roughly split into three degrees. The first of these is primary involvement, in which the audience is solely concentrating on consuming the media text. For example, they are sitting down solely to watch their favorite program on television. Secondary involvement is when an audience's concentration is split between the media text and another distraction. For example, working on the computer while watching television. Tertiary involvement is when the media text is merely in the background, with no real concentration upon it at all. For example, glancing at a newspaper on a crowded train.

While this theory is somewhat simplistic, it provides a clear and probable explanation as to the changes in audience reception. Perhaps the most widely accepted theory on audience reception is Denis McQuail's Uses and Gratifications model. This places emphasis on why audiences consume media. The first reason outlined in the model are the need to reinforce your own behaviour by identifying with roles, values and sex presented in the media. Secondly, we need to feel some kind of interaction with other people; this is offered by text such as soap operas and lifestyle magazines. The third reason is the need for security in our lives. Media offer us a window to the world that allows education and the acquisition of information. The final reason is the need for entertainment through both escapism and the need for emotional release, such as laughter. A strength of this theory is the emphasis on the audience as active in the reception of media. However, this would suggest no passivity within the audience whatsoever. A person may, for example, be too lazy to turn off their television and so consume any media that is available. This theory also pays little attention to the short term and long term effects of media on the audience.

David Gauntlett, the Professor of Media and Communications at the University of Westminster, proposed ten criticisms of the Media Effects model. First, that media effects researchers go about their research starting with the assumption that media does in fact cause violence, and thus producing studies where media is administered and violent reactions are looked for, whereas, Gauntlett prefers that things should be done the other way around. To explain the problem of violence in society, researchers should begin with that social violence and seek to explain it with reference, quite obviously, to those who engage in it: their identity, background, character and so on.

Gauntlett goes on to criticise studies that focus on children by stating that they do not utilize adults as a control group, and that the studies are conducted primarily to further a "barely-concealed conservative ideology", and counters the premise of these studies with the concept that not all depictions of violence are even bad to witness. M.I.T. Professor Henry Jenkins, for instance, suggested in his speech to congress that The Basketball Diaries utilizes violence in a form of social commentary that provides clear social benefit. David Gauntlett explains further that defining objects that are "violent" or "anti-social" may not be such in the minds of the viewer, tend to be viewed in artificial circumstances, are furthermore based on previous studies with flawed methodology, and are not grounded in theory.

Additionally, he claims that the effects model makes no attempt to understand the *meanings* of media.

- Historical criticisms situate the 'meta-narrative' of effects theory within a long history of distrust of new forms of media, dating as far back as Socrates's objections to the deleterious effects due to the written alphabet.
- Political criticisms pose an alternative conception of humans as rational, critical subjects, who are alert to genre norms and adept at interpreting and critiquing media representations, not passively absorbing them.

Supporters of effects theory contend that commercials, advertising and voter campaigns prove that the media influences people's behaviour. In the 20th century aggressive media attention and negative depictions of trials revolving around celebrities as Roscoe Fatty Arbuckle or Michael Jackson have influenced the general public's opinion, before the trials effectively started. However, these critics do point out that while the media could have an effect on people's behaviour this isn't necessarily always the case. Critics of the media effects theory point out that many copycat murders, suicides and other violent acts nearly always happen in abnormal upbringings.

They were raised in a violent, emotionally neglected or aggressive environment which influenced their behaviour more rather than watching certain programs, films or listening to certain music. Most people who carry out these acts are also mentally unstable to begin with. Critics also point out that just because an audience sees acts of violence on TV, etc, this does not mean they will actually do it themselves. Of the millions of people who watch violent films, only a small number have carried out acts of violence as a direct result. People regularly exposed to violent media usually grow up to be completely normal people. If there are any effects from media, they only affect a very small number of people.

Also there are other thinkers who criticize effects based research, such as Terry Flew and Sal Humphreys, Barker and Freedman. Martin Barker (2001) criticised Elizabeth Newson who alleged link between media violence and real life violence in her report in 1994, Brooke (2003-07),for example talks about this in details., and the report gained the media concerns and attentions when it claimed that the horror film *Child's Play 3* had influenced 10 years old boys behaviours and led to murder of James Bulger in Feb 1993. After examining and assessing Newson's report case studies in his research and other researches, it was apparent that there is no clear link between film and crime. Bulger case was one of examples of her case studies in the report and which was contested by Barker. Critics criticized her report by pointing out that her case studies was very reliant on press accounts and opinions rather than independent research. However, Newsons report was influential, it has influenced public and institutions and result in more concern on censorship on videos and more concern from the British Board of Film classification on Psychological effects of media violence.

The attention and question become whether they were watching violent media. But Barker (2001) doesn't agree with Elizabeth Newson. He reject her claim about the connection between media violence and real life violence, in his argument he justifies his position, he indicates that there was not a scrap of evidence that the boys had seen the movie and Child Play 3 is a moral film. '

He also criticized anti media campaigns and described them as ignorant and disguised political campaigns. He states that these claims are represented by media and most of people have no chance to check the credibility of them, he also points out that these films including child play 3 are often attacked because they deal with political issues. Moreover, he lists real cases, for example "a man takes a gun and shoots his entire family after watching the news, arrested and tried, he explains his actions on the basis that the world news was so bad there seemed no point anyone going on living".

Barker suggests that this case for example is no different that other putative cases of media a causing violence, Barker said that we should not always blindly blame the media because people are not copycats, instead we should be aware of someone mental state and take other factors into account before making such claims. For example, in his case he states that the man reaction was abnormal. Therefore, his behaviour could not be explained by suggesting "the effects of the news". There are other social and cultural factors in criminal acts in which the media are not the basic influence.

Barker also suggests 'that we must look beyond a specific film to think about the specific context in which it has been consumed, and the wider social background of the people' according to Barker there is no such thing called violence in the media that either could or could not cause violence, we should rather pay attention to how social factors and background make some people consume media in specific way, for instance, even the news also show lots of violence, so people should rather pay attention to how social factors and background make some people consume media in particular way. In addition Barker (2001) proposes further research, he suggests that the theory of media violence connection must be tested because identification with particular element in a film is not something can be seen. He also noted problem with campaigners treating delinquents as normal people who become influenced by the media. Therefore, he suggests further research on how these people understand and consume media.

Critics of effects based research see no connection between exposure to media violence and real life violence, because human are not copycats and they can realize what is wrong and what is right. Although some research states claims that heavy exposure to media violence can lead to more aggressive behaviour, but not criminal violence and even in these researches it has been suggested that exposure alone does not cause a child to commit violence and media alone are not seen to be the main influence, also the ones that claim such connection are rare.

Flew and Humphreys (2005) said that the assumptions of effects researches are frequently flawed. According to Flew and Humphreys, Freedman (2001) and Goldstein (2001) have found that the number of studies on games and violence is small and the research suffers from flawed methodologies and ambiguous results which do very little to prove a direct link. Terry Flew and Sal Humphreys also state 'that differing context of consumption will always mean we need to take account of the particularities of players and how and why they play, effects researches often give insufficient account to the relevance of cultural contexts and the way in which media are actually implicated in the circulation of meanings in our cultures'.

Freedman (2007) is another thinker who rejects this idea, in reference to the FCC 'the Federal Communications Commission in US' report that suggests link between media violence and real life violence, Freedman indicates the lack of discussion and states that the FCC does not make a sufficient distinction between people's opinions, intuitions and musings on the one hand, and the hard scientific data on the other, and he indicates the lack of discussion of one of the strongest arguments against the idea that media violence causes aggression.

According to Freedman the rate of violent crime in the United states increased sharply from 1965 to 1980 and some people blamed that increase on media. The rate of violent crime leveled off until about 1992, since that time, television continued to have violent programs, there was also more scenes and media showing more violence, if exposure to violent media cause real violence one would surely expect the rate of violent crime to have increased sharply, yet, since 1992 there has been a dramatic drop in violent crime, it seems clear that media violence did not cause the earlier increase. Therefore, it is widely accepted that there is no convincing evidence that prove that media violence cause violent crime or any type of real life violence.

Political

Certain groups tend to argue for media effects in an effort to promote a political cause. Demands for the banning of certain songs or the labeling of obscene albums came specifically from conservative political groups in the United States. However, it is important to note that Mary Elizabeth (Tipper) Aitcheson Gore, the wife of Al Gore, was the founder of the Parent's Music Resource Center, and was the main figure in pushing for warning labels on music although she does not fit into the conservative demographic. They argued — without evidence — that such material had simple and identifiable effects on children, and this should be banned/labeled.

Priming and Framing

The agenda setting process is partly one which is an almost unavoidable function of the process involved in newsgathering by the large organisations which make up much of the mass media. (Just four main news agencies - AP, UPI, Reuters and Agence-France-Presse - claim together to provide 90% of the total news output of the world's press, radio and television.) Stuart Hall points out that because some of the media produce material which often is good, impartial, and serious, they are accorded a high degree of respect and authority. But in practice the ethic of the press and television is closely related to that of the homogeneous establishment, providing a vital support for the existing order. But independence (eg of the BBC) is not "a mere cover, it is central to the way power and ideology are mediated in societies like ours." The public are bribed with good radio, television and newspapers into an acceptance of the biased, the misleading, and the status quo.

The media are not, according to this approach, crude agents of propaganda. They organise public understanding. However, the overall interpretations they provide in the long run are those which are most preferred by, and least challenging to, those with economic power. Greg Philo demonstrates this in his 1991 article, "Seeing is Believing", in which he showed that recollections of the 1984 miners' strike were strongly correlated with the media's original presentation of the event, including the perception of the picketing as largely violent (violence was rare), and the use of phrases which had appeared originally in the media of the time. McCombs and Shaw (1972) demonstrate the agenda-setting effect at work in a study conducted in Chapel Hill, North Carolina, USA during the 1968 presidential elections.

Having selected a representative sample of undecided voters, they were asked to outline the key issues of the election as they perceived them. Concurrently, the mass media serving these subjects were collected and analysed as regards their content. The results showed a definite correlation between the two accounts of predominant issues. "The evidence in this study that voters tend to share the media's composite definition of what is important strongly suggests an agenda-setting function of the mass media."

New Media

Theorists such as Louis Wirth and Talcott Parsons have emphasised the importance of mass media as instruments of social control. In the twenty-first century, with the rise of the internet, the two-way relationship between mass media and public opinion is beginning to change, with the advent of new technologies such as blogging. Mander's theory is related to Jean Baudrillard's concept of 'hyperreality'. We can take the

1994 O.J. Simpson trial as an example, where the reality reported on was merely the catalyst for the simulacra (images) created, which defined the trial as a global event and made the trial more than it was. Essentially, hyperreality is the concept that the media is not merely a window on to the world (as if a visiting alien were watching TV), but is itself part of the reality it describes.

Hence (although additionally there is the question of navel-gazing) the media's obsession with media-created events. It is this which lead Marshall McLuhan in the 1960s to say that "the medium is the message", and to suggest that mass media was increasingly creating a "global village". Thus, for example, there is evidence that Western media influences in Asia are the driving force behind rapid social change: "it is as if the 1960s and the 1990s were compressed together." A notable example is the recent introduction of television to Bhutan, with dramatic effects in terms of very rapid Westernization. This raises questions of 'cultural imperialism' (Schiller) - the de facto imposition, through economic and political power and through the media, of Western (and in particular US) culture.

An Instrument for Social Control

Social scientists have made efforts to integrate the study of the mass media as instrument of control with the study of political and economic developments in the Afro-Asian countries. David Lerner(1958) has emphasised the general pattern of increase in standard of living, urbanization, literacy and exposure to the mass media during the process of transition from traditional to modern society. According to Lerner, while there is a heavy emphasis on the expanding of the mass media in developing societies, the penetration of the central authority into the daily consciousness of the mass has to overcome profound resistance.

Government and Mass Media

They include licensing in advance, censorship of offending

material before publication, seizure of offending material, injunctions against publication of a newspaper or book or of specified content, requirement of surety bonds against libel or other offense, compulsory disclosure of ownership and authority, post publication criminal penalties for objectionable matter, post publication collection of damages in a civil action, post publication correction of libel and other mis-statements, discrimination in granting access to news source and facilities, discrimination and denial in the use of communications facilities for distribution, taxes, discriminatory subsidies, and interference with buying, reading and listening.

PUBLIC SPHERE

Structural Transformation

Habermas believed that society becomes increasingly polarised into spheres of "public authority" - referring to the emergence of the state and associated political activity - and the "private" - the intimate domain of private relationships and the family. Jürgen Habermas believed that the development of mass media was a crucial factor in the transition from an absolutist regime to liberal-democratic society.

With the invention of the printing press and then the availability of newspapers and other forms of printed literature, Habermas claimed the emergence of an intermediate sphere which according to him is the bourgeois public sphere. This space will provide individuals with a chance to gather together to critically access, discuss and evaluate important contemporary issues of utmost importance for the people. He claimed that this will resemble the Greek agora. Habermas claims that this public use of reason not only acts as a regulatory mechanism over the state, which is now highly visible, but also as a catalyst for the replacement of the absolutist regime with a liberal democratic government.

The Frankfurt School came into existence in order to explain the success of Nazism in Weimar Germany. It sees the loss of individuality through decline of privacy as the main cause of dependence on great mass organisations. Habermas to a certain extent depends on some early critiques of the media from the 'Frankfurt School', such as that of Max Horkheimer use. For these three, media was a 'culture industry' which was creating an impact on passive individuals. These individuals merely absorb any information they are exposed to. (A clear influence of Karl Marx can be seen here, with links to the theory of alienation.)

According to Thompson, the cause of this is the commodification of art and culture, which allows the possibility of "manipulation by demagogues".Emile Durkheim claimed that the interdependence of highly specialised individuals, or what is known as 'organic solidarity', is seen as being succeeded by a new and barbarous homogeneity. Due to this, only a 'mechanical' cohesion is possible, dependent on similarity and standardisation. Horkheimer thus argued that, paradoxically, individuality was impaired by the decline in the impulse for collective action.

According to him, 'As the ordinary man withdraws from participating in political affairs, society tends to revert to the law of the jungle, which crushes all vestiges of individuality.' In this analysis the Frankfurt school saw totalitarianism emerging as a result of corrupt social institutions and the decline of liberal principles. Thus Oppenheimer claimed that: "Just as the slogans of rugged individualism are seeking exemption from social control, so in mass culture the rhetoric of individuality, by imposing patterns for collective imitation, subverts the very principle to which it gives lip service." Adorno in *The Jargon of Authenticity* claimed that "mass media can create an aura which makes the spectator seem to experience a non-existent actuality". Thus a mass-produced, artificial culture replaces what went before.

Mass Media and Modern Public Sphere

In political behaviour, opinion leading tends to correlate positively with status, whereas this is not the case in consumer behaviour . So for political behaviour, the general conclusion that the media merely fixes (confirms) people's opinion is not supported. Hovland, using experimental psychology, found significant effects of information on longer-term behaviour and attitudes, particularly in areas where most people have little direct experience (e.g. politics) and have a high degree of trust in the source (e.g. broadcasting). Since class has become a less reliable indicator of party (since the surveys of the 40s and 50s) the floating voter today is no longer the apathetic voter, but likely to be more well-informed than the consistent voter – and this mainly through the media.

There is also some very persuasive and empirical evidence suggesting that it is 'personal contact, not media persuasiveness' which counts. For example, Trenaman and McQuail (1961) found that 'don't knows' were less well informed than consistent voters, appearing uninterested, showing a general lack of information, and not just ignorance of particular policies or policies of one particular party. During the 1940 presidential election, a similar view was expressed by Katz and Lazarsfeld's theory of the two-step flow of communication, based on a study of electoral practices of the citizens of Erie County, Ohio.

This examined the political propaganda prevalent in the media at the time during the campaign period to see whether it plays an integral role in influencing people's voting. (In terms of generalising their results, one should note that there are questions about short term versus long term influence). The results contradict this: Lazarsfeld et al. (1944) find evidence for the Weberian theory of party, and identify certain factors, such as socio-economic circumstances, religious affiliation and area of residence, which together determine political orientation. The study claims that political propaganda serves to reaffirm the individual's predisposed orientation rather than to influence or change one's voting behaviour.

Thompson does not see 'mediated quasi-interaction' (the monological, mainly one-way communication of the mass media) as dominant, but rather as intermingling with traditional face-to-face interactions and mediated interactions (such as telephone conversations). Contrary to Habermas' pessimistic view, this allows both more information and discussion to come into the public domain (of mediated quasi-interaction) and more to be discussed within the private domain (since the media provides information individuals would not otherwise have access to).

Mass Media in a Free Enterprise Society

Although a sizeable portion of mass media offerings - particularly news, commentaries, documentaries, and other informational programmes - deal with highly controversial subjects, the major portion of mass media offerings are designed to serve an entertainment function. These programmes tend to avoid controversial issues and reflect beliefs and values sanctified by mass audience. This course is followed by Television networks, whose investment and production costs are high. Jerry Mander's work has highlighted this particular outlook. According to him, the atomised individuals of mass society lose their souls to the phantom delights of the film, the soap opera, and the variety show.

They fall into a stupor, or apathetic hypnosis, that Lazarsfeld called the 'narcotizing dysfunction' of exposure to mass media. Individuals become 'irrational victims of false wants' - the wants which corporations have thrust upon them, and continue to thrust upon them, through both the advertising in the media (with its continual exhortation to consume) and through the individualist consumption culture it promulgates. Thus, according to the Frankfurt School, leisure has been industrialised. The production of culture had become standardised and dominated by the profit motive as in other industries. In a mass society leisure is constantly used to induce the appropriate values and motives in the public. The modern media train the young for consumption. 'Leisure had ceased to be the opposite of work, and had become a preparation for it.'

Mass Media, Mass Culture and Elite

The relation of the mass media to contemporary popular culture is commonly conceived in terms of dissemination from the elite to the mass. The long-term consequences of this are significant in conjunction with the continuing concentration of ownership and control of the media, leading to accusations of a 'media elite' having a form of 'cultural dictatorship'. Thus the continuing debate about the influence of 'media barons' such as Conrad Black and Rupert Murdoch. For example, the UK *Observer* (March 1st 1998) reported the Murdoch-owned HarperCollins' refusal to publish Chris Patten's *East and West*, because of the former Hong Kong Governor's description of the Chinese leadership as "faceless Stalinists" possibly being damaging to Murdoch's Chinese broadcasting interests.

In this case, the author was able to have the book accepted by another publisher, but this kind of censorship may point the way to the future. A related, but more insidious, form is that of self-censorship by members of the media in the interests of the owner, in the interests of their careers. It has become something of a cliché to observe that despite many decades of research and hundreds of studies, the connections between people's consumption of the mass media and their subsequent behaviour have remained persistently elusive. Indeed, researchers have enjoyed an unusual degree of patience from both their scholarly and more public audiences.

But the time comes when we must take a step back from this murky lack of consensus and ask - why? Why are there no clear answers on media effects? There is a choice of two conclusions which can be drawn from any detailed analysis of the research. The first is that if, after over sixty years of a considerable amount of research effort, direct effects of media upon behaviour have not been clearly identified, then we should conclude that they are simply *not there to be found*. The media effects research has quite consistently taken the *wrong approach* to the mass media, its audiences, and society in general.

Effects Model Tackles Social Problems 'Backwards'

To explain the problem of violence in society, researchers should begin with that social violence and seek to explain it with reference, quite obviously, to those who engage in it: their identity, background, character and so on. The 'media effects' approach, in this sense, comes at the problem *backwards*, by starting with the media and then trying to lasso connections from there on to social beings, rather than the other way around. This is an important distinction. Criminologists, in their professional attempts to explain crime and violence, consistently turn for explanations not to the mass media but to social factors such as poverty, unemployment, housing, and the behaviour of family and peers.

In a study which *did* start at what we would recognise as the correct end - by interviewing 78 violent teenage offenders and then tracing their behaviour back towards media usage, in comparison with a group of over 500 'ordinary' school pupils of the same age - Hagell & Newburn (1994) found only that the young offenders watched *less* television and video than their counterparts, had less access to the technology in the first place, had no particular interest in specifically violent programmes, and either enjoyed the same material as non-offending teenagers or were simply *uninterested*.

This point was demonstrated very clearly when the offenders were asked, 'If you had the chance to be someone who appears on television, who would you choose to be?':

'The offenders felt particularly uncomfortable with this question and appeared to have difficulty in understanding why one might want to be such a person... In several interviews, the offenders had already stated that they watched little television, could not remember their favourite programmes and, consequently, could not think of anyone to be. In these cases, their obvious failure to identify with any television characters seemed to be part of a general lack of engagement with television'.

Thus we can see that studies which take the perpetrators

of actual violence as their first point of reference, rather than the media, come to rather different conclusions (and there is certainly a need for more such research). The point that effects studies take the media as their starting point, however, should not be taken to suggest that they involve sensitive examinations of the mass media. As will be noted below, the studies have typically taken a stereotyped, almost parodic view of media content. In more general terms, the 'backwards' approach involves the mistake of looking at individuals, rather than society, in relation to the mass media.

The narrowly individualistic approach of some psychologists leads them to argue that, because of their belief that particular individuals at certain times in specific circumstances may be negatively affected by one bit of media, the removal of such media from society would be a positive step. '

This approach is rather like arguing that the solution to the number of road traffic accidents in Britain would be to lock away one famously poor driver from Cornwall; that is, a blinkered approach which tackles a real problem from the wrong end, involves cosmetic rather than relevant changes, and fails to look in any way at the 'bigger picture'.

Effects Model Treats Children as Inadequate

The individualism of the psychological discipline has also had a significant impact on the way in which children are regarded in effects research. Whilst sociology in recent decades has typically regarded childhood as a social construction, demarcated by attitudes, traditions and rituals which vary between different societies and different time periods, the psychology of childhood - developmental psychology - has remained more tied to the idea of a universal individual who must develop through particular stages before reaching adult maturity, as established by Piaget. The developmental stages are arranged as a hierarchy, from incompetent childhood through to rational, logical adulthood, and progression through these stages is characterised by an 'achievement ethic'.

In psychology, then, children are often considered not so

much in terms of what they *can* do, as what they (apparently) cannot. Negatively defined as non-adults, the research subjects are regarded as the 'other', a strange breed whose failure to match generally middle-class adult norms must be charted and discussed.

Most laboratory studies of children and the media presume, for example, that their findings apply only to children, but fail to run parallel studies with adult groups to confirm this. We might speculate that this is because if adults were found to respond to laboratory pressures in the same way as children, the 'common sense' validity of the experiments would be undermined.

In her valuable examination of the way in which academic studies have constructed and maintained a particular perspective on childhood, Christine Griffin (1993) has recorded the ways in which studies produced by psychologists, in particular, have tended to 'blame the victim', to represent social problems as the consequence of the deficiencies or inadequacies of young people, and to 'psychologize inequalities, obscuring structural relations of domination behind a focus on individual "deficient" working-class young people and/or young people of colour, their families or cultural backgrounds'. Problems such as unemployment and the failure of education systems are thereby traced to individual psychology traits.

The same kinds of approach are readily observed in media effects studies, the production of which has undoubtedly been dominated by psychologically-oriented researchers, who - whilst, one imagines, having nothing other than benevolent intentions - have carefully exposed the full range of ways in which young media users can be seen as the inept victims of products which, whilst obviously puerile and transparent to adults, can trick children into all kinds of ill-advised behaviour. This situation is clearly exposed by research which seeks to establish what children can and do understand about and from the mass media. Such projects have shown that children can talk intelligently and indeed cynically about the mass media, and that children as young as seven can make thoughtful, critical and 'media literate' video productions themselves.

BARELY-CONCEALED CONSERVATIVE IDEOLOGY

The systematic derision of children's resistant capacities can be seen as part of a broader conservative project to position the more contemporary and challenging aspects of the mass media, rather than other social factors, as the major threat to social stability today. American effects studies, in particular, tend to assume a level of television violence which - as Barrie Gunter shows in this volume - is simply not applicable in other countries such as Britain. George Gerbner's view, for example, that 'We are awash in a tide of violent representations unlike any the world has ever seen... drenching every home with graphic scenes of expertly choreographed brutality', both reflects his hyperbolic view of the media in America and the extent to which findings cannot be simplistically transferred across the Atlantic. Whilst it is certainly possible that gratuitous depictions of violence might reach a level in American screen media which could be seen as unpleasant and unnecessary, it cannot always be assumed that violence is shown for 'bad' reasons or in an uncritical light.

Even the most obviously 'gratuitous' acts of violence, such as those committed by Beavis and Butt-Head in their eponymous MTV series, can be interpreted as rationally resistant reactions to an oppressive world which has little to offer them. The condemnation of generalised screen 'violence' by conservative critics, supported by the 'findings' of the effects studies - if we disregard their precarious foundations - can often be traced to concerns such as 'disrespect for authority' and 'anti-patriotic sentiments'. Programmes which do not necessarily contain any greater *quantity* of violent, sexual or other controversial depictions than others, can be seen to be objected to because they take a more challenging socio-political stance. This was illustrated by a study of over 2,200 complaints about British TV and radio which were sent to the Broadcasting Standards Council over an 18 month period from July 1993 to December 1994. This showed that a relatively narrow range of most complained-of programmes were taken by complainants to characterise a much broader decline in the morals of both broadcasting in particular and the nation in general.

This view of a section of the public is clearly reflected in a large number of the effects studies which presume that 'antisocial' behaviour is an objective category which can be observed in numerous programmes and which will negatively affect those children who see it portrayed. This dark view is constructed with the support of content analysis studies which appear almost designed to incriminate the media. Even today, expensive and avowedly 'scientific' content analyses such as the well-publicised US National Television Violence Study, for example, include odd tests such as whether violent acts are punished *within* the same scene - a strange requirement for dramas - making it easier to support views such as that 'there are substantial risks of harmful effects from viewing violence throughout the television environment'. This study also reflects the continuing willingness of researchers to impute *effects* from a count-up of content.

INDEQUATELY DEFINES ITS OWN OBJECTS OF STUDY

The flaws numbered four to six in this list are more straightforwardly methodological, although they are connected to the previous and subsequent points. The first of these is that effects studies have generally taken for granted the definitions of media material, such as 'antisocial' and 'prosocial' programming, as well as characterisations of behaviour in the real world, such as 'antisocial' and 'prosocial' action. The point has already been made that these can be ideological value judgements; throwing down a book in disgust, smashing a nuclear missile, or - to use a *Beavis and Butt-Head* example - sabotaging activities at one's burger bar workplace, will always be interpreted in effects studies as 'antisocial', not 'prosocial'.

Furthermore, actions such as verbal aggression or hitting an inanimate object are recorded as acts of violence, just as TV murders are, leading to terrifically (and irretrievably) murky data. It is usually impossible to discern whether very minor or extremely serious acts of 'violence' depicted in the media are being said to have led to quite severe or merely trivial acts in the real world. More significant, perhaps, is the fact that this is rarely seen as a problem: in the media effects field, dodgy 'findings' are accepted with an uncommon hospitality.

Based on Artificial Studies

Since careful sociological studies of media effects require amounts of time and money which limit their abundance, they are heavily outnumbered by simpler studies which are usually characterised by elements of artificiality. Such studies typically take place in a laboratory, or in a 'natural' setting such as a classroom but where a researcher has conspicuously shown up and instigated activities, neither of which are typical environments. Instead of a full and naturally-viewed television diet, research subjects are likely to be shown selected or specially-recorded clips which lack the narrative meaning inherent in everyday TV productions.

They may then be observed in simulations of real life presented to them as a game, in relation to inanimate objects such as Bandura's famous 'bobo' doll, or as they respond to questionnaires, all of which are unlike interpersonal interaction, cannot be equated with it, and are likely to be associated with the previous viewing experience in the mind of the subject, rendering the study invalid. Such studies also rely on the idea that subjects will not alter their behaviour or stated attitudes as a response to being observed or questioned. This naive belief has been shown to be false by researchers such as Borden (1975) who have demonstrated that the presence, appearance and gender of an observer can radically affect children's behaviour.

BASED ON STUDIES WITH MISAPPLIED METHODOLOGY

Many of the studies which do not rely on an experimental method, and so may evade the flaws mentioned in the previous section, fall down instead by applying a methodological procedure wrongly, or by drawing inappropriate conclusions from particular methods. The widely-cited longitudinal panel study by Huesmann, Eron and colleagues, for example, has been less famously slated for failing to keep to the procedures, such as assessing aggressivity or TV viewing with the same measures at different points in time, which are necessary for their statistical findings to have any validity. The same researchers have also failed to adequately account for why the findings of this study and those of another of their own studies absolutely contradict each other, with the former concluding that the media has a marginal effect on boys but no effect on girls, and the latter arguing the exact opposite (no effect on boys, but a small effect for girls).

They also seem to ignore the fact that their own follow-up of their original set of subjects 22 years later suggested that a number of biological, developmental and environmental factors contributed to levels of aggression, whilst the mass media was not even given a mention. These astounding inconsistencies, unapologetically presented by perhaps the best-known researchers in this area, must be cause for considerable unease about the effects model. More *careful* use of the same methods, such as in the three-year panel study involving over 3,000 young people conducted by Milavsky, Kessler, Stipp & Rubens, has only indicated that significant media effects are not to be found.

Another misuse of method occurs when studies which are simply unable to show that one thing causes another are treated as if they have done so. Correlation studies are typically used for this purpose. Their finding that a particular personality type is also the kind of person who enjoys a certain kind of media, is quite unable to show that the latter *causes* the former, although psychologists such as Van Evra (1990) have casually assumed that this is probably the case. There is a logical coherence to the idea that children whose behaviour is antisocial and disruptional will also have a greater interest in the more violent and noisy television programmes, whereas the idea that the behaviour is a *product* of these programmes lacks both this rational consistency, and the support of the studies.

MEDIA DEPICTIONS OF VIOLENCE

In addition to the point that 'antisocial' acts are ideologically defined in effects studies, we can also note that the media depictions of 'violence' which the effects model typically condemns are limited to fictional productions. The acts of violence which appear on a daily basis on news and serious factual programmes are seen as somehow exempt.

The point here is not that depictions of violence in the news should necessarily be condemned in just the same, blinkered way, but rather to draw attention to another philosophical inconsistency which the model cannot account for. If the antisocial acts shown in drama series and films are expected to have an effect on the behaviour of viewers, even though such acts are almost always ultimately punished or have other negative consequences for the perpetrator, there is no obvious reason why the antisocial activities which are always in the news, and which frequently do *not* have such apparent consequences for their agents, should not have similar effects.

ASSUMES SUPERIORITY TO THE MASSES

Surveys typically show that whilst a certain proportion of the public feel that the media may cause other people to engage in antisocial behaviour, almost no-one ever says that they have been affected in that way themselves. This view is taken to extremes by researchers and campaigners whose work brings them into regular contact with the supposedly corrupting material, but who are unconcerned for their own well-being as they implicitly 'know' that the effects will only be on 'other people'. Insofar as these others are defined as children or 'unstable' individuals, their approach may seem not unreasonable; it is fair enough that such questions should be explored. Nonetheless, the idea that it is unruly 'others' who will be affected - the uneducated? the working class? - remains at the heart of the effects paradigm, and is reflected in its texts (as well, presumably, as in the researchers' overenthusiastic interpretation of weak or flawed data).

George Gerbner and his colleagues, for example, write about 'heavy' television viewers as if this media consumption has necessarily had the opposite effect on the weightiness of their brains. Such people are assumed to have no selectivity or critical skills, and their habits are explicitly contrasted with preferred activities: 'Most viewers watch by the clock and either do not know what they will watch when they turn on the set, or follow established routines rather than choose each program as they would choose a book, a movie or an article'. This view, which knowingly makes inappropriate comparisons by ignoring the serial nature of many TV programmes, and which is unable to account for the widespread use of TV guides and VCRs with which audiences plan and arrange their viewing, reveals the kind of elitism and snobbishness which often seems to underpin such research. The point here is not that the content of the mass media must not be criticised, but rather that the mass audience themselves are not well served by studies which are willing to treat them as potential savages or actual fools.

NO ATTEMPT TO UNDERSTAND MEANINGS OF THE MEDIA

A further fundamental flaw, is that the effects model *necessarily* rests on a base of reductive assumptions and unjustified stereotypes regarding media content. To assert that, say, 'media violence' will bring negative consequences is not only to presume that depictions of violence in the media will always be promoting antisocial behaviour, and that such a category exists and makes sense, as noted above, but also assumes that the medium holds a singular message which will be carried unproblematically to the audience.

The effects model therefore performs the double deception

of presuming (a) that the media presents a singular and clear-cut 'message', and (b) that the proponents of the effects model are in a position to identify what that message is. The meanings of media content are ignored in the simple sense that assumptions are made based on the appearance of elements removed from their context (for example, woman hitting man equals violence equals bad), and in the more sophisticated sense that even *in* context the meanings may be different for different viewers (woman hitting man equals an unpleasant act of aggression, *or* appropriate self-defence, *or* a triumphant act of revenge, *or* a refreshing change, *or* is simply uninteresting, *or* any of many further alternative readings).

In-depth qualitative studies have unsurprisingly given support to the view that media audiences routinely arrive at their own, often heterogeneous, interpretations of everyday media texts. Since the effects model rides roughshod over both the meanings that actions have for characters in dramas *and* the meanings which those depicted acts may have for the audience members, it can retain little credibility with those who consider popular entertainment to be more than just a set of very basic propaganda messages flashed at the audience in the simplest possible terms.

NOT GROUNDED IN THEORY

Finally, and underlying many of the points made above, is the fundamental problem that the entire argument of the 'effects model' is substantiated with no theoretical reasoning beyond the bald assertions that particular kinds of effects *will* be produced by the media. The basic question of *why* the media should induce people to imitate its content has never been adequately tackled, beyond the simple idea that particular actions are 'glamorised'. (Obviously, *antisocial* actions are shown really *positively* so infrequently that this is an inadequate explanation). Similarly, the question of how merely seeing an activity in the media would be translated into an actual *motive* which would prompt an individual to behave in a particular way is just as unresolved.

The lack of firm theory has led to the effects model being based in the variety of assumptions outlined above - that the media (rather than people) is the unproblematic starting-point for research; that children will be unable to 'cope' with the media; that the categories of 'violence' or 'antisocial behaviour' are clear and self-evident; that the model's predictions can be verified by scientific research; that screen fictions are of concern, whilst news pictures are not; that researchers have the unique capacity to observe and classify social behaviour and its meanings, but that those researchers need not attend to the various possible meanings which media content may have for the audience. Each of these very substantial problems has its roots in the failure of media effects commentators to found their model in any coherent theory.

Future for Research on Media influences

The effects model, we have seen, has remarkably little going for it as an explanation of human behaviour, or of the media in society. Whilst any challenging or apparently illogical theory or model reserves the right to demonstrate its validity through empirical data, the effects model has failed also in that respect. Its continued survival is indefensible and unfortunate.

However, the failure of this particular *model* does not mean that the impact of the mass media can no longer be considered or investigated. The studies by Greg Philo and Glasgow University Media Group colleagues, for example, have used often imaginative methods to explore the influence of media presentations upon perceptions and interpretations of factual matters. We have realised rather late that our own study in which children made videos about the environment, which were used as a way of understanding the discourses and perspectives on environmentalism which the children had acquired from the media, can be seen as falling broadly within this tradition.

The strength of this work is that it operates on a terrain different from that occupied by the effects model; even at the most obvious level, it is about *influences* and *perceptions*, rather than *effects* and *behaviour*. However, whilst such studies may provide valuable reflections on the relationship between mass media and audiences, they cannot - for the same reason - directly challenge claims made from within the 'effects model' paradigm. This is not a weakness of these studies, of course; the effects paradigm should be left to bury itself whilst prudent media researchers move on to explore these other areas.

Any paradigm which is able to avoid the flaws and assumptions which have inevitably and quite rightly ruined the effects model is likely to have some advantages. With the rise of qualitative studies which actually listen to media audiences, we are seeing the advancement of a more forward-thinking, sensible and compassionate view of those who enjoy the mass media. After decades of stunted and rather irresponsible talk about media 'effects', the emphasis is hopefully changing towards a more sensitive but rational approach to media scholarship.

COMMUNICATION THEORY

There is much discussion in the academic world of communication as to what actually constitutes communication.

Currently, many definitions of communication are used in order to conceptualize the processes by which people navigate and assign meaning. Communication is also understood as the exchanging of understanding. Additionally the biocommunication theory investigates communicative processes within and among non-humans such as bacteria, animals, fungi and plants.

We might say that communication consists of transmitting information from one person to another. In fact, many scholars of communication take this as a working definition, and use Lasswell's maxim, "who says what to whom in what channel with what effect," as a means of circumscribing the field of communication theory. Other commentators suggest that a ritual process of communication exists, one not artificially divorceable from a particular historical and social context.

Communication stands so deeply rooted in human behaviours and the structures of society that scholars have difficulty thinking of it while excluding social or behavioural events. Because communication theory remains a relatively young field of inquiry and integrates itself with other disciplines such as philosophy, psychology, and sociology, one probably cannot yet[update] expect a consensus conceptualization of communication across disciplines. Currently, there is no paradigm from which communi-cation scholars may work. One of the issues facing scholars is the possibility that establishing a communication metatheory will negate their research and stifle the broad body of knowledge in which communication functions.

Communication as a named and unified discipline has a history of contestation that goes back to the Socratic dialogues, in many ways making it the first and most contestatory of all early sciences and philosophies. Aristotle first addressed the problem of communication and attempted to work out a theory of it in *The Rhetoric*.

He was primarily focused on the art of persuasion. A monologue (speak to self) is also a method of communication even if the person involved does not have any audition but himself. Humanistic and rhetorical viewpoints and theories dominated the discipline prior to the twentieth century, when more scientific methodologies and insights from psychology, sociology, linguistics and advertising began to influence communication thought and practice. Seeking to define "communication" as a static word or unified discipline may not be as important as understanding communication as a family of resemblances with a plurality of definitions as Ludwig Wittgenstein had put forth.

Theory Framework

It is helpful to examine communication and communi-cation theory through one of the following viewpoints:

- ***Mechanistic*** : This view considers communication to be a perfect transaction of a message from the sender to the receiver.

- ***Psychological:*** This view considers communication as the act of sending a message to a receiver, and the feelings and thoughts of the receiver upon interpreting the message.
- ***Social Constructionist (Symbolic Interactionist):*** This view considers communication to be the product of the interactants sharing and creating meaning.
- *Systemic:* This view considers communication to be the new messages created via "through-put", or what happens as the message is being interpreted and re-interpreted as it travels through people.
- *Critical:* This view considers communication as a source of power and oppression of individuals and social groups.

Inspection of a particular theory on this level will provide a framework on the nature of communication as seen within the confines of that theory.

Theories can also be studied and organized according to the ontological, epistemological, and axiological framework imposed by the theorist. Ontology essentially poses the question of what, exactly, it is the theorist is examining. One must consider the very nature of reality. The answer usually falls in one of three realms depending on whether the theorist sees the phenomena through the lens of a realist, nominalist, or social constructionist. Realist perspective views the world objectively, believing that there is a world outside of our own experience and cognitions. Nominalists see the world subjectively, claiming that everything outside of one's cognitions is simply names and labels. Social constructionists straddle the fence between objective and subjective reality, claiming that reality is what we create together.

Epistemology is an examination of how the theorist studies the chosen phenomena. In studying epistemology, objective knowledge is said to be the result of a systematic look at the causal relationships of phenomena. This knowledge is usually attained through use of the scientific method. Scholars often think that empirical evidence collected in an objective manner is most likely to reflect truth in the findings. Theories of this ilk are usually created to predict a phenomenon. Subjective theory holds that understanding is based on situated knowledge, typically found using interpretative methodology such as ethnography and interviews. Subjective theories are typically developed to explain or understand phenomena in the social world. Axiology is concerned with what values drive a theorist to develop a theory. Theorists must be mindful of potential biases so that they will not influence or skew their findings.

Mapping the Theoretical landscape

A discipline gets defined in large part by its theoretical structure. Communication studies often borrow theories from other social sciences. This theoretical variation makes it difficult to come to terms with the field as a whole. That said, some common taxonomies exist that serve to divide up the range of communication research. Two common mappings involve contexts and assumptions. Many authors and researchers divide communication by what they sometimes called "contexts" or "levels", but which more often represent institutional histories. The study of communication in the US, while occurring within departments of psychology, sociology, linguistics, and anthropology (among others), generally developed from schools of rhetoric and from schools of journalism.

While many of these have become "departments of communication", they often retain their historical roots, adhering largely to theories from speech communication in the former case, and from mass media in the latter.

The great divide between speech communication and mass communication becomes complicated by a number of smaller sub-areas of communication research, including intercultural and international communication, small group communication, communication technology, policy and legal studies of communication, telecommunication, and work done under a variety of other labels. Some of these departments take a largely social-scientific perspective, others tend more heavily toward the humanities, and still others gear themselves more toward production and professional preparation. These "levels" of communication provide some way of grouping communication theories, but inevitably, some theories and concepts leak from one area to another, or fail to find a home at all.

Another way of dividing up the communication field emphasizes the assumptions that undergird particular theories, models, and approaches. While this approach also tends to have as its basis institutional divisions, theories within each of the seven "traditions" of communication theory that Robert Craig suggests tend to reinforce one another, and retain the same ground epistemological and axiological assumptions. His traditions include:

- ***Rhetorical:*** Practical art of discourse
- ***Semiotic:*** Intersubjective mediation through signs in order to mediate between different perspectives
- ***Phenomenological:*** Experience of otherness, dialogue
- *Cybernetic:* Information processing and explains how all kinds of complex systems, whether living or nonliving, macro or micro, are able to function, and why they often malfunction
- ***Sociopsychological:*** Expression, interaction and influence
- ***Critical:*** Discursive reflection
- ***Sociocultural:*** Reproduction of social order (Miller, 13)

Craig finds each of these clearly defined against the others, and remaining cohesive approaches to describing communicative behaviour. As a taxonomic aid, these labels help to organize theory by its assumptions, and help researchers to understand why some theories may seem incommensurable. While communication theorists very commonly use these two approaches, theorists decentralize the place of language and machines as communicative technologies. The idea (as argued by Vygotsky) of communication as the primary tool of a species defined by its tools remains on the outskirts of communication theory.

It finds some representation in the Toronto School of communication theory (alternatively sometimes called medium theory) as represented by the work of Innis, McLuhan, and others. It seems that the ways in which individuals and groups use the technologies of communication – and in some cases are used by them – remain central to what communication researchers do. The ideas that surround this, and in particular the place of persuasion, remain constants across both the "traditions" and "levels" of communication theory.

4

Media and Research for Social Causes

MEDIA VIOLENCE RESEARCH

Media and violence research attempts to determine whether a link between consuming media violence and subsequent aggressive and violent behaviour exists. Although many social scientists support this link, methodological and theoretical problems with the existing literature limit interpretation of findings in this area. Media violence researchers investigate whether the popular media is one potential cause of aggressive behaviour. Some have claimed that media violence research effect sizes are similar to those seen in smoking/lung cancer research . This claim was recently challenged when it was noted that the authors had miscalculated the effect size for smoking and lung cancer as much lower than it actually is. Some authors also conclude that the effect size for media violence research has been greatly exaggerated.

Few media researchers would claim that media is the only cause of aggression. However, there is debate and concern among some scholars that media researchers may have exaggerated effects. Media violence researcher Rowell Huesmann has said: "Serious aggressive behaviour only occurs when there is a convergence of multiple predisposing and precipitating factors". Many other explanations of aggressive behaviour exist; for example, some researchers have suggested that the pathway to aggression is largely biological/genetic, and others have suggested that aggression can be explained by principles of evolutionary psychology.

Complaints over the possible deleterious effects of various media are nothing new. Plato complained about the effects of plays on youth. Various media including comic books, jazz and rock and roll, Dungeons and Dragons and dime novels have all caused speculation that consumers of such media may become more aggressive, rebellious or immoral. The advent of television prompted research into the effects of this new medium in the 1960s. Much of research has been guided by social learning theory developed by Albert Bandura. Social learning theory suggests that one way in which human beings learn is by the process of modeling. Social learning theory is compatible with a variety of other theories of aggression and a diversity of research methods, for instance, neurophysiological theory and research.

Mechanisms

Models of a causal connection between media consump-tion and behaviour include mechanisms underlying both short-term and long-term effects of media violence exposure. In the short term, it is theorized that media violence exposure increases arousal, primes aggressive scripts and cognitions, and activates the tendency to automatically imitate. When models in the media respond violently, this activates violent cognitive scripts in the viewer's mind, primes the individual's network of aggressive concepts, and increases the individuals level of physiological arousal; all increasing the likelihood in an increase in their subsequent aggression level (meaning an increase in aggressive thoughts, beliefs, and behaviours). It is hypothesized that as arousal increases, the ability to inhibit the imitative tendency decreases (Hurley, forthcoming). The process of excitation transfer is also theorized to play a role in short-term effects.

Such theories claim that in the long term, media violence exposure leads to the acquisition and elaboration of aggressive scripts, aggressive interpretational schemas, aggressive beliefs about the world and social behaviour, and desensitizes individuals to violent stimuli . However critics contend that most effects demonstrated by media violence research have been inconsistent and small. According to McQuail's theory (2002), violence from media, especially television is encoded in the cognitive map of viewers, and subsequent viewing of television violence helps to maintain aggressive thoughts, ideas and behaviours. Boyatzis, Matillo and Nesbit investigated the children's reaction to the popular series Mighty Morphin Power Rangers to prove that children became more aggressive in their styles of play after watching an episode from this program.

The research was as follows: "Fifty-two elementary-school girls and boys, aged between 5 and 11 years were randomly assigned either to watch an episode of Power Rangers or to a control group which did not see the episode. All the children were observed both before and after the programme while playing in their classroom. The researchers reported that children who had watched the Power Rangers episode exhibited a greater number of aggressive acts the next day at play than did children who had not been shown the episode. Indeed, children who had watched the episode committed seven times as many actions classed as aggressive as did the other children."

Those children displayed aggressive acts after watching the Power Rangers and tried to act certain scenes from the television program out while being the hero and carrying a gun because it is "cool" to fight against enemies. It is worth noting however that this study, like many others did not distinguish between aggression meant to harm others, and "aggressive play" in which children mutually enjoy acting out scenes from a show. Although skeptics claim that such research does not give enough evidence to indicate a direct causal connection between media and violence, it demonstrates the creation of the aggressive social scripts that are then available for use in actual future decisions and behaviours. Although the relevance of socio-cultural contexts wasn't evaluated in this sort of study, some like Flew and Humphreys (2005) believe that it can not be easily demonstrated that media violence causes aggression.

Media violence research methods include laboratory experiments, correlational studies, and longitudinal studies. Experimental studies expose volunteers to violent media and then measure their aggression in a laboratory setting. However, some critics cite methodological flaws in these studies, leading some researchers to be skeptical of the literature which demonstrates a causal effect. The cognitive psychologist Steven Pinker in his (2002) book, *The Blank Slate* criticizes this body of work for its methodological and theoretical flaws. Correlational studies measure exposure to media violence and associate these exposure levels with aggressive behaviour but rarely with serious violent criminal behaviour. Findings from longitudinal studies have been inconsistent in correlating early exposure to media violence with later aggressiveness beyond what is predicted from early aggressiveness alone.

Within these studies some measures are "statistically significant" whereas others are not (or results may vary between groups of participants) making interpretation difficult and often subject to who is interpreting the findings (people advocating a causal link versus skeptics of a causal link). Court cases regarding media violence (most recently regarding video games) have generally not been positive regarding the convincing nature of the findings. Most court cases find that such research does not meet standards of admissibility (e.g. Daubert standard) or fail to convincingly show harm. Similarly a recent Surgeon General's report minimized the importance of media effects in contributing to youth violence. By contrast however, most American scientific organizations such as the American Psychological Association and American Academy of Pediatrics are supportive of a link between media violence and aggression.

Critisms of Media Violence Research

Although organizations such as the American Academy of Pediatrics and the American Psychological Association have suggested that thousands (3500 according to the AAP) of studies have been conducted confirming this link, others have argued that this information is incorrect. Rather, only about two hundred studies (confirmed by meta-analyses such as Paik and Comstock, 1994) have been conducted in peer-reviewed scientific journals on television, movie, music and video game violence effects. Critics argue that about half find some link between media and subsequent aggression (but not violent crime), whereas the other half do not find a link between consuming violent media and subsequent aggression of any kind.

Criticisms of the media violence link focus on a number of methodological and theoretical problems including (but not limited to) the following:

1. ***Failure to employ standardized, reliable and valid measures of aggression and media violence exposure:*** Although measurement of psychological variables is always tricky at best, it is generally accepted that measurement techniques should be standardized, reliable and valid, as demonstrated empirically. However, a read of the studies involved notes that the measurement tools involved are often unstandardized, sloppily employed and fail to report reliability coefficients. Examples include the "Competitive Reaction Time Test" in which participants believe that they are punishing an opponent for losing in a reaction time test by subjecting the opponent to noise blasts or electric shocks. There is no standardized way of employing this task, raising the possibility that authors may manipulate the results to support their conclusions. This task may produce dozens of different possible ways to measure "aggression", all from a single participant's data. Without a standardized way of employing and measuring aggression using this task, there is no way of

knowing whether the results reported are a valid measure of aggression, or were selected from among the possible alternatives simply because they produced positive findings where other alternatives did not. However, developing newer, valid measures of aggression has proven difficult.

2. ***Failure to report negative findings:*** Many of the articles that purport positive findings regarding a link between media violence and subsequent aggression, on a closer read, actually have negative or inconclusive results. One example is the experimental portion of Anderson & Dill (2000; with video games) which measures aggression four separate ways (using an unstandardized, unreliable and unvalidated measure of aggression, the Competitive Reaction Time Test mentioned above) and finds significance for only one of those measures. Had a statistical adjustment known as a Bonferroni correction been properly employed, that fourth finding also would have been insignificant. This issue of selective reporting differs from the "file drawer" effect in which journals fail to publish articles with negative findings. Rather, this is due to authors finding a "mixed bag" of results and discussing only the supportive findings and ignoring the negative findings within a single manuscript. The problem of non-reporting of non-significant findings (the so-called "file cabinet effect") is a problem throughout all areas of science but may be a particular issue for publicized areas such as media violence.
3. ***Failure to account for "third" variables:*** Media violence studies regularly fail to account for other variables such as genetics, personality and exposure to family violence that may explain both why some people become violent and why those same people may choose to expose themselves to violent media.
4. ***Failure to adequately define "aggression":*** Experimental measures of aggression have been questioned by critics. The main concern of critics has been the issue of the

external validity of experimental measures of aggression. The validity of the concept of aggression itself, however, is rarely questioned. Highly detailed taxonomies of different forms of aggression do exist. Whether or not researchers agree on the particular terminology used to indicate the particular sub-types of aggression (i.e. relational versus social aggression), concepts of aggression are always operationally defined in peer-reviewed journals. However many of these operational definitions of aggression are specifically criticized. Many experimental measures of aggression are rather questionable. Other studies fail to differentiate between "aggression" aimed at causing harm to another person, and "aggressive play" in which two individuals (usually children) may pretend to engage in aggressive behaviour, but do so consensually for the purpose of mutual enjoyment.

5. ***Small "effects" sizes:*** In the research world, the meaning of "statistical significance" can be ambiguous. A measure of effect size can aid in the interpretation of statistical significance. In a meta-analysis of 217 studies by Paik and Comstock (1994), effect sizes for experiments were r = .37 and r = .19 for surveys, which are small to moderate effects. Most of these studies however did not actually measure aggression against another person. Paik and Comstock note that when aggression toward another person, and particularly actual violent crime is considered, the relationship between media violence and these outcomes is near zero. Effects can vary according to their size (for example the effects of eating bananas on your mood could very well be "statistically significant" but would be tiny, almost imperceptible, where as the effect of a death in the immediate family would also be "statistically significant" but obviously much larger). Media violence studies usually produce very small, transient effects that do not translate into large effects in the real world. Media violence researchers often defend this by stating that many medical studies also produce small effects (although as Block and Crain, 2007, note,

these researchers may have miscalculated the effect sizes from medical research).

6. ***Media violence rates are not correlated with violent crime rates:*** Ultimately the biggest problem for this body of literature is that for this theory to be true, media violence (which appears to have been consistently and unfailingly on the rise since the 1950s) should be well correlated with violent crime (which has been cycling up and down throughout human history). By discussing only the data from the 1950s through the 1990s, media violence researchers create the illusion that there is a correlation, when in fact there is not. Large spikes in violent crime in the United States occurred without associated media violence spikes during the 1880s (when records were first kept) and 1930s. The homicide rate in the United States has never been higher than during the 1930s. Similarly, this theory fails to explain why violent crime rates (including among juveniles) dramatically fell in the mid 1990s and have stayed low, during a time when media violence has continued to increase, and saw the addition of violent video games. Lastly media violence researchers can not explain why many countries with media violence rates similar to or equal to the U.S. (such as Norway, Canada, Japan, etc.) have much lower violent crime rates. Huesmann & Eron's own cross-national study (which is often cited in support of media violence effects) failed to find a link between television violence and aggressive behaviour in most of the countries included in the analysis (including America, and even in studies on American boys).

MEDIA VIOLENCE RESEARCHERS' RESPONSE TO CRITICISMS

Regarding instruments used to measure aggression, media researchers note that better measures are often not readily available and most critics of media violence research do not appear to offer alternatives. That is, a type II error may be made in denying the importance of research findings that suggest a connection. Also measuring "violent criminal behaviour" in laboratory studies would clearly be unethical, much the same way as experimental studies of smoking and lung cancer would have been unethical. Regarding the inconclusive nature of some findings, media researchers often contend that it is the critics who are misinterpreting or selectively reporting studies. It may be that both sides of the debate are highlighting separate findings that are most favorable to their own "cause".

Regarding "third" variables, media violence researchers acknowledge that other variables may play a role in aggression and that aggression is due to a confluence of variables. These variables are known as "third variables" and if found, would probably be *mediator* variables (which differ from *moderator* variables). As of yet, no third variable has been shown to explain away media violence effects, although this may be because media violence researchers have consistently failed to control for variables such as family violence, genetics or personality. Confusion commonly arises among non-scientists in the interpretation of medialional versus moderational (interaction) effects. A mediator variable could 'explain away' media violence effects, whereas a moderator variable cannot. For instance, trait aggressiveness has been demon-strated to moderate media violence effects (Bushman), but is commonly misunderstood as a variable that 'explains away' the causal link between exposure and behaviour, although in some studies "trait aggression" does appear to account for any link between media violence exposure and aggression.

Other variables have also been found to moderate media violence effects. Another point of confusion in understanding the media violence literature is the way researchers deal with potential confounding variables. Researchers use random assignment to neutralize the effects of what commonly are cited as third variables (i.e. gender, trait aggressiveness, preference for violent media). Because experimental designs employ random assignment to conditions, the effect of such attributive variables on experimental results is assumed to be random (not systematic). However, the same can not be said for correlational studies, and failure to control for such variables in correlational studies limits the interpretation of such studies. Often, something as simple as gender proves capable of "mediating" media violence effects. Definitions of aggression have improved with time.

Most researchers agree that aggression, as a construct involves willful intent to cause harm or intent to another person who would wish to avoid the same. As such the problem may have less to do with the definition of aggression, but rather how aggression is measured in studies, and how aggression and violent crime are used interchangeably in the public eye. Much of the debate on this issue seems to revolve around ambiguity regarding what is considered a "small" effect. Media violence researchers contend that effect sizes noted in media violence effects are similar to those found in some medical research which is considered important by the medical community, although medical research may suffer from some of the same interpretational flaws as social science.

Also Block & Crain (2007) recently found that social scientists had been miscalculating some medical effect sizes. The interpretation of effect size in both medical and social science remains in its infancy. More recently, media violence experts have acknowledged that societal media consumption and violent crime rates are not well associated, but claim that this is likely due to other variable that are poorly understood. However, this effect remains poorly explained by current media violent theories, and media violence researchers may need to be more careful not to retreat to an unfalsifiable theory - one that cannot be disproven.

MEDIA TRANSPARENCY

Media Transparency is the concept of determining how and why information is conveyed through various means. This is a specific case of the topic, Transparency (humanities). As used in the humanities, it implies openness and accountability. It is a metaphorical extension of the meaning used as "transparent" object is one that can be seen through.

In communication studies, Media is transparent when:

- There are many, often competing, sources of information
- Much is known about the method of information delivery
- The funding of media production is publicly available

Aspects of transparent media include open source documentation, open meetings, financial disclosure statements, the freedom of information legislation, budgetary review, audit, peer review, etc. Some organisations and networks insist that not only the ordinary information of interest to the community is made freely available, but that all (or nearly all) meta-levels of organising and decision-making are themselves also published. This is known as radical transparency.

These organizations include: Wikipedia, the GNU/Linux community, and Indymedia. When an organization (corporate, government, non-profit, or other) holds a meeting and the proceedings are open to the public and the press, and the meeting is publicized via one or more of the following methods, there is less opportunity for the organization to abuse the system of information delivery in their own interest:

- broadcast over radio
- reviewed on television
- reported in newsprint
- journalized on weblogs

This assumes, of course, that the organization does not own or otherwise affect the media conveying the information.

MEDIA BIAS

Media bias is a term used to describe a real or perceived bias of journalists and news producers within the mass media, in the selection of which events will be reported and how they are covered. The term "media bias" usually refers to a pervasive or widespread bias contravening the standards of journalism, rather than the perspective of an individual journalist or article. The direction and degree of media bias in various countries is widely disputed, although its causes are both practical and theoretical. Practical limitations to media neutrality include the inability of journalists to report all available stories and facts, and the requirement that selected facts be linked into a coherent narrative.

Since it is impossible to report everything, some selectivity is inevitable. Government influence, including overt and covert censorship, biases the media in some countries. Market forces that can result in a biased presentation include the ownership of the news source, the selection of staff, the preferences of an intended audience, pressure from advertisers, or reduced funding due to lower ratings or governmental funding cuts. Political affiliations arise from ideological positions of media owners and journalists. The space or air time available for reports, as well as deadlines needing to be met, can lead to incomplete and apparently biased stories.

Types of bias:

- Ethnic or racial bias, including racism, nationalism.
- Corporate bias, coverage' of political campaigns in such a way as to favor or oppose corporate interests, and the reporting of issues to favor the interests of the owners of the news media or its advertisers. Some critics view the financing of news outlets through advertisers as an inherent bias.
- Class bias, including bias favoring one social class and bias ignoring (or exaggerating) social or class divisions.
- Political bias, including bias in favor of or against a particular political party, candidate, or policy. Other complaints are: the American media has an "either or" view by only focusing on Republicans or Democrats, and ignoring other lines of thought such as socialism and libertarianism.

- Religious and cultural bias, including bias in which one religious or non-religious viewpoint is given preference over others.
- Bias based on sex, age, background, education, language, among others. (For instance woman's issues are rarely featured in mainstream news, and a poorly written letter won't make it into the Letters to the Editor section.)
- Sensationalism, bias in favor of the exceptional over the ordinary. This includes the practice whereby exceptional news may be overemphasized, distorted or fabricated to boost commercial ratings; entertainment news is often subjected to sensationalism.
- Exaggerated influence of minority views: Like sensationalism, this is a tendency to emphasize the new and the different over the *status quo* or existing consensus. This may be done in an attempt to be "fair", or to find something worth reporting.
- Bias toward ease or expediency: This can be a tendency to present information which is already widely reported in other news media, i.e. "jumping on the bandwagon" or "following the leader", presentation of "fluff pieces" which are of questionable journalistic merit (such as coverage in news media of the personal lives of celebrities, or "news you can use"-style reporting which offers consumer advice which is widely viewed as common sense), and over representation of crime reporting, particularly street crime. This type of bias is largely attributed to the relatively low cost of presenting these stories (compared to investigative journalism which tends to require more time and research, and thus more money, to produce), competition between commercial news media for consumers, ratings and ad revenue, and a 24-hour news cycle which demands constant output.
- "Accidental bias" which could include errors and misinformation (re: expediency) or editors accidentally reinterpreting a reporter's work.

Sources of Media Bias

Whether or not media bias exists is a seemingly endless debate. Yet valid questions remain about media performance and the role of public communications practitioners in shaping perception. There are some researchers who use a "social construction of reality" framework to analyze media and the ways in which information is filtered. According to scholar Richard Alan Nelson's (2003) study Tracking Propaganda to the Source: Tools for Analyzing Media Bias, media effects findings suggest that when bias occurs it stems from a combination of 10 factors:

- The media are neither objective nor completely honest in their portrayal of important issues.
- Framing devices are employed in stories by featuring some angles and downplaying others.
- The news is a product not only of deliberate manipulation, but of the ideological and economic conditions under which the media operate.
- While appearing independent, the news media are institutions that are controlled or heavily influenced by government and business interests experienced with manufacturing of consent/consensus.
- Reporters' sources frequently dominate the flow of information as a way of furthering their own overt and hidden agendas. In particular, the heavy reliance on political officials and other government related experts occurs through a preferential sourcing selection process which excludes dissident voices.
- Journalists widely accept the faulty premise that the government's collective intentions are benevolent, despite occasional mistakes.
- The regular use of the word "we" by journalists in referring to their government's actions implies nationalistic complicity with those policies.
- There is an absence of historical context and contemporary comparisons in reportage which would make news more meaningful.

- The failure to provide follow up assessment is further evidence of a pack journalism mentality that at the conclusion of a "feeding frenzy" wants to move on to other stories.
- Citizens must avoid self-censorship by reading divergent sources and maintaining a critical perspective on the media in order to make informed choices and participate effectively in the public policy process.

Scholarly Treatment

Media bias is studied at schools of journalism, university departments (including Media studies, Cultural studies and Peace studies) and by many independent watchdog groups from various parts of the political spectrum. In the United States, many of these studies focus on issues of a conservative/liberal balance in the media. Other focuses include international differences in reporting, as well as bias in reporting of particular issues such as economic class or environmental interests. A widely-cited public opinion study documents a correlation between news source and certain misconceptions about the Iraq war. Conducted by the Program on International Policy Attitudes in October 2003, the poll asked Americans whether they believed statements about the Iraq war that were known to be false. Respondents were also asked which was their primary news source: Fox News, CBS, NBC, ABC, CNN, "Print sources," or NPR .

By cross referencing the responses according to primary news source, the study showed that higher numbers of Fox News watchers held certain misconceptions about the Iraq war. The director of Program on International Policy (PIPA), Stephen Kull said, "While we cannot assert that these misconceptions created the support for going to war with Iraq, it does appear likely that support for the war would be substantially lower if fewer members of the public had these misperceptions."

The Glasgow Media Group carried out the Bad News Studies, a series of detailed analyses of television broadcasts (and later newspaper coverage) in the United Kingdom.

(Eldridge, 2000). Published between 1976 and 1985, the Bad News Studies used content analysis, interviews and covert participant observation to conclude that news was biased against trade unions, blaming them for breaking wage negotiating guidelines and causing high inflation.

Martin Harrison's *TV News: Whose Bias?* (1985) criticized the methodology of the Glasgow Media Group, arguing that the GMG identified bias selectively, via their own preconceptions about what phrases qualify as biased descriptions. For example, the GMG sees the word "idle" to describe striking workers as pejorative, despite the word being used by strikers themselves.

Herman and Chomsky (1988) proposed a propaganda model hypothesizing systematic biases of U.S. media from structural economic causes. They hypothesize media ownership by corporations, funding from advertising, the use of official sources, efforts to discredit independent media ("flak"), and "anti-communist" ideology as the filters that bias news in favor of U.S. corporate interests.

Their propaganda model first and foremost disuses self censorship through the corporate system; that reporters and especially editors share and/or acquire values with corporate elites in order to further their careers. Those that don't are usually weeded out or marginalized. Such examples have been dramatized in fact based movie dramas as "Good Night, and Good Luck" and "The Insider" or demonstrated in the documentary "The Corporation". George Orwell originally wrote a preface for his book "Animal Farm", which focuses on British self censorship. "The sinister fact about literary censorship in England is that it is largely voluntary. ... [Things are] kept right out of the British press, not because the Government intervened but because of a general tacit agreement that 'it wouldn't do' to mention that particular fact." As if to prove the point, the preface itself was censored and is not published with most copies of the book.

The propaganda model posits that advertising dollars are essential for funding most media sources and clearly have an effect on the content of the media. For example, according to Fair, 'When Al Gore proposed launching a progressive TV network, a Fox News executive told Advertising Age (10/13/03): "The problem with being associated as liberal is that they wouldn't be going in a direction that advertisers are really interested in.... If you go out and say that you are a liberal network, you are cutting your potential audience, and certainly your potential advertising pool, right off the bat."

Furthermore "an internal memo from ABC Radio Networks to its affiliates reveals scores of powerful sponsors have a standing order that their commercials never be placed on syndicated Air America programming that airs on ABC affiliates.... The list, totaling 90 advertisers, includes some of largest and most well-known corporations advertising in the U.S.: Wal-Mart, GE, Exxon Mobil, Microsoft, Bank of America, Fed-Ex, Visa, Allstate, McDonald's, Sony and Johnson & Johnson. The U.S. Postal Service and the U.S. Navy are also listed as advertisers who don't want their commercials to air on Air America."

The academic study cited most frequently by critics of a "liberal media bias" in American journalism is *The Media Elite,* a 1986 book co-authored by political scientists Robert Lichter, Stanley Rothman, and Linda Lichter. They surveyed journalists at national media outlets such as the New York Times, Washington Post, and the broadcast networks. The survey found that most of these journalists were Democratic voters whose attitudes were well to the left of the general public on a variety of topics, including such hot-button social issues such as abortion, affirmative action, and gay rights. Then they compared journalists' attitudes to their coverage of controversial issues such as the safety of nuclear power, school busing to promote racial integration, and the energy crisis of the 1970s.

The book's most thorough case study involved nuclear energy. The survey of journalists showed that most were highly skeptical about nuclear safety. However, the authors conducted a separate survey of scientists in energy related fields, who were much more sanguine about nuclear safety issues. They then conducted a content analysis of nuclear energy coverage in the media outlets they had surveyed. They found that the opinions of sources who were cited as scientific experts reflected the antinuclear sentiments of journalists, rather than the more pro-nuclear perspectives held by most energy scientists.

The authors concluded that journalists' coverage of controversial issues reflected their own attitudes, and the predominance of political liberals in newsrooms therefore pushed news coverage in a liberal direction. They presented this tilt as a mostly unconscious process of like-minded individuals projecting their shared assumptions onto their interpretations of reality. At the time the study was embraced mainly by conservative columnists and politicians, who adopted the findings as scientific proof of liberal media bias.

Many of the positions in the preceding study are supported by a 2002 study by Jim A. Kuypers: Press Bias and Politics: How the Media Frame Controversial Issues. In this study of 116 mainstream US papers (including The New York Times, the Washington Post, Los Angeles Times, and the San Francisco Chronicle), Kuypers found that the mainstream print press in America operate within a narrow range of liberal beliefs. Those who expressed points of view further to the left were generally ignored, whereas those who expressed moderate or conservative points of view were often actively denigrated or labeled as holding a minority point of view. In short, if a political leader, regardless of party, spoke within the press-supported range of acceptable discourse, he or she would receive positive press coverage.

If a politician, again regardless of party, were to speak outside of this range, he or she would receive negative press or be ignored. Kuypers also found that the liberal points of view expressed in editorial and opinion pages were found in hard news coverage of the same issues. Although focusing primarily on the issues of race and homosexuality, Kuypers found that the press injected opinion into its news coverage of other issues such as welfare reform, environmental protection, and gun control; in all cases favoring a liberal point of view.

There is also a growing economics literature on mass media bias, both on the theoretical and the empirical side. On the theoretical side the focus is on understanding to what extent the political positioning of mass media outlets is mainly driven by demand or supply factors. According to Dan Sutter of the University of Oklahoma, a systematic liberal bias in the U.S. media could depend on the fact that owners and/or journalists typically lean to the left.

Along the same lines, David Baron of Stanford GSB presents a game-theoretic model of mass media behaviour in which, given that the pool of journalists systematically leans towards the left or the right, mass media outlets maximise their profits by providing content that is biased in the same direction. They can do so, because it is cheaper to hire journalists that write stories which are consistent with their political position. A concurrent theory would be that supply and demand would cause media to attain a neutral balance because consumers would of course gravitate towards the media they agreed with. This argument fails in considering the imbalance in self-reported political allegiances by journalists themselves, that distort any market analogy as regards offer: (...) *Indeed, in 1982, 85 percent of Columbia Graduate School of Journalism students identified themselves as liberal, versus 11 percent conservative"*, quoted in Sutter, 2001.

This same argument would have news outlets in equal numbers increasing profits of a more balanced media far more than the slight increase in costs to hire unbiased journalists, notwithstanding the extreme rarity of self-reported conservative journalists.

As mentioned above, Tim Groseclose of UCLA and Jeff Milyo of the University of Missouri at Columbia use think tank quotes, in order to estimate the relative position of mass media outlets in the political spectrum. The idea is to trace out which think tanks are quoted by various mass media outlets within news stories, and to match these think tanks with the political position of members of the U.S. Congress who quote them in a non-negative way. Using this procedure, Groseclose and Milyo obtain the stark result that all sampled news providers -except Fox News' Special Report and the Washington Times- are located to the left of the average Congress member, i.e. there are signs of a liberal bias in the US news media. However, the news media also show a remarkable degree of centrism, just because all outlets but one are located -from an ideological point of view- between the average Democrat and average Republican in Congress.

The methods Groseclose and Milyo used to calculate this bias have been criticized by Mark Liberman, a professor of Computer Science at the University of Pennsylvania. Liberman concludes by saying he thinks "that many if not most of the complaints directed against G&M are motivated in part by ideological disagreement — just as much of the praise for their work is motivated by ideological agreement. It would be nice if there were a less politically fraught body of data on which such modeling exercises could be explored."

Sendhil Mullainathan and Andrei Shleifer of Harvard University construct a behavioural model, which is built around the assumption that readers and viewers hold beliefs that they would like to see confirmed by news providers. When news customers share common beliefs, profit-maximizing media outlets find it optimal to select and/or frame stories in order to pander to those beliefs. On the other hand, when beliefs are heterogeneous, news providers differentiate their offer and segment the market, by providing news stories that are slanted towards the two extreme positions in the spectrum of beliefs.

Matthew Gentzkow and Jesse Shapiro of Chicago GSB present another demand-driven theory of mass media bias. If readers and viewers have a priori views on the current state of affairs and are uncertain about the quality of the information about it being provided by media outlets, then the latter have an incentive to slant stories towards their customers' prior beliefs, in order to build and keep a reputation for high-quality journalism.

The reason for this is that rational agents would tend to believe that pieces of information that go against their prior beliefs in fact originate from low-quality news providers. The economics empirical literature on mass media bias mainly focuses on the United States.

Steve Ansolabehere, Rebecca Lessem and Jim Snyder of the Massachusetts Institute of Technology analyze the political orientation of endorsements by U.S. newspapers. They find an upward trend in the average propensity to endorse a candidate, and in particular an incumbent one. There are also some changes in the average ideological slant of endorsements: while in the 40s and in the 50s there was a clear advantage to Republican candidates, this advantage continuously eroded in subsequent decades, to the extent that in the 90s the authors find a slight Democratic lead in the average endorsement choice.

John Lott and Kevin Hassett of the American Enterprise Institute study the coverage of economic news by looking at a panel of 389 U.S. newspapers from 1991 to 2004, and from 1985 to 2004 for a subsample comprising the top 10 newspapers and the Associated Press. For each release of official data about a set of economic indicators, the authors analyze how newspapers decide to report on them, as reflected by the tone of the related headlines. The idea is to check whether newspapers display some kind of partisan bias, by giving more positive or negative coverage to the same economic figure, as a function of the political affiliation of the incumbent President. Controlling for the economic data being released, the authors find that there are between 9.6 and 14.7 percent fewer positive stories when the incumbent President is a Republican.

Riccardo Puglisi of the Massachusetts Institute of Technology looks at the editorial choices of the *New York Times* from 1946 to 1997. He finds that the *Times* displays Democratic partisanship, with some watchdog aspects. This is the case, because during presidential campaigns the Times systematically gives more coverage to Democratic topics of civil rights, health care, labor and social welfare, but only when the incumbent president is a Republican. These topics are classified as Democratic ones, because Gallup polls show that on average U.S. citizens think that Democratic candidates would be better at handling problems related to them. According to Puglisi, in the post-1960 period the Times displays a more symmetric type of watchdog behaviour, just because during presidential campaigns it also gives more coverage to the typically Republican issue of Defense when the incumbent President is a Democrat, and less so when the incumbent is a Republican.

Alan Gerber and Dean Karlan of Yale University use an experimental approach to examine not whether the media are biased, but whether the media influence political decisions and attitudes. They conduct a randomized control trial just prior to the November 2005 gubernatorial election in Virginia and randomly assign individuals in Northern Virginia to (a) a treatment group that receives a free subscription to the Washington Post, (b) a treatment group that receives a free subscription to the Washington Times, or (c) a control group. They find that those who are assigned to the Washington Post treatment group are eight percentage points more likely to vote for the Democrat in the elections. The report also found that "exposure to either newspaper was weakly linked to a movement away from the Bush administration and Republicans."

Another unaffiliated group, Media Study Group, established seven categories of poor journalistic practice: for example, the journalist stating personal opinion in a report, asserting incorrect facts, applying unequal space or treatment to two sides of a controversial issue; then analyzed The Age Newspaper (Melbourne Australia) for the frequency of infraction of this code of practice. The resultant instances were then analyzed statistically with respect to the frequency they supported one or other side of the two-sided controversial issue under consideration. The goal of this group was to establish a quantitative methodology for the study of bias.

A self-described progressive media watchdog group, Fairness and Accuracy in Reporting, in consultation with the Survey and Evaluation Research Laboratory at Virginia Commonwealth University, sponsored a rigorous academic study in which journalists were asked a range of questions about how they did their work and about how they viewed the quality of media coverage in the broad area of politics and economic policy. "They were asked for their opinions and views about a range of recent policy issues and debates. Finally, they were asked for demographic and identifying information, including their political orientation". They then compared to the say or similar questions posed with "the public" based on Gallup, and Pew Trust polls. Their study concluded that a majority of journalists, although relatively liberal on social policies, were significantly to the right of the public on economic, labor, health care and foreign policy issues.

This study continues: "we learn much more about the political orientation of news content by looking at sourcing patterns rather than journalists' personal views. As this survey shows, it is government officials and business representatives to whom journalists "nearly always" turn when covering economic policy. Labor representatives and consumer advocates were at the bottom of the list. This is consistent with earlier research on sources. For example, analysts from the centrist Brookings Institution and conservative think tanks such as the Heritage Foundation and the American Enterprise Institute are those most quoted in mainstream news accounts; liberal think tanks are often invisible. When it comes to sources, 'liberal bias' is nowhere to be found."

Experimenter Bias

A major problem in studies is experimenter bias. Research into studies of media bias in the United States shows that Liberal experimenters tend to get results that say the media has a conservative bias, while conservatives experimenters tend to get results that say the media has a liberal bias, and those who do not identify themselves as either liberal or conservative get results indicating little bias, or mixed bias. This same problem with experimenter bias extends to the studies of experimenter bias, of course. Whether bias is toward the left or the right depends on where you stand. The study "A Measure of Media Bias" by political scientist Timothy J. Groseclose of UCLA and economist Jeffrey D. Milyo of the University of Missouri-Columbia, purports to rank news organisations in terms of identifying with liberal or conservative values relative to each other.

They used the Americans for Democratic Action (ADA) scores as a quantitative proxy for political leanings of the referential organizations. Thus their definition of "liberal" includes the RAND Corporation, a nonprofit research organization with strong ties to the Defense Department. According to Media Matters for America (a non-profit progressive research and information center), "the study employed a measure of "bias" so problematic that its findings are next to useless". What is "liberal" in the United States may not be "liberal" by world standards. FAIR suggests that a benchmark for each country be set by scientific polling of a cross-section of the citizens. Another source of bias is the fact that some studies are reported by the media, and other stories are not. The case study "A Measure of Media Bias" discussed above was widely reported in the United States. George Orwell pointed out that in the UK during the last century businesses did not undermine their own interests by reporting leftist (anti business or pro-labor) information. In the United States Ben Bagdikian documents a long history of advertisers pulling out support when media content becomes too controversial.

Tools for Measuring and Evaluating Media Bias

Richard Alan Nelson's (2003) study cited above on *Tracking Propaganda to the Source: Tools for Analyzing Media Bias* reports there are at least 12 methods used to analyze the existence of and quantify bias:

1. Surveys of the political/cultural attitudes of journalists, particularly members of the media elite, and of journalism students.
2. Studies of journalists' previous professional connections.

3. Collections of quotations in which prominent journalists reveal their beliefs about politics and/or the proper role of their profession.
4. Computer word-use and topic analysis searches to determine content and labeling.
5. Studies of policies recommended in news stories.
6. Comparisons of the agenda of the news and entertainment media with agendas of political candidates or other activists.
7. Positive/negative coverage analysis.
8. Reviews of the personal demographics of media decision makers.
9. Comparisons of advertising sources/content which influence information/entertainment content.
10. Analyses of the extent of government propaganda and public relations (PR) industry impact on media.
11. Studies of the use of experts and spokespersons etc. by media vs. those not selected to determine the interest groups and ideologies represented vs. those excluded.
12. Research into payments of journalists by corporations and trade associations to speak before their groups and the impact that may have on coverage.

Efforts to Correct Bias

One technique used to avoid bias is the "point/counterpoint" or "round table," an adversarial format in which representatives of opposing views comment on an issue. This approach theoretically allows diverse views to appear in the media. However, the person organizing the report still has the responsibility to choose people who really represent the breadth of opinion, to ask them non-prejudicial questions, and to edit or arbitrate their comments fairly. When done carelessly, a point/counterpoint can be as unfair as a simple biased report, by suggesting that the "losing" side lost on its merits.

The Skeptics Society has accused reporters of misusing

the point/counterpoint format by giving more time to superstitions than to their scientific rebuttals. Using this format can also lead to accusations that the reporter has created a misleading appearance that viewpoints have equal validity (sometimes called "false balance"). This may happen when a taboo exists around one of the viewpoints, or when one of the representatives habitually makes claims that are easily shown to be inaccurate.

One such allegation of misleading balance came from Mark Halperin, political director of ABC News. He stated in an internal e-mail message that reporters should not "artificially hold [George W. Bush and John Kerry] 'equally' accountable" to the public interest, and that complaints from Bush supporters were an attempt to "get away with ... renewed efforts to win the election by destroying Senator Kerry." When the Drudge Report published this message, many Bush supporters viewed it as "smoking gun" evidence that Halperin was using ABC to propagandize against Bush to Kerry's benefit, by interfering with reporters' attempts to avoid bias. An academic content analysis of election news later found that coverage at ABC, CBS, and NBC was more favorable toward Kerry than Bush, while coverage at Fox News Channel was more favorable toward Bush.

Scott Norvell is London bureau chief for Fox News. On May 20 in an interview with the Wall Street Journal he said, "Even we at Fox News manage to get some lefties on the air occasionally, and often let them finish their sentences before we club them to death and feed the scraps to Karl Rove and Bill O'Reilly.

And those who hate us can take solace in the fact that they aren't subsidizing Bill's bombast; we payers of the BBC license fee don't enjoy that peace of mind. Fox News is, after all, a private channel and our presenters are quite open about where they stand on particular stories. That's our appeal. People watch us because they know what they are getting. The Beeb's (British Broadcasting Corporation) (BBC) institutionalized leftism would be easier to tolerate if the corporation was a little more honest about it". With the release of the 2008 book *What*

Happened: Inside the Bush White House and Washington's Culture of Deception by George W. Bush's press secretary Scott McClellan, there are some who contend that this is evidence of Mark Halperin being correct instead of biased. In his book, McClellan admits to lying to the media, and describes the contempt he felt for reporters who so easily believed his lies, and were cowed by the fear that if they exposed the lies, they would be accused of "liberal bias". Another technique used to avoid bias is disclosure of affiliations that may be considered a possible conflict of interest. This is especially apparent when a news organization is reporting a story with some relevancy to the news organization itself or to its ownership individuals or conglomerate.

Often this disclosure is mandated by the laws or regulations pertaining to stocks and securities. Commentators on news stories involving stocks are often required to disclose any ownership interest in those corporations or in its competitors. In rare cases, a news organization may dismiss or reassign staff members who appear biased. This approach was used in the Killian documents affair and after Peter Arnett's interview with the Iraqi press. This approach is presumed to have been employed in the case of Dan Rather over a heavily biased story that he ran on 60 Minutes in the month prior to the 2004 election that attempted to impugn the military record of George W. Bush by relying on obviously fake documents that were provided by a Democrat Party operative.

Finally, some countries have laws enforcing balance in state-owned media. Since 1991, the CBC and Radio Canada, its Francophone counterpart, are governed by the Broadcasting Act. This act states, amongst other things: The programming provided by the Canadian broadcasting system should (i) be varied and comprehensive, providing a balance of information, enlightenment and entertainment for men, women and children of all ages, interests and tastes, (ii) provide a reasonable opportunity for the public to be exposed to the expression of differing views on matters of public concern.

Political bias has been a feature of the mass media since

its birth with the invention of the printing press. The expense of early printing equipment restricted media production to a limited number of people. Historians have found that publishers often served the interests of powerful social groups. John Milton's pamphlet *Areopagitica, a Speech for the Liberty of Unlicensed Printing*, published in 1644, was one of the first publications advocating freedom of the press.

In the nineteenth century, journalists began to recognize the concept of unbiased reporting as an integral part of journalistic ethics. This coincided with the rise of journalism as a powerful social force. Even today, though, the most conscientiously objective journalists cannot avoid accusations of bias. Like newspapers, the broadcast media (radio and television) have been used as a mechanism for propaganda from their earliest days, a tendency made more pronounced by the initial ownership of broadcast spectrum by national governments. Although a process of media deregulation has placed the majority of the western broadcast media in private hands, there still exists a strong government presence, or even monopoly, in the broadcast media of many countries across the globe. At the same time, the concentration of media in private hands, and frequently amongst a comparatively small number of individuals, has also lead to accusations of media bias.

There are many examples of accusations of bias being used as a political tool, sometimes resulting in government censorship. In the United States, in 1798, Congress passed the Alien and Sedition Acts, which prohibited newspapers from publishing "false, scandalous, or malicious writing" against the government, including any public opposition to any law or presidential act. This act was in effect until 1801. During the American Civil War, President Abraham Lincoln accused newspapers in the border states of bias in favor of the Southern cause, and ordered many newspapers closed.

Chancellor Adolf Hitler of Germany, in the years leading up to World War II, accused newspapers of Marxist bias, an accusation echoed by pro-German media in England and the

United States. Politicians who favored the United States entering World War II on the German side asserted that the international media were controlled by Jews, and that reports of German mistreatment of Jews were biased and without foundation. Hollywood was said to be a hotbed of Jewish bias, and films such as Charlie Chaplin's The Great Dictator were offered as proof.

In the 1980s, the government of South Africa accused newspapers of liberal bias and instituted government censorship. In 1989, the newspaper *New Nation* was closed by the government for three months for publishing anti-apartheid propaganda. Other newspapers were not closed, but were extensively censored. Some published the censored sections blacked out, to demonstrate the extent of government censorship. In the USA during the labor union movement and the civil rights movement, newspapers supporting liberal social reform were accused by conservative newspapers of communist bias.

Film and television media were accused of bias in favor of mixing of the races, and many television programs with racially mixed casts, such as *I Spy* and *Star Trek*, were not aired on Southern stations. During the war between the United States and North Vietnam, Vice President Spiro Agnew accused newspapers of anti-American bias, and in a famous speech delivered in San Diego in 1970, called anti-war protesters "The nattering nabobs of negativism." Not all accusations of bias are political. Science writer Martin Gardner has accused the entertainment media of anti-science bias. He claims that television programs such as *The X-Files* promote superstition. In contrast, the Competitive Enterprise Institute accuses the media of being biased in favor of science and against business interests, and of credulously reporting science that purports to show that greenhouse gasses cause global warming.

Role of Language

Mass media, despite its ability to project worldwide, is limited in its cross-ethnic compatibility by one simple attribute - language. Ethnicity, being largely developed by a divergence in geography, language, culture, genes and similarly, point of view, has the potential to be countered by a common source of information. Therefore, language, in the absence of translation, comprises a barrier to a worldwide community of debate and opinion, although it is also true that media within any given society may be split along class, political or regional lines. Furthermore, if the language is translated, the translator has room to shift a bias by choosing weighed words for translation.

Language may also be seen as a political factor in mass media, particularly in instances where a society is characterized by a large number of languages spoken by its populace. The choice of language of mass media may represent a bias towards the group most likely to speak that language, and can limit the public participation by those who do not speak the language. On the other hand, there have also been attempts to use a common-language mass media to reach out to a large, geographically dispersed population, such as in the use of Arabic language by news channel Al Jazeera.

Many media theorists concerned with language and media bias point towards the media of the United States, a large country where English is spoken by the vast majority of the population. Some theorists argue that the common language is not homogenizing; and that there still remain strong differences expressed within the mass media. This viewpoint asserts that moderate views are bolstered by drawing influences from the extremes of the political spectrum. In the United States, the national news therefore contributes to a sense of cohesion within the society, proceeding from a similarly informed population. According to this model, most views within society are freely expressed, and the mass media are accountable to the people and tends to reflect the spectrum of opinion.

Language may also be a more subtle form of bias. Use of a word with positive or negative connotations rather than a more neutral synonym can form a biased picture in the audience's mind. It makes a difference whether the media calls a group "terrorist" or "freedom fighters" or "insurgents". For example, a 2005 memo to the staff of the CBC states:

Rather than calling assailants "terrorists," we can refer to them as bombers, hijackers, gunmen (if we're sure no women were in the group), militants, extremists, attackers or some other appropriate noun. In a widely criticized episode, initial online BBC reports of the 7 July 2005 London bombings identified the perpetrators as terrorists, in contradiction to the BBC's internal policy. But by the next day, Tom Gross and many others noted that the online articles had been edited, replacing "terrorists" by "bombers". In another case, March 28, 2007, the broadcaster paid almost $400,000 in legal fees in a London court to keep an internal memo dealing with alleged anti-Israeli bias from becoming public. BBC was accused of pro-Palestinian bias over a documentary about Israel developing a nuclear weapon during the second Palestinian intifada in 2000.

National and Ethnic Viewpoint

Many news organizations reflect or are perceived to reflect in some way the viewpoint of the geographic, ethnic, and national population that they primarily serve. Media within countries is sometimes seen as being sycophantic or unquestioning about the country's government. Western media are often criticized in the rest of the world (including eastern Europe, Asia, Africa, and the Middle East) as being pro-Western with regard to a variety of political, cultural and economic issues. Al Jazeera has been frequently criticized in the West about its coverage of Arab world issues. The Israeli-Palestinian conflict and wider Arab-Israeli issues are a particularly controversial area, and nearly all coverage of any kind generates accusation of bias from one or both sides.

Anglophone Bias in the World Media

It has been observed that the world's principal suppliers of news, the news agencies, and the main buyers of news are Anglophone corporations and this gives an Anglophone bias to the selection and depiction of events. Anglophone definitions of what constitutes news are paramount; the news provided originates in Anglophone capitals and responds first to their own rich domestic markets. Despite the plethora of news services, most news printed and broadcast throughout the world each day comes from only a few major agencies, the three largest of which are the Associated Press, Reuters and Agence France-Presse.

Although these agencies are 'global' in the sense of their activities, they each retain significant associations with particular nations, namely France (AFP), the United States (AP) and the United Kingdom (Reuters). Chambers and Tinckell suggest that the so-called global media are agents of Anglophone values which privilege norms of 'competitive individualism, laissez faire capitalism, parliamentary democracy and consumerism.' They see the presentation of the English language as international as a further feature of Anglophone dominance.

Vis-a-Vis Religious Issues

Media bias towards religion is most obvious in countries where the media are controlled by the state, which is in turn dominated by a particular religion. In these instances, bias against other faiths can be explicit and virulent. But even in countries with freedom of religion and a free press, the dominant religion exerts some amount of influence on the media. In nations where Christianity is the majority faith, reporters tend to focus on the activities of the Christian community, to the exclusion of other faiths. But the opposite may also occur, with media self-consciously avoiding reporting on any religious matters at all in order to avoid the appearance of favoring one faith over another, or presenting religious faith and phenomenon in a negative light.

This type of bias is often seen with reporting on new religious movements. It is often the case that the only view the public gets of a new religious movement, controversial group or purported cult is a negative and sensationalized report by the media. For example, most new or minority religious movements only receive media coverage when something sensational occurs, e.g. the mass suicide of a cult or illegal activities of a leader in the religious movement. According to the Encyclopedia of Social Work (19th edition), the news media play an influential role in the general public's perception of cults.

As reported in several studies, the media have depicted cults as problematic, controversial, and threatening from the beginning, tending to favor sensationalistic stories over balanced public debates. It furthers the analysis that media reports on cults rely heavily on police officials and cult "experts" who portray cult activity as dangerous and destructive, and when divergent views are presented, they are often overshadowed by horrific stories of ritualistic torture, sexual abuse, mind control, etc. Furthermore, unfounded allegations, when proved untrue, receive little or no media attention.

Other Influences

The apparent bias of media is not always specifically political in nature. The news media tend to appeal to a specific audience, which means that stories that affect a large number of people on a global scale often receive less coverage in some markets than local stories, such as a public school shootings, a celebrity wedding, a plane crash, or similarly glamorous or shocking stories. For example, the deaths of millions of people in an ethnic conflict in Africa might be afforded scant mention in American media, while the shooting of five people in a high school is analyzed in depth. The reason for this type of bias is a function of what the public wants to watch and/or what producers and publishers believe the public wants to watch.

Bias has also been claimed in instances referred to as conflict of interest, whereby the owners of media outlets have vested interests in other commercial enterprises or political parties. In such cases in the United States, the media outlet is required to disclose the conflict of interest. However, the decisions of the editorial department of a newspaper and the corporate parent frequently are not connected, as the editorial staff retains freedom to decide what is covered as well as what isn't. Biases, real or implied, frequently arise when it comes to deciding what stories will be covered and who will be called for those stories.

Accusations that a source is biased, if accepted, may cause media consumers to distrust certain kinds of statements, and place added confidence on others. For example, if readers believe that a particular newspaper is conservatively biased, they may feel that a pro-liberal article in that paper *must* be true. Conversely, they may assume that a pro-conservative article in that paper is suspect. Because of the possibility of influencing the public in this way, accusations about which media outlets are biased, and how, have become a very common occurrence.

Evidence from Tobacco Control

There is widespread appreciation that the media has an influence on health behaviours. In most instances, the perception among public health advocates is that this impact is primarily negative (such as tobacco use, obesity, violence). In a few other cases, the media framing of a health problem is less contentious; what is debated is how to harness the media for improving public health. In the past year, I have heard repeatedly from international HIV prevention experts that *what we need to do is launch the same type of media campaigns to change social norms that the tobacco control community has done.* Unfortunately, this call is then followed by a riff on the need for 'hard-hitting, fear-arousal'-types of efforts. What is unfortunate is that these experts do not appreciate the multiplicity of media efforts that have gone into developing tobacco control media activities – they have not simply been emotional television ads.

The National Cancer Institute has published the monograph *The role of the media in preventing and reducing tobacco use.* It should be required reading for anyone using, or considering using, the mass media in any of its forms to address public health issues from obesity to mental illness to climate change. The monograph is a collection of chapters reviewing the empirical evidence on the role of mass media on tobacco use including industry marketing and promotion practices (often the playbook for other industries), tobacco portrayal in news and entertainment media, tobacco control media interventions, and the use of the media by the industry to weaken tobacco control efforts (pay attention to this one too).

Here's a sampling of some of the conclusions, pulled from the Executive Summary (pdf file), to start your thinking. The key in reading this list, and the monograph, is to make the inference to your own issue and the players and practice that you face. I write this remembering a nutrition professional who after listening to me talk about tobacco advertising and promotion practices and their influence on tobacco use raised her hand and innocently asked: could the food industry do the same thing to encourage excessive consumption, and therefore obesity? Yes they (and others) DO.

- The total weight of evidence - from multiple types of studies, conducted by investigators from different disciplines, and using data from many countries - demonstrates a causal relationship between tobacco advertising and promotion and increased tobacco use.
- Tobacco advertising has been dominated by three themes: providing satisfaction (taste, freshness, mildness, etc.), assuaging anxieties about the dangers of smoking, and creating associations between smoking and desirable outcomes (independence, social success, sexual attraction, thinness, etc.).
- Targeting various population groups - including men, women, youth and young adults, specific racial and ethnic populations, religious groups, the working class, and gay and lesbian populations - has been strategically important to the tobacco industry.
- Substantial evidence exists from the United States and several other countries that tobacco companies typically respond to partial advertising bans in ways that undermine the ban's effectiveness. These responses

include shifting promotional expenditures from "banned" media to "permitted" media (which may include emerging technologies and "new" media), changing the types and targets of advertising in permitted media, using tobacco-product brand names for nontobacco products and services,

- Corporate sponsorship of events and social causes represents a key public relations strategy for major tobacco companies, which spent more than $360 million on these efforts in 2003. Key targets included sporting events, antihunger organizations, and arts and minority organizations. These efforts have been used, in certain cases, to influence opinion leaders who benefit from such sponsorship.
- Corporate image campaigns by tobacco companies have highlighted their charitable work in the community and have promoted their youth smoking prevention programs; at times, corporate spending on these campaigns has vastly exceeded the amount actually given to the charities. These campaigns have reduced perceptions among adolescents and adults that tobacco companies are dishonest and culpable for adolescent smoking, and among adults, have increased perceptions of responsible marketing practices and favorable ratings for the individual companies.
- Strong and consistent evidence from longitudinal studies indicates that exposure to cigarette advertising influences nonsmoking adolescents to initiate smoking and to move toward regular smoking.
- The studies of tobacco advertising bans in various countries show that comprehensive bans reduce tobacco consumption. Noncomprehensive restrictions generally induce an increase in expenditures for advertising in "nonbanned" media and for other marketing activities, which offset the effect of the partial ban so that any net change in consumption is minimal or undetectable.

- News coverage that supports tobacco control has been shown to set the agenda for further change at the community, state, and national levels. Despite this, organized media advocacy efforts on behalf of tobacco control issues remain an underutilized area of activity within public health.
- Experimental studies show that images of cigarette smoking in film can influence adolescent and adult viewers' beliefs about social norms for smoking, beliefs about the function and consequences of smoking, and their personal intentions to smoke. Protobacco movie content (e.g., stars smoking, absence of health consequences portrayed) appears to promote prosmoking beliefs and intentions. The effects observed for experimental studies of smoking in movies on viewers' smoking-related beliefs are of a similar magnitude as those observed in experimental media research on other health topics (e.g., effects of media violence on viewers' aggression).
- The total weight of evidence from cross-sectional, longitudinal, and experimental studies, combined with the high theoretical plausibility from the perspective of social influences, indicates a causal relationship between exposure to movie smoking depictions and youth smoking initiation.
- Numerous studies have shown consistently that advertising carrying strong negative messages about health consequences performs better in affecting target audience appraisals and indicators of message processing (such as recall of the advertisement, thinking more about it, discussing it) compared with other forms of advertising, such as humorous or emotionally neutral advertisements. Some of these negative advertisements also portray deception on the part of the tobacco industry. Advertisements for smoking cessation products and tobacco-industry sponsored smoking prevention advertising have been shown to elicit significantly poorer target audience appraisals than do advertisements based on negative health consequences.

- Population-based studies of antitobacco mass media campaigns that were only one component of multicomponent tobacco control programs provide considerable evidence for reduced use of tobacco by youth and adults. The antitobacco mass media campaign and the other program components together may have reduced smoking more than did any single component alone. The relative contributions of various components to program effectiveness are difficult to determine, but some of the controlled field experiments showed a dose-response relationship between reduced smoking and an increased number of program components.
- Increasing consumer awareness of tobacco industry activities to counteract public-health-sponsored campaigns designed to reduce tobacco use can be an important component of effective media interventions.
- The tobacco industry consistently has used several primary themes to defeat state tobacco tax increase initiatives. These include suggestions that the measures would impose unfair taxes and that tax revenues would not be spent on health care or tobacco control programs as intended. Secondary themes used consistently over an 18-year time span include that the measures would increase "big government" and wasteful spending, discriminate against smokers, and increase crime and smuggling. Other, less frequent themes were that the measures would be a tax cut for the rich, impede economic growth, fail to solve state budget problems, restrict personal choice, and violate antitrust laws.

The point here is with a research base that is probably the most extensive with respect to the role of the media and a health behaviour (well, with the exception of the portrayal of aggression on television and violent behaviours which we have known about since the early 1960s), you have to think about media in the broadest possible way – including new media, movies, news coverage, editorial pages and the public policies that govern them. It is not just advertisements, entertainment-education or mass media campaigns. Research in this area is also finding that it is the exposures to multiple channels, rather than the magic bullet, that is most likely to lead to behaviour change. If researchers would stop asking the wrong question of "which one is it" among a multi-component program and focus instead on how to maximize the impact of media multiplexity, we will move further along the path of developing better interventions across channels that are relevant to our priority audience. Changing social norms is an admirable goal, but unless behaviours change and policies are in place to encourage, reinforce and sustain the changes and normative shifts, we are undertaking a Sisyphean task: the norms will always roll back on us after short-lived gains.

5

Social Change and Participatory Communications

We stand for democracy that strengthens human spirits and communities, for consistent democracy that addresses injustices and inequalities of power. Organizers also recognize that an individual person or organization may escape or overcome power inequalities, but s/he can rarely change them. We say, "If it takes a whole village to raise a child, it takes a whole social movement to raise an issue." Social justice organizing—the layering of relationships and networks around a shared vision of a more just world—is inseparable from the act of communicating. At heart, organizing is about communication. Organizer foster dialogs through which people come to a shared vision, a shared strategy, and a shared plan for executing that strategy. Dialogs establish networks that can gather resources, set priorities, resolve differences, and draw lessons. A group's communications strategy defines the many ways that an organization connects, that is, communicates with important members, allies, broader publics and even target institutions—anyone needed to achieve its vision.

Mass-mediated societies present particular challenges to social justice movements. We describe those challenges below. After defining what we mean by power and collective action, we describe our participatory communication model. It grew from our two decades of collaboration with global north movement organizations but resonates with movement-building approaches common in the global south. We summarize its core elements and suggest how movement organizations can incorporate them in their organizing. In concluding, we caution that many debates among media activists pit forms of media activism against each other although these forms could be retooled to work synergistically to build movement strength and simultaneously broaden needed support for the media reform movement. We conclude with a ten-step practical guide.

Populist pundit, Kevin Philips suggests, "Power is the ability to say what the issue is and who the good guys and bad guys are. That is power." The ability to promote and reinforce what the issue is and who's responsible (framing) assumes, however, control over webs of institutionalized power relations—interacting layers of agenda-setting, rule-making, rule enforcement as well as resource allocation. It takes resources to run the media machines that shape meaning (public opinion). Publics' opinions, in turn, affect the election of rule-makers, the legislators who pose agendas, make laws and oversee their enforcement by agencies such as Federal Communication Commission (FCC) which controls the country's airwaves. Within organizations, leaders exercise communicative power in direct and mass media formats to translate political strategy into a communication strategy. A communication strategy sets audiences priorities, frames messages and chooses how to engage prioritized audiences, i.e., the communities whose support can help move the issue at hand.

Organizers build collective actors—ever widening networks of people committed to a common mission. Working from the core and moving out, organizers use each layer of contacts to establish the next, each layer making the next layer of contact much easier. The value of organizing from the inside out is that there is always a place to start. Every group needs to create a solid foundation, a safe space from which to operate by taking its core members seriously and working from that safe space. Regardless of what happens on a regional and national level, local organizations can begin to work within their own organizations and/or coalitions. A communications strategy maps how an organization communicates its mission and vision to the range of communities whose support is desired. Thus, communications strategy builds from an organization's mission and overall strategy. If a group lacks a clear strategy, the media spotlight will highlight precisely that lack of direction. There is no communication strategy until there is an organizing strategy.

Mass media form the master forum of our historical time, the space to which publics look to follow political debates. In choosing what the issues are, whom to quote and whom to ignore, mass media outlets through editors and reporters acting as gatekeepers exerting power —they decide whose accounts count. Accounts that count gain visibility; the accounts' sponsors use that visibility to gain political ground. Accounts that don't count lack visibility; these accounts' sponsors face marginalization. Given mass media's power, most social movements struggle to achieve media standing even as they build independent communication capacity. The problem of media marginalization is, again, about power. No message gets transmitted without active sponsorship, and sustained, active sponsorship requires resources and organization.

Only by forming collective actors can marginalized communities accrue and focus the resources needed to create and maintain communications infrastructure— media data bases, regular news monitoring, rapid response capacity, messaging systems, etc. Without such infrastructure, communication might be initiated but not sustained. Even when, movement organizers have few illusions of gaining routine access to mass media, they hesitate to give opponents free reign in such an important arena of social contest. Activists operate from the "hope at least of breaking the appearance of unanimity which is the greater part of the symbolic force of the dominant discourse."

Media criticism and independent media play essential roles in breaking the appearance of consensus. Given the importance of mass media as a convening system through which Americans talk politics, most activists also engage with mass media MMRAP's experiences with many partnering social movement organizations suggests that in the U.S. context, most movement communications strategies must integrate three components—independent media, media monitoring and criticism, and mass media.

Engaging with Mass Media

Additionally, we argue that many debates about communication among progressive groups have been misplaced debates pitting different forms of media activism against one another rather than seeing them as parts of a synergistic whole. What holds the disparate parts together is a world view—a shared understanding or vision of a more just society. This shared vision as practiced by MMRAP (Movement Media Research Action Project) and its movement and community partners has five core elements. Focus on power inequalities. Communication arenas embody the same power inequalities as the rest of social life. We organize against marginalization here as in other social arenas. Those marginalized by power inequalities must be at the table in communication planning. Build collective action. While individuals and individual organizations can gain standing in media institutions, only movements—fields of collective actors— can change media institutions.

All organizing entails short-term wars of maneuver within longer term wars of position. (Gramsci) Communication campaigns serve longer-term strategic goals. Be reflexive. Learning builds as collective actors engage in cycles of dialog, action and reflection with potential allies. Social movement organizations are learning communities. Develop self critical governance to build a more just world; we seek to eliminate institutionalized inequalities of power. We begin by creating consistent democratic practices internally, in coalitions, and in public arenas. Racism, sexism, homophobia, class & nat'l inequalities are ours to solve. Take as a whole, these core elements comprise a justice-centered, power-sensitive world view that puts various approaches to media organizing into perspective. It also makes it possible to move beyond polarization (mass media or independent media) so that activists can integrate multiple media approaches in the service of social justice movements.

Social marketing, for instance, offers useful tools for assessing existing opinion but falls short in focusing on individual rather than institutional change. Media advocacy proponents add social policy to a social marketing approach, but media advocacy often fails to open strategic decision-making to those directly affected. (To advocate, is to speak for another, not to empower). Civic journalism, similarly, reinvigorates journalists' as social critics and community builders. But just as with media advocates, civic journalists in their enthusiasm to achieve a short-term institutional goal, can forget to embed a reform in empowerment and movement building. In sum, we urge organizers to use all encounters with media to extend movement building.

Only in this way, can we widen and deepen support for democratic media reforms such as those proposed by the media reform movement. It will take collective action to democratize mass media. We embrace a holistic approach that includes independent media, media criticism and engagement with mainstream media. We link communication strategy both to political strategy for individual movements and to strategies for reforming the media as a critical social arena in itself. We will accomplish this by creating conscious collective actors grounding action in dialog and reflection. In cycles of dialog, action and reflection we will develop needed power analyses and strategy, then modify these based on our lived experiences.

AN INTEGRATED MODEL OF COMMUNICATION FOR SOCIAL CHANGE

The guiding philosophy of communication for social change can readily be traced to the work of Paulo Freire (1970),the Brazilian educator who conceived of communication as dialogue and participation for the purpose of creating cultural identity, trust, commitment, ownership and empowerment (in today's term).

The proposed model builds on this principle and a broad literature on development communication developed by practitioners, communication activists and scholars (such as Beltran, Díaz Bordenave, Calvelo, Shirley White, Prieto Castillo, Everett Rogers, Mata, Simpson, Servaes, Portales and Kincaid), as well as on theories of communication, dialogue and conflict resolution. In bringing together the work of practitioners and scholars we have found that there is considerable agreement on the role of communication in development even though at various times over the last 30 years the two groups have diverged. In this sense, special recognition should be given to the practitioners convened by the Rockefeller initiative for reigniting the dialogue and re-examination of the role of communication in development.

We are also indebted to other issue-framing activities, such as the recent UNAIDS communication framework, that was developed through a worldwide process that brought together communication specialists and practitioners working in the field of HIV/AIDS prevention. Many of the practitioners and scholars involved in these activities also participate actively in online debate through the Communication Initiative's Drumbeat. This interaction between theory and practice, through the dialogue among practitioners and scholars, will undoubtedly produce valuable contributions and insights for the field of development communication. It is inappropriate to base a model of communication for social change on a linear model of communication that describes what happens when an individual source transmits a message to a receiver or group of receivers with some desired and predetermined individual effect.

For social change, a model of communication is required that is cyclical and relational and leads to an outcome of mutual change rather than one-sided, individual change. In this section we provide a brief description of such a model: communication as dialogue rather than monologue, as a cyclical process of information sharing which leads to mutual understanding, mutual agreement and collective action. This alternative model serves as the foundation upon which the Communication for Social Change Model is based. The community as defined in this document is a multilevel concept ranging from local, geographically defined entities, such as villages, cities and nations, to international entities widely dispersed in space and time, such as activists organized by means of the Internet to protest the World Trade Organization. It also includes issue-related groups, such as the gay community, professional organizations and even the development communication community itself.

The model also recognizes that communities are not homogeneous entities but are comprised of subgroups with social strata and divergent interests. As a consequence, disagreement and conflict are also incorporated into the communication for social-change model. The full layout of the model is presented in this section. The model also acknowledges that external constraints and supports often hinder or facilitate community dialogue and collective action.

Communication as Dialogue

Theories are not right or wrong, only appropriate or inappropriate given the circumstances and nature of the phenomenon to which they are applied. For example, the theory of reasoned action, the health-belief model, and the stages of change model may all work quite well for communication projects designed to persuade individuals to reduce unsaturated fat in their diet, quit smoking and drinking, and practice safer sex, especially in situations where external constraints (social or physical) do not prevent or discourage individuals from taking action by themselves. Even in these situations, however, models of individual change reach their own, inherent limitations. For example, when the research shows that social influence and peer pressure are the major determinants of smoking and drinking, then finding the best rational arguments against smoking and drinking are simply not sufficient.

Collective, institutional changes, policies and laws – such as the smoke-free workplace and a maximum, legal blood-alcohol level – are also necessary. In other situations, the prevention of a disease may only be possible by means of collective action. The risk of getting dengue fever can be reduced by eliminating all of the standing water sources (e.g., tin cans, old tires, etc.) around one's house. This individual behaviour is ineffective; however, if none of one's neighbors within the range of flight of mosquitoes eliminates the standing water around their houses as well. If everyone does not do it, what is the point of anyone doing it? The response must be collective. Some type of community dialogue and collective, cooperative action is required to solve the problem.

Even in cases where individual change is extremely difficult to achieve, such as the reduction of HIV/AIDS by means of safer sex practices, it is still fruitful to adopt a social-change strategy in addition to an individual one. The individual-change strategy may simply not be sufficient by itself. Individual-change strategies also have a habit of succeeding with one segment of a population (often the "haves") while failing with another (the "have-nots").

The unintended outcome may be an increase in the pre-existing gap or inequality in the population due to unequal access to education, mass media, employment and health care. In addition to failing to change as expected and then lagging further behind, these same individuals may even be blamed for a program's failure. Personal or individual blame is to some extent a natural consequence of doing individual, psychological research on problems that are fundamentally social problems. The communication literature also contains criticisms of the dominant, individual approach to communication theory.

Early models of communication were linear, one-way processes from sources to receivers, usually for the purpose of having an effect on individual receivers. When feedback was included in these models, it was treated as "knowledge of effects." Even though the diffusion model identified a "diffusion effect" in the adoption "S" curve due to interpersonal communication with satisfied adopters, communication was still assumed to serve primarily a function of information dissemination and persuasion. During the 1970s, criticism of one-way, top-down, persuasive models of communication was well articulated by Latin American scholars such as Beltran.

As a consequence of this growing dissatisfaction, emphasis began to shift from audience members as individual objects to audiences as social groups, and from the action of sources on receivers to the relationships among participants, to mutual understanding, and to convergence within communication networks.

In spite of this initial effort to shift the paradigm from action to transaction, by the end of the 1990s it became apparent that transmission and persuasive models still continue to dominate the design of strategic communication, at least in the field of health. Communication practitioners, however, have not let go of this important issue. The call for a model of development communication based on dialogue versus monologue, horizontal versus vertical information sharing, equitable participation, local ownership, empowerment, and social versus individual change continues to be heard and, if anything, has grown stronger with the rapid decentralization of authority and increased access to new communication technology that occurred during the 1990s.

What would an alternative paradigm look like? At least two key features are necessary. It needs to be based on a model of communication that describes a process of dialogue, information sharing, mutual understanding and agreement, and collective action. Second, it needs a model of social change based on community dialogue and collective action that clearly specifies social outcomes as well as individual outcomes. The convergence/network model of communication meets the first requirement. It represents communication as a process of horizontal sharing between two or more participants within social networks. It is beyond the scope of the present paper to present this model in detail, but a brief description is necessary to understand how community dialogue fits into a model of social change. The first noticeable feature of the model is that information is shared or exchanged between two or more individuals rather that transmitted from one to the other.

All participants act on the same information; none are passive receivers of information. The information can be created by the action of any participant, or it may originate from a third source such as television or radio, or a person or institution not directly participating such as church, school, nongovernmental agency and so forth. The second feature of the model is that it stresses the important role of the perception and interpretation of participants, and thus draws upon the principles of semiotics and the hermeneutics, which treats understanding in terms of a dialogue or ongoing cultural conversation. The third feature of the model is that it represents a horizontal, symmetrical relationship among two or more participants (A,B,... n) that is created by sharing information.

The outcomes of information processing by the participants are social – mutual understanding, agreement and collective action, as well as individual – perceiving, interpreting, understanding and believing. And finally, the model implies a continuous, cyclical process as participants take turns creating information to share with one another and then interpreting and reinterpreting its meaning until a sufficient degree of mutual understanding and agreement has been reached for collective action to take place. "Information" is preferred over the term "message" to allow for both verbal and nonverbal information, unintended as well as intended information.

For example, if women suddenly show up at a community meeting for the first time, this action by itself conveys information that can be stronger than all of the verbal comments made about "allowing women to participate." Each participant perceives and arrives at her/his own unique interpretation, understanding and beliefs (defined as the validity of one's interpretation) about information that is shared. Once reached, each person understands and beliefs can then be expressed to others. In the diagram, talking (self-expression) is one type of action that follows from, and is based on, each person's own under- standing and beliefs. Any action creates new information, which potentially can be interpreted by the other participants. For instance, this means walking out of a meeting is also a form of information that can be interpreted.

In a dialogue, a process of turn taking occurs as each participant seeks to clarify what others believe and understand as well as one's own understanding and beliefs. And that turn taking constitutes a minimal form of collective action: joint action in the form of two or more persons engaging in dialogue. But dialogue must mean more than just endless turn taking. The underlying assumption of dialogue is that all participants are willing to listen and change not just one of the parties. Communities that have a long history of conflict may not be able to engage even in this minimal form of collective action – talking to one another. This turn taking (conversation, dialogue) constitutes a feedback process for each participant which, if effective, leads to a "series of diminishing mistakes – a dwindling series of under-and-over corrections converging on a goal".

The common experience of "ah...so that's what you mean," indicates a process in which participants gradually converge toward a greater degree of mutual understanding and agreement (shared beliefs).The initial, relatively unique understanding and beliefs of each individual gradually become more similar and share more in common with those of others. Convergence does not imply perfect agreement, only the direction of movement. The inherent properties of this process suggest that over time most groups will converge toward a state of greater internal uniformity, also referred to as "local culture". The convergence theory is valid in part because of the important roles played by boundaries. Within the boundaries created by the dialogue itself, convergence occurs because those who do not see an issue the same way nor agree with other participants tend to stop participating in the dialogue and then "drop out" of the group.

Simply leaving a group (moving outside the boundaries created by the dialogue) automatically ensures greater uniformity among those who remain within the group. In communities, this process of divergence describes the formation of factions. The existence of factions/subgroups within a group (culture) implies two simultaneous processes: convergence among members within each bounded subgroup and divergence between subgroups over time. Boundaries determine who is included and who is excluded within a dialogue. Boundaries can be determined by observation and self- report, and by mapping the social networks within a community. Splitting communities into factions with different points of view reduces the overall social cohesion of a community and hence its capacity to solve mutual problems through collective action.

If severe, it can bring cooperative action among groups within a community to a halt. Ironically, dialogue itself is one of the primary means of overcoming such divisions. Effective dialogue occurs when participants with differing points of view listen to one another, as indicated by paraphrasing the other's point of view to the other's satisfaction, when each one acknowledges the conditions under which the other's point of view can be accepted as valid, and when each one acknowledges the overlap or similarity of both points of view. But sometimes dialogue can lead to disagreement and divergence, especially when the dialogue makes it clear each individual's true interests and values are in conflict.

Other models are needed to add this level of complexity. The social-change model described below considers these missing elements. The convergence model of communication implies symmetry in the relationship of participants and equity of information sharing (action). Real groups and communities are sometimes far from this ideal. Power relationships substantially affect the communication process. Power may be exercised by means of authority (threat or use of positive and negative sanctions), influence (persuasiveness of participants), pre-existing social norms or all three. So, power and conflict represent another means for overcoming differences and opposition within a group. But even in cases where a community leader or outsider coerces recalcitrant individuals and subgroups to cooperate in a project, some minimal level of mutual understanding and agreement is still required for them to comply and engage in collective action.

Negotiation represents a third means of overcoming opposition and conflict. Leaders of opposing factions can propose trade-offs and agree to compromises in order to obtain sufficient mutual agreement for collective action to proceed. For example, the subgroup within a village that wants to build latrines rather than new wells can agree to cooperate with building the wells first if the other subgroups agree to help with latrines later and if some of the wells are located close to their houses. Third- party arbitration or mediation provides another alternative to conflict if dialogue and negotiation fail. In summary, some initial amount of communication within a community or group is required to identify areas of agreement and disagreement among those participating.

When different points of view and beliefs arise (divergence), further communication is required to reduce the level of diversity (convergence) to the point where there is a sufficient level of mutual understanding and agreement to engage in collective action and solve mutual problems. The method used to reach consensus is usually determined by leaders within the community. The communication for social-change model describes a process by which leaders guide community members through dialogue and collective action in order to resolve mutual problems for themselves.

Community Dialogue and Collective Action

The Integrated Model of Communication for Social Change (IMCFSC) describes an iterative process where "community dialogue" and "collective action" work together to produce social change in a community that improves the health and welfare of all of its members. The development of a community can occur through a variety of change processes: Externally generated change, such as the construction of potable water systems, roads and health clinics by outsiders that leads to a reduction in the prevalence of disease within the communities affected. Individual behaviour change, such as the adoption of chlorinated water, oral rehydration solutions for diarrhea and visits to local health clinics that, when aggregated, leads to a reduction in the prevalence of disease within the communities which experience sufficient individual change.

Social influence for individual behaviour changes where individuals who adopt a new health behaviour publicly advocate its adoption to other individuals, so that the rate of change (decline) in the prevalence of disease increases. Community dialogue and collective action in which members of a community take action as a group to solve a common problem, such as high rates of diarrhea, lack of potable water and so forth, which leads not only to a reduction in the prevalence of disease within the community but also to social change that increases the collective capacity to solve new problems. The IMCFSC was developed to describe the last type of change: community dialogue and collective action. The four types of change are not mutually exclusive.

For example, externally-generated, government-development projects can also involve individual adoption of new behaviour with social influence. A collective-action project, such as getting every household to eliminate stagnant water sources to eradicate the spread of dengue fever by mosquitoes, may require individual behaviour change as a result of social pressure from neighbors. The integrated model draws from a broad literature on development communication that has developed in the early 1960s.In particular, the work of Latin American theorists and communication activists was used for its clarity and rich recommendations for a more people-inclusive, integrated approach for using communication for development. Likewise, theories of group dynamics, conflict resolution, leadership, quality improvement, and future search, as well as the network/convergence theory of communication have been used to develop the model.

CATALYST

The model describes a dynamic, iterative process that starts with a "catalyst/stimulus" that can be external or internal to the community. This catalyst leads to a dialogue within the community that when effective, leads to collective action and the resolution of a common problem. The model identifies six potential catalysts:

1. An internal stimulus may be discovery of high levels of arsenic in the village wells, the onset of an epidemic such as AIDS, noticeable increases in maternal mortality or, perhaps, the suggestions of a local leader that stimulates members of the community to talk to one another about a health problem.
2. A change agent, such as the ones used in most NGO community interventions, may visit a community to initiate a discussion of "felt needs" or of a specific health problem in order to induce the community to take some type of collective action.
3. An innovation, such as a new oral rehydration solution, a new vaccine or the availability of a new type of chlorine water disinfectant, may stimulate a community to talk about its adoption.
4. Policies that prompt the community to act, such as a new law that requires all children to complete primary education.
5. Availability of technology, such as the injectable method of contraception or mechanical digging equipment, may stimulate a community to talk about family planning or to reconsider the construction of new wells.
6. Mass media, including messages designed to promote individual behaviour or collective action, may stimulate members of a community to adopt the behaviour or to emulate other communities that have achieved some common goal by working together.

The catalyst in the model represents the particular trigger that initiates the community dialogue about a specific issue of concern or interest to the community. This catalyst is a missing piece in most of the literature about development communication. Much of the existing literature implies that the community spontaneously initiates dialogue and action or that an external change agent visits the community to mobilize the community. Experience has shown that communities rarely initiate a dialogue about a problem spontaneously, and that some do take action on their own without being visited by external change agents. Some authors like Juan Díaz Bordenave (1998) initiate the description of a community process with the "identification of the problem."

One could ask how a problem is identified in contexts where "a problem" is seen in the community as something "normal"? For example, it may be normal that children under the age of 1 often die or that mothers die during pregnancy. What the model implies is that some type of catalyst is usually necessary to stimulate a community to consider and discuss a problem. Once this discussion is initiated it may unfold in several directions: from simply creating a greater sense of dissatisfaction, to inciting a community conflict or to cooperative action that helps solve the problem.

The Community Dialogue and Action box of the model describes a sequential process or series of steps that can take place within the community, some of them simultaneously, and which lead to the solution to a common problem. The literature and previous experience indicate that if these steps are successfully completed, community action is more likely to be successful. In this sense, it is a descriptive model, one that could be used to describe and explain why previous community projects were successful or unsuccessful.

In another sense, it is a prescriptive model, one that can be used by local leaders and external change agents to increase the likelihood that community action will be successful. Each small box in the model represents a step that may or may not happen in a specific context or case. At some points, when a particular step is not successfully completed the group may "loop back" to an earlier point in the process and reconsider earlier decisions.

Community Dialogue

The 10 steps of community dialogue are:

1. ***Recognition of a Problem:*** As result of a catalyst, someone in the community becomes aware of the existence of a problem. For example, a group of women who wash clothes together discover that all of their children are suddenly having unusually severe episodes of diarrhea. The women ask each other why this is happening.
2. ***Identification and Involvement of Leaders and Stakeholders:*** Some of the women talk to their husbands and elders about the problem. Perhaps they visit the leader of their own women's development group. Eventually, someone exercises leadership and takes responsibility for solving the problem. Through a process of sequential networking (going from house to house) or small group meetings, the leader(s) identifies other opinion leaders and resource persons who can help in the process for solving the problem. A midwife or volunteer health worker may live in the community that can be consulted. Men or women who frequently travel outside the community are asked to consult with health providers at local clinics. Once the problem is labeled (say) as diarrhea and dehydration, informal community leaders may call a meeting to discuss the problem. Members of the community who are most affected by the problem (stakeholders), such as mothers with children under 5, are asked to come to the meeting.
3. ***Clarification of Perceptions:*** It is possible that different perceptions of the problem exist among different members of the community. For example, some people may think that the problem is being caused by the food supply, while others think that the water is being contaminated. Someone else may see it as a problem of inadequate hand washing because of the current drought or a lack of soap. Unless a consensus can be reached regarding the nature of the problem and its causes, it will be difficult for the

group to find an adequate course of action that is acceptable to everyone. Dialogue is necessary to create a mutual understanding (common framework) with which to solve the problem. Only after such perceptions have been clarified and different points of view rectified can the process move forward with a clear understanding of how the problem should be addressed.

4. ***Expression of Individual and Shared Needs:*** One key element that community projects have to keep in check is the involvement of those individuals that are among the most disadvantaged in the community. Otherwise, projects run the risk of involving groups that may not be representative of those in the bottom of the scale and whose perception of the problem and needs may be different. Not everyone will experience the problem with the same level of severity. For example, better-off families may not experience as high a frequency of diarrhea. They may believe that diarrhea is a problem for each individual family, and not something that the whole community should get involved in. Someone else may think that the lack of good latrines combined with contaminated water is something that involves everyone: everyone is part of the problem, so the solution has to come from everyone. In order to resolve problems successfully it is important that all affected in the community get the chance to express their own views and needs. If any conflict or dissatisfaction arises, then community leaders have to resolve the conflict before much progress can be made with the problem. The potential for this conflict/ dissatisfaction is reflected, in the model, by the dotted line coming out from this box. To resolve the conflict, more clarification may be needed (arrow into the clarification box) or new leaders and stakeholders may have to get involved (arrow into the leaders' box) so that a majority can convince a reluctant minority to go along.

5. ***Vision of the Future:*** This box represents the ideal "picture" of how the community wants to see itself in the future. This will be the answer to the question: Where do

we want to be in a year from now, with respect to the problem? It is important that this vision involves representatives of all affected groups (stakeholders) in the community so that it becomes inclusive of all interests. The common vision expresses all of the changes that will occur and the benefits that everyone expects to receive.

6. ***Assessment of Current Status:*** To be able to set clear goals of where to go and to assess accomplishments, the community should have an objective measurement of the size of the problem. The shared vision expresses where the group wants to go; assessment of current status tells them where they are *now*. Answers to this question can be qualitative and quantitative. Quantification of the problem will give a clear idea of the size of the problem, for example, the number of children who got diarrhea in the last week, the number of children that died from diarrhea in the last three months, the number of mothers that have died during delivery in the last year, the number of new orphans resulting from AIDS and so forth. Qualitative assessment would consider what kind of diarrhea is occurring and how it differs from previous years and if it responds at all to antibiotics and oral rehydration therapy. Unless a clear measure of the problem is established it will be difficult to set goals for action, and then determine if any progress is being made later.
7. ***Setting Objectives:*** With the current status clearly stated and shared by community members, the next question is: What is a reasonable expectation about what the group itself can do about the problem? Can the number of children and adults experiencing diarrhea be cut in half in three months if a certain number of families take the appropriate action? Can it be eliminated altogether? Turned into a rare rather than a common event? The act of comparing one's current status with one's desired status and then setting realistic goals is the source of group motivation. Research has shown that if the goal is set too high, and hence is unrealistic, then motivation will be low.

The group will not have a sufficient sense of self- efficacy or confidence that anything they do will make a difference. If the goal is set too low, then it can be reached with hardly any action, and motivation will also be low. Moderate goal setting that is achievable creates the high level of group motivation that is required for people to take sufficient action to solve the problem.

8. ***Options for Action:*** This box is the answer to the question: What different kinds of action can be taken to accomplish the objectives with which everyone agreed? This implies the identification of resources both inside and outside the community as well as persons or groups that can carry them out. Following the example of diarrhea, the community needs to decide whether to build new latrines, establish locations further from the village for defecation, get community members to wash their hands appropriately after defecation and before preparing and handling food, increasing water treatment or boiling, new well construction, etc. One or all of the above? In what order of priority? Getting a consensus on action can also lead to conflict or a lack of commitment. If a sufficient consensus cannot be reached, then the objectives and/or the courses of action may have to be discussed all over again. If not handled successfully, the whole community dialogue process may break down for good, and the problem may persist or worsen while nothing is done.
9. ***Consensus on Action:*** Once a detailed plan is at hand, a new process of getting consensus among the community needs to take place. Getting consensus is important not only for summing up resources but also for getting people to volunteer or for assigning courses of action to various members of the community. The more the community participates and sees the proposed actions as "theirs," the more likely that they will take action. Likewise, the more a community is "involved and committed" the higher the empowerment and sense of collective self-efficacy that the community will develop.
10. ***Action Plan:*** A specific timetable for when each activity

has to be accomplished will help the community to have clear deadlines for effectively moving toward the solution of the problem. This box will be the answer to the question: Who does what and when do we need to do each activity and organize ourselves to accomplish our goals?

Collective Action

The collective action portion of the model describes the process of effectively executing the action plan and the evaluation of its outcomes. The model identifies five key action steps:

1. *Assignment of Responsibilities:* To convert a plan into action, specific people must take responsibility to accomplish specific tasks within specified periods of time. Leaders must ask for volunteers or else assign tasks to individuals and/or community subgroups (existent or newly created for executing the action plan).Someone must take responsibility for each of the activities identified in the action plan. Depending on the complexity of the problem it may be necessary to create community task forces focused on specific project goals and subgoals.
2. *Mobilization of Organizations:* It may not be necessary for members of the community to take responsibility for all of the tasks that need to be accomplished, especially if there are existing organizations inside and outside the community that can help. Thus, one of the assigned tasks may be to obtain the support and help of pre-existing community resources. For example, in most health interventions, health providers and schools should be asked to contribute. In the experience of many communication activists, communication through the local media can be an invaluable resource for mobilizing community support and activity. Díaz Bordenave (1998) lists several ways in which the media can facilitate the dialogue and action process.

   In the *dialogue phase* (a) it can support the diagnosis of problem situations and the presentation of the problem to the community (there are many examples of how radio or radio tapes have assisted in getting the "voices" of community groups in the dialogue process), (b) it can stimulate community deliberation and the prioritizing of problems,(c) it can support the exchange of ideas and experiences among distant communities,(d) it can help community organizations find solutions to problems, and in the *action phase* communication and local media can contribute by (e) informing the community about available services and how to gain access to them,(f) training community members how to use the media to inform the general public about their needs,(g) helping communities to obtain legitimization and support from authorities, (h) providing feedback to the community about the progress and achievements of community projects, and (i) praising/rewarding communities for their achievements and thereby enhancing member's self-esteem and sense of collective self-efficacy.

3. ***Implementation:*** This step refers to the actual execution of the action plan and its monitoring. No plan can be successful if the required work is not done. Furthermore, leaders, members and/or subgroups should take responsibility for monitoring all the tasks that have been assigned making sure that activities are moving according to the timetable and everyone is fulfilling their responsibilities.
4. ***Outcomes:*** This step refers to the actual results that the community is able to achieve given the resources, organization and mobilization process specified by the action plan and then carried out. If the problem was an unacceptable level of diarrhea among children under 5, then the solution – the action taken – should be followed by a reduction in diarrhea among that group. If a certain number of tube wells were planned for the preceding year, then how many were actually constructed? To know the results of community projects, some type of observation and/or counting of events/incidents need to be done to measure the level of achievement.
5. ***Participatory Evaluation:*** The achieved outcomes may or

may not be what the community originally planned in their specification objectives. The comparison of the outcomes to the shared vision and original objectives is an important *self-evaluation* process. For purposes of group motivation and reward, it is important that most of the community participate in the evaluation process so that the lessons learned about what worked and why can be shared throughout the community. The result of the participatory evaluation should be a *new reassessment of the current status* of the community with respect to the problem. This is shown in the diagram by the arrow moving back up to the shared vision and the assessment of current status boxes in the model. From here, the community is ready to renew the process, moving forward into further action for the same problem, perhaps, or on to a different problem. It is by means of this reassessment process that the community reinforces its sense of collective self-efficacy, which in turn leads to and increases the community's belief in and *value for continual improvement*. This improvement is shown in the model as one of the primary outcomes of continual reassessment of the current status followed by a renewal of community dialogue and collective action.

External Constraints and Support refers to any factor outside the control of community members that can either inhibit or enhance dialogue and collective action. Extreme poverty, the drastic consequences of a flood or famine, or even the distance between homes in a community make it difficult to engage in a participatory process. It is easier to announce and get women to come to a group meeting in a densely packed Korean village, for example, than in the geographically dispersed housing pattern of a coconut plantation in certain areas of the Philippines. It was not possible for women to meet in *jiggasha* discussion groups in Bangladesh where the norms of *purdah* (modesty) and their husbands do not allow it.

On the other hand, government construction of a community schoolhouse or meeting house can greatly enhance the capacity of a community to meet to discuss common problems. The model shows two-way arrows from community dialogue and collective action to external constraints and support implying that *over the long run* community action itself can be taken to remove external constraints and to obtain external support. Government field workers can persuade husbands to allow their wives to participate in group meetings; communities can construct their own meeting halls.

The state of the community in terms of the status of the individuals who comprise it as well as the community as a whole can be measured at any time before, during and after a development project has been undertaken. The differences between individual or social characteristics of a community from one point of time to another provide an indication of the *change* that has occurred while the community was engaged in community dialogue and collective action. The lower left-hand side of the model lists the most prevalent types of individual change that can occur, which are based in stage models of behaviour change and ideation models of behaviour. A thorough discussion of individual change is beyond the scope of this report.

The potential outcomes of dialogue and collective action *for the individuals who participate* include:

- Improvement in skills necessary to perform new behaviours;
- Ideational factors such as knowledge, beliefs, values, perceived risk, subjective norms and even self-image; emotional responses such as feelings of solidarity, empathy and confidence; and increase in social support and influence *from* others as well as increased advocacy *to* others;
- Intention to engage in new behaviour in the future; and
- Specific behaviours related to the problem addressed by the dialogue and collective action. The model also indicates that these individual outcomes can be the result of the direct influence of one of the external catalysts identified in the model, such as mass-media messages that promote specific health practices and the introduction of

health clinics near a community. The right-hand side of the model lists seven possible outcomes of social change that may occur.

Many of the individual and social change outcomes are related and can affect one another. For example, the knowledge that individual participants have about a health problem is aggregated at the community level to determine the average level and distribution (equity) of that type of knowledge in the community. Where the perceived social norm is that both men and women are expected to participate in community meetings, we would expect to find a majority of women saying that they think, "Most of my friends expect me to come to the meeting and participate."If this behaviour is encouraged and rewarded during collective action, we would expect a greater number of women to report afterwards that they did indeed participate (an individual outcome),leading to an overall increase in the degree and equity of participation with the community (a social outcome). There is no better example of the relationship between social and individual change than the case of malaria prevention by removing stagnant water sources in the area around one's own home.

If only a few individuals in a community do this on their own, their (individual) behaviour will have little impact on the mosquito population. However, if through dialogue a consensus is reached among everyone (or a critical mass of community members) and they all take *joint action* at the same time (social behaviour),then the strategy can lead to an effective, long- term solution to the problem of mosquito-born diseases. The primary focus of *Communication for Social Change* is on the social outcomes of dialogue and collective action. If a community effectively completes the steps outlined in the model and then accomplishes one or more of the objectives it sets for itself, then we would expect some potentially profound social outcomes within the community, above and beyond what happens to the individual members who participate or benefit.

For example, if leaders successfully engage the requisite number of stakeholders, facilitate the expression of individual and shared interests, resolve conflicts, and help create a vision for the future in ways that they have never used before, then those leaders *learn* something that they can use again. In one sense these are individual leadership skills, but leadership cannot be practiced in isolation from followers. Leadership is a joint behaviour that takes place between leaders and their followers, and hence is a characteristic of the group or community in which it occurs. In other words, an improvement in leadership is an indication of *social change* as well as change in the individual behaviour of specific leaders. The same implication applies to followers as well.

Participative leadership and an increase in the shared decision making and power within a community require followers to change their behaviour as well. Although it may appear that a greater burden falls on leaders, the 15 steps specified in the model require effective *followership* – the appropriate response and cooperation of other members of the community. In many cultures, for example, where women, following long-held traditional norms, have not attended community meetings or have attended without speaking, it would be very difficult for a leader *by himself* to suddenly ask for women to participate actively and on an equal basis with men. Doing so could easily turn into a "token effort" that results in a reinforcement of the shared belief (stereotype) that women really do not want to participate or are simply unable to do so.

On the other hand, a leader who identifies the most influential women and who meets with them beforehand to plan and prepare for their participation is much more likely to succeed. He/she is developing a change in the relationship before asking for change in the behaviour of particular individuals and for a change in the norms governing behaviour in community meetings. *Leadership* and *followership* is a characteristic of the community as a whole because it is based on the *relationship* between leaders and followers rather than on a set of traits possessed by either one alone. In the same sense, while we can measure individual gains in knowledge about a problem and its solution, individual levels of knowledge can be aggregated as the proportion of community members who are knowledgeable or as the average level of knowledge of all the members.

The average level of knowledge can be high in a situation where (say) half the people have a lot of knowledge and the rest have hardly any. Statistically, this is a bipolar distribution. Since one of the implied social goals of the social change model is knowledge equity, then emphasis must be placed on the extent to which the knowledge is *shared* within the community as opposed to hoarded or monopolized by just a few. The width of the distribution (standard deviation) around the average level of knowledge offers an indication of how widespread knowledge is as well as its average level. Changes in the frequency of participation and the proportion of community members who participate in dialogue, decision making and implementation, along with the diversity of participants in terms of education, occupation, gender, ethnicity, and so forth, provide a measure of social change of the community in terms of *degree and equity of participation.*

Such a change is a desirable outcome of a participatory development project in and of itself, regardless of expected changes in individual health behaviour and status, because such changes at the community level are expected to have a positive impact on the success of the project and on the *capacity* of a community to deal with its next problem. Perceived ownership, cohesion and a value for continual improvement is also expected to follow from increased participation and shared decision making.

When community dialogue and collective action are implemented in the manner specified by the model (the 15 steps), we expect not only an improvement in the health status of community's members, but also an increase in the following:

- Community's sense of *collective self-efficacy:* The confidence that *together* they can succeed in future projects,
- *Sense of ownership:* The degree to which they perceive themselves as responsible for the project's success and thus feel that they deserve the credit and benefits from

the project,

- *Social cohesion:* The extent to which members want to cooperate in another community project and the degree to which the social network of the community is interconnected as opposed to divided into cliques and factions,
- *Social norms* – the accepted rules for participation, especially regarding who should or should not speak up and share in decision making and "fairness" regarding contribution and sharing of benefits, and, finally,
- *Collective capacity:* The overall ability of a community to engage in effective dialogue and collective action that is a consequence of all of the social change indicators specified by the model. Social scientists have developed the concept of "social capital" to account for a community's capacity to cooperate for mutual benefit.

Putnam (1993) defines social capital as the "features of social organization, such as networks, norms and trust that facilitate coordination and cooperation for mutual benefit." The concept can be traced back to James Coleman (1988), who proposed that social capital consists of a variety of different entities with two elements in common: some aspect of *social structure* that facilitates the *actions* of actors within the structure. Like economic and human capital, "social capital is productive, making possible the achievement of certain ends that would not be attainable in its absence, but unlike other forms of capital, social capital inheres in the structure of relations between persons and among persons. It is lodged neither in individuals nor in physical implements of production".

Nan Lin defines social capital as "investment in social relations by individuals through which they gain access to embedded resources to enhance expected returns of instrumental or expressive actions." To qualify as a type of capital, the social capital of a group must be capable of being increased by means of some type of investment (in resources and work).Social capital as a form of surplus value, must be capable of being increased and captured by means of some process.

Thus, from the perspective of social capital, the dialogue and collective-action process described in our model is a *learning process*, in which individual members through their participation in community projects increase their capacity for cooperative action with one another and form social structures – networks, teams, leader-follower relationships – which increase the community's overall capacity for future collective action. Information sharing, coordination of activities by leaders, joint decision making and the equitable distribution of participation and benefits all provide an incentive for further cooperative action, increase the productivity of the community as a whole and create a shared value for continual improvement.

Individual and Social Change

For health, as well as many other areas of development, individual and social changes are both necessary for attaining sustained health improvement. Individual change by itself is usually the expected outcome of health promotion programs, especially those dedicated to a single health problem such as the use of oral- rehydration therapy to reduce childhood diarrhea, immunization programs, family planning programs, condom promotion for HIV/AIDS prevention, and mosquito-net use. The urgency of the problem, the initiative taken by centralized agencies, the concentration of resources, the specific focus, and the concrete and limited nature of the behaviour to be changed, all increase the efficiency and likelihood of success. It is not surprising to find, therefore, that individual behaviour-change programs are quite common in the field of public health.

By design, however, the outcomes are limited to a single, specific aspect of health. As a consequence, some individual behavioural change may even be limited to a short duration in time unless other measures are taken to ensure that such changes are institutionalized and self-sustaining. In a situation where only social change occurs, the capacity or potential for improvement in health or other areas of development may increase but with little impact if not accompanied by the required changes in individual behaviour. Changing a community's leadership patterns, initiating a dialogue about problems that resonate with everyone and even jointly deciding on a course of action may all improve a community's capacity to solve problems, but if it is not accompanied by the required changes in the behaviour of individual members, then very little progress will be made on specific problems.

Ironically, communities may have to conduct their own internal health-promotion programs to get their members to adopt the appropriate behaviour. If neither social nor individual change occurs, then we would expect the existing *status quo* to be maintained. The ideal change process would result in social change and in the requisite individual change. We expect the interaction of these two types of change to result in *self- sustained* improvement in health and other problems faced by a community. Every time a community goes through the dialogue and collective-action process and actually achieves a set of shared objectives, its *potential* to cooperate effectively in the future is also expected to increase. If the process also leads to the changes necessary in individual behaviour for a community to *achieve* its objectives, then the success of the community reinforces both collective and individual behaviour.

The likelihood of a community continuing to solve problems together in the future is expected to increase. Furthermore, the confidence of the community to undertake collective action increases and the value for continual improvement is strengthened and institutionalized. The possibility for self-sustained, continual improvement can become a reality. The question of which type of change should receive the highest priority is sometimes very controversial. We must keep in mind that we should not expect every local community to invent its own solutions to every problem, especially for problems in which specific technology such as vaccinations, antibiotics or contraceptives can be made available from outside authorities in the "larger community," such as local and national governments or international development agencies.

Even in this obvious situation of individual adoption, however, a community response may be necessary to obtain such technologies from the outside. Oral rehydration solution (ORS) for the treatment of diarrhea, a leading cause of infant mortality, underscores these issues.

ORS has saved millions of lives, but the alternative solution of hand washing with soap, improvement of latrines and clean water within the *community as a whole* would be expected to have a greater impact on childhood diarrhea than the treatment of one child at a time with ORS after an infection occurs, especially if some of the ingredients of ORS are not always available. Both external policymakers and local community leaders have to find the appropriate balance between social and individual approaches to change, a balance that best fits the problem itself and the needs of the members of the community.

6

Social Change Process Indicators

In addition to specific measures for each stage, two summary matrices are provided as well, one for dialogue and one for collective action. The matrices give a "snap- shot" of exactly how a particular community has acted: who and how many engaged in dialogue and participated in decisions, whether or not measurable objectives were identified, whether specific people were assigned to each task and if outside resources used. But first we address the question of *who* uses the model for evaluation and *for what purpose.* Assessment and evaluation of the process and its outcomes can be conducted by, three different groups:

- Members of the community who want to know how well their effort has achieved the objectives they set for themselves and how much more needs to be done,
- External change agents involved in the process who need to document how well a community has performed, and
- Social scientists who want to conduct a systematic analysis of the relationship between the process and its outcomes across a sample of communities.

The distinctions made across the three types of evaluators reflect the difference in goals that each one has, and these differences also determine which indicators described below are used, and how they are reported. For members of the community, the dialogue in which they have participated should have led to a clearer vision of the future, and assessment of community's status when they begin, and some concrete and measurable objectives to accomplish. In the final stage of the collective-action process, the community needs to reassess its status in terms of the objectives that it set for itself.

This is identical to assessment of the current state, which should occur in the dialogue process, but which also involves comparing the initial state of the community to its (new) current state after the project is completed. Did they reach or exceed these objectives? What contributed to, or prevented, their reaching these objectives? If community wells were built how many were finished and, more importantly, how many and which community members benefited from having them? The degree of success is crucial for *motivating* the community to continue working on problems together and for developing a belief in and greater value for *continual improvement.*

This is why it is so important that they do this assessment themselves, for themselves. If for some reason they do not reassess their situation, nothing will be learned and the likelihood that further action would be taken will diminish. This type of self-evaluation is central to the participatory development communication. In practice, *self-evaluation* is often skipped over, especially when projects are initiated by outside agents who hold a rigid notion of evaluation or an anti-participatory ideology. The communication for social-change model explicitly incorporates participatory evaluation into the process itself rather than leaving it for others to do at another time.

Outside agents, if they have taken responsibility for initiating the dialogue and action process, often have obligations to their own funding sources to provide feedback regarding how well their goals are being met. In this situation, the model and its indicators can be used to collect additional information required by the project. For example, change agents may have a goal of increasing the level of participation, equity of information and decision making that initially some community members may not have. By measuring previous levels of participation and styles of leadership, and then documenting how the project influenced and changed these features of the community, the change agent may also change the way community members view the collective-action process itself.

Especially if greater participation and sharing of responsibility contributed to the success of the project, then community members may endorse these aspects of the process as goals themselves and strive to improve them in their next round of dialogue and action. For this to happen, the change agent needs to provide *feedback* to the community about these issues and encourage them to work on these issues. If the information is buried in the agent's own report, then the likelihood of development in this respect would be expected to diminish substantially, even if community members have some vague idea about how things took place. And finally, a rigorous, systematic investigation of the process and outcomes may be undertaken by social scientists in cooperation with change agents.

Participative observation, extensive in-depth interviews with knowledgeable informants, systematic focus-group discussions with subgroups within the community, and even surveys with statistical analysis may be conducted using the indicators described below. In addition to providing more details about the process and outcomes to community members and external funding agencies, such an extensive, systematic investigation – especially if it is done over a number of communities – would provide the opportunity to increase the general knowledge about dialogue and collective action. The results would have implications for both practice and theory. For example, the theory that greater motivation (and hence, action) occurs when moderate, feasible goals are set versus goals that are either too easy or impossible to achieve, can be tested and confirmed by examining a wide range of community experiences.

In fact, such an analysis may be the only way to establish what constitutes a "moderate, feasible" set of objectives in a particular situation. Other aspects of the model would benefit from this type of analysis as well. In a particular culture, what balance of strong authoritative leadership and participatory decision making leads to the greatest satisfaction among community members as well as the most successful collective action? What type leads to greater motivation to participate in another project? These are difficult, complex questions that require more information than community members would normally obtain for their own purposes, or that change agents would obtain to meet their own reporting obligations. The knowledge gained from such an analysis could lead to better training programs, more effective guidance by change agents and more effective dialogue and action within communities.

Community Definition

Social change refers to characteristics of a *group* of individuals that change over time, as opposed to changes in the individual members of a group. To measure social change in a group it is first necessary to define the group:

- To determine what criteria are used by community members to define themselves as a group, and
- To establish the *boundaries* that determine who is inside and who is outside of the group. A community is often defined by geographical and legal/governmental criteria. Using location as the criterion, a *community* is defined as a group of people who reside in the same locality.

For groups in which members do not reside in the same location, community is defined as a group of individuals who share a common interest. A professional group, an Internet chat group or labor-union members meet this criterion for membership. But interest alone may not be sufficient. To qualify as an active member of an interest group it is also necessary to know which individuals communicate with one another about the issue, that is, who is a member of the *communication network* that addresses the issue. The network can be defined by face-to-face interpersonal communication or mediated communication by means of the telephone, the Internet, etc. Establishing the geographical boundaries of a local residential community (village, neighborhood, etc.) is not always simple and straight forward. The members who reside in a neighborhood may themselves have different ideas regarding its geographical boundaries.

Needless to say, the boundary issue needs to be resolved before it is possible to measure accurately the social aspects of any type of community. The resulting definition can then be used to measure characteristics of the group. To proceed, a community profile needs to be constructed by means of a series of focus-group discussions with knowledgeable, key informants in the community before conducting the study of its social characteristics. In addition to preparing for the main study, these initial group interviews will establish a *consensus definition* of the "community" in which the remaining research is to be conducted. These focus-group discussions can also be used to draw a community map, which specifies the boundaries and indicates all of the community resources, such as wells, common land and meeting houses.

The discussions can also be used to obtain an initial list of all of the formal and informal groups, organizations and institutions that exist in the community, along with a list of the leaders of each one. Techniques are available that allow focus-group discussions to place all of the relevant community groups and organizations on various-sized pieces of paper. Then they can be moved around on a large sheet of paper or table in a manner that indicates the closeness of each group to each of the others. Once a consensus is reached on this set of relationships, the same focus-group discussions can then draw lines between pairs of groups/organizations that frequently interact and cooperate with one another.

The resulting interorganizational diagram can then be photographed and used later to calculate indices of *intergroup network cohesion*. This community definition and mapping procedure is important for the rest of the community study, so more than one focus-group discussion should be conducted. The number of focus-group discussions to be conducted for this purpose depends on the degree of diversity in the community. At least one focus-group discussion for men and one for women should be conducted separately. Groups representing different ethnicity or religions, residential areas or age groups may also be conducted. To reach a consensus on community boundaries, groups/organizations and leaders, a spokesperson from each of the groups can meet afterward to establish a consensus among the groups. Difficulty or inability to reach such a consensus is the first evidence of potential divisions in the community that may reduce its overall capacity for community dialogue and collective action.

Social Change Process

The following indicators correspond to the community dialogue and collective-action process as described previously. These indicators have the purpose of assessing how the community is advancing in its collective effort in the undertaking of a program or solution to a problem affecting the community. These indicators are complementary to the outcome indicators described later. Note, also, that these indicators intend to measure the extent and mechanisms of the participation so that the effort (dialogue and action) is inclusive of all community members. Likewise, they intend to assess whether there is conflict and how does the community deal with it, so that the conflict empowers the community rather than preventing the program from advancing.

Recognition of a Problem

The process of problem identification is complex, may take a great deal of time and may be catalyzed internally or externally. Within the dialogue process "recognition of a problem" may occur simultaneously with "clarification of perceptions" (identification of the root causes and the potential solutions to the problem) and with the "expression of individual and shared interests" (conflict and opposition). These stages, however, have been assigned to individual boxes in the IMCFSC because of the importance of wider participation by the affected groups. These stages are presented separately with separate indicators, but they may, in fact, be all integral parts to the problem identification and clarification process.

These indicators together with "social change" indicators of "information equity" and "sense of ownership," should be considered in assessing a community's progress towards addressing the problem. The first stage in the process of social change is the recognition by the larger community or by a smaller subset of the community that there is a problem that limits their current quality of life, constrains their aspirations for the future, or has the potential to hurt the community or members of the community. This stage is so fundamental that it is unlikely that any process would be implemented before there is a basic recognition of a problem.

Indicators to measure early-stage awareness of the problem are:

- Has the community recognized the issue as a problem?
- What are (have been) the catalyst(s)?
- Which groups and people have been involved in the recognition of the problem? Implicit in the identification of a problem is the *identification of a solution.*

If there is not a solution, it is rare that people would think of the issue as a problem. Excess fertility, while a serious threat to a woman's health, became the problem of unwanted fertility only when women could control their fertility. The identification of a solution should be clearer as result of the "clarification of perceptions" by the wider community and not just by the initial groups aware of the problem. Another important element of the problem identification stage is the *recognition of the opposition to change.* The opposition may be based on tradition, economics, control and power, ethnicity, competition or just fear of change. Empowering women may be a good strategy for promoting condom use to prevent AIDS, but that empowerment comes at the expense of men's power and control.

Potable water systems may be a good solution to prevention of diarrheal disease, but it is a threat to the income of the water haulers. Ending the practice of female genital cutting has a positive health impact, but is an attack on traditional values and denies an income to the traditional practitioners who do the operation. Possible opposition to a program/solution of a problem may be resolved during the community's stage of "expression of shared interests" and "involvement of leaders and stakeholders." An evaluator faced with opposition to the solutions should first assess what resources (such as additional key stakeholders/leaders who can address opposition) have been mobilized to overcome the barriers.

Identification and Involvement

The problem or issue to be addressed next should logically produce some kind of leadership structure. This leadership structure can take many forms:

- Spontaneously generated from within the group vs. externally appointed.
- Leadership comes from an existing cadre of community leaders vs. leaders that evolve to address a specific problem (often first-time leaders).
- Traditional or cultural leaders vs. political or externally appointed leaders.
- Group leadership vs. individual leadership.
- Casual and/or dynamic leadership structure vs. more formal or structured (often hierarchical) leadership.
- Stable vs. constantly changing leadership structures.
- Leadership based on capacity vs. interest vs. random selection.
- Ongoing vs. specialized or one-time leadership.
- Participatory vs. autocratic leadership.
- Open opportunity vs. selected leadership.

The leadership that evolves in any community may be described using a number of the above descriptors. It is important to note that the above types of leadership do not have an inherent value – that is, one type is not better than another in producing the desired outcome. Special attention should be paid to ensure that the leadership structure created to tackle the issue does not reproduce an existing inequitable power structure in the community. For equitable leadership to happen, a fair representation of all community groups affected by the problem should be in place and endorsed or approved by these community groups.

It should be noted that a mechanism that provides opportunities for active participation for leadership is more likely to convey social change as it provides reinforcement and renewal of the existing leadership. The indicators for this stage are:

- How were leaders (individual or groups) on the issue/ program elected?
- Proportion of different interest groups or factions in the community represented in the leadership (individual or group)?
- Number of individual leaders or groups working on the particular issue/program?

Stakeholders

Participation of those who are most affected by the problem (stakeholders/beneficiaries) is a characteristic of community/ social-change intervention. This involvement may be direct (work on the solution) or indirect (advocate or support for facilitating the solution or removing opposition).Besides direct beneficiaries, stakeholders can also be family/friends of direct beneficiaries, potential future beneficiaries, or people with an interest in the issue but no expectation of benefit (altruistic).

Indicators of stakeholders' involvement can be qualified by answering the following questions:

- Describe what was done to get stakeholder and beneficiaries involved in the program (posters, public meetings, speaker, truck, referrals, etc.).
- What was the mechanism for involving the larger community to discuss the issues and obtain representation?
- Who was involved in the discussion of the problem and

possible solutions of the problem: – Persons from outside the community? – Small leadership group (look for fair representation of affected members)? – Members of the community (this is the response that indicates how equitable the participation by stakeholders is)?

Clarification of Perceptions

When this stage of community dialogue has occurred, there should be a greater degree of unanimity and understanding over the nature of the problems (root cause/s), possible solutions and associated actions. This stage can be transitional and may be skipped over if the root cause(s) of the problem is widely recognized and the solution(s) clear (e.g., household spraying for malaria), or if it has been resolved in the "recognition of a problem" stage. Potential indicators for assessing whether the community is moving toward a clear understanding of what are the causes and solutions to the problem are the following:

- Mechanisms for clarifying perceptions that involve the whole community,
- Proportion of most affected groups in the community effectively participating in discussions regarding the issue, and
- Level of agreement regarding the root causes of the problem and or solution.

Expression of Individual and Share Interests

One of the goals of community dialogue is to maximize participation in the issue, while balancing the needs of a consensus. Another goal of dialogue is to balance the interests of individuals with the larger interests of the community. A problem that effects a small number of members of the community, or a solution that helps a small proportion of the community at risk, must be considered in light of the communities needs and the potential impact across the range of community members. This stage, like "clarification of perceptions," is transitional in the dialogue process, meaning that these transitional steps may have occurred earlier, or they may have occurred in the context of another step (e.g., involvement of leaders).

It is important to remember that the IMCFSC, *while laid out linearly does not function in a linear manner*. The best indicator for participation is the degree to which all in the community are involved, including those who might be excluded. It is possible to identify if the community is allowing for "expression of interests" with the following indicators:

- Was anything done to identify all the beneficiaries, and include them in the planning process?
- What are the mechanisms being used for all community members to communicate their interests at the different structural levels in the community?
- Proportion of relevant groups expressing their needs or interests with regard to the issue.
- Was the design of the project changed to increase the number of beneficiaries?
- Were there any relevant groups (those most affected) in the community that refused to participate?

Conflict and Dissatisfaction

Balancing the interests of individuals with the larger interests of the community may result in conflict. Besides existing power structures within the community that may bias the direction of the program or that may represent opposition, there may be undeniable conflicts of interest among community groups in dealing with solutions to the problem. This is a critical stage that may terminate a program or, if dealt with effectively, can render an empowered community. For effectively dealing with conflict more/other leaders or stakeholders may be consulted to provide additional support/evidence and/or persuade/influence reticent groups.

Vision of the Future

Once a community has passed through the previous stages it would be ready to plan *where* it wants to be in the future (five years from now, one year from now) and to figure out the ways for getting there. As in the previous stages, broader community participation will ensure that the defined "vision" is inclusive of all community member's hopes and aspirations:

- What has been the representation of community members and affected groups in defining the vision?
- How has the community articulated its "dream" (generally, this takes the form of a statement that includes the ideal (feasible) scenario of where the community wants to be with respect to the problem/issue?

Assessment of Current Status

At this stage, the community may be already motivated (if not, it should be encouraged) to assess the extent/magnitude of the problem so that a plan of action can be defined. This assessment can be quantitative as well as qualitative. This may require gathering information about the problem from either an available source, such as the health center, or from members within the community. If information gathering within the community is necessary, the community should decide how to organize to get the data. It could be through periodic community meetings where the affected groups have member representatives to report, or by visiting those households in the community affected by the problem.

Information gathering through group meetings may prove better as it facilitates sharing of knowledge and progress on the issue. An indicator for assessing whether the community is working on this stage is the mechanism used : Existing mechanism for information gathering about the extent of the problem in the community and the changes over time. This tracking mechanism should allow the community to answer questions such as: How many children in the community had diarrhea last week? How are these events similar or different from previous years? Resources, inside and outside of the community, being used to track changes in the number of cases and other qualifications related to the issue/problem.

Setting Objectives

A shared vision should allow the community to list the goals/objectives it wants to achieve. The community, together with the leaders and/or change agent, should evaluate how realistic the goals are and should try to set moderate goals in order to avoid either a sense of failure (if goals are unrealistic, too high),or lack of motivation (if goals are too low).Goals that are challenging but feasible should be preferred. Potential indicators to assess this stage of the process are the following:

- How are (were) the goals/objectives set up (participatory goal setting, in principle, would secure wide support and action)?
- What are the goals set up by the community to deal with the problem (generally, a list of goals should exist, that describes what the community wants to see accomplished at the end of the program)?
- Level of agreement of leaders/group members on the goals/objectives set up.

Options for Action

The goal-setting stage should naturally give place to the actual planning process of what different kinds of actions can be taken to accomplish the objectives with which everyone has agreed. This implies the identification of resources both inside and outside the community, as well as persons or groups that can carry them out. A change agent can assist the community by making sure it has considered all feasible options.

If the change agent believes a feasible option hasn't been considered it should be brought to the attention of the community and explored as to why the community did not decide on that option.

Consensus on Action

Getting a consensus on action can also lead to conflict or a lack of commitment. The important measurement at this stage is that the community continues to seek resources and deals with conflict positively to advance the solution to their problem:

- Has any conflict arisen in reaching consensus?
- How is the community dealing with conflict on actions and how is conflict being resolved?
- Has consensus been reached on any action plan?
- How was the consensus reached on the final action plan?
- Who participated in reaching consensus?
- Does a document exist that specifies what the community-action plan is?

Action Plan: A specific timetable for when each activity needs to be accomplished will help the community to have clear deadlines for effectively moving toward the solution of the problem:

- Does a written community action plan exist (Yes/No)?

  Verification of following data in the action plan:

- Who is responsible for each activity?
- What resources are needed (people and other material resources)?
- When is the activity going to be implemented?
- Where will the activity be implemented?
- How will the activity be monitored?
- What is the expected result?

Assignment of Responsibilities

Specific people and groups should take responsibility for conducting each activity as defined in the action plan. Indicators for assessing this stage are as follows:

- How were the actual responsibilities assigned (leaders assigned, volunteers, other)?
- Level of agreement (by leaders, community groups) with the assignment of responsibilities?
- Level of representation of interest groups on the assignment of responsibilities?

- Are there any new task forces/groups created to carry out different activities under the action plan (Yes/No)?
- If yes, a listing of the different groups/task forces created.
- Are leaders (individuals or groups) sharing in responsibility for implementing the action plan?

Mobilisation of Organizations

Depending on the size and nature of the problem, existing organizations inside and outside the community can be called upon to join the community-action effort. It is likely that the higher the resources mobilized by the community, the higher the commitment to the program/solution of problem by the community.

The extent of the participation by the different groups in the community should also influence the sense of ownership of the program and social cohesion:

- Magnitude of resources mobilized within and outside the community (a listing of all organizations contacted will give evidence of the size of the network accessed by the community).
- Type of internal and external organizations/resources contacted (extent of networking; look for involvement of the local media).
- Representation of affected groups in the community in the participating resources and organizations.

Implementation

This step refers to the actual execution of the action plan and its monitoring. Actions should be put in place for back-up activities so that the whole action plan does not get truncated if some activities do not work according to the original plan. Indicators for this stage are:

- How is the implementation being monitored?
- Who is monitoring the implementation of the activities?
- Has each activity specified in the action plan been implemented as intended (documentation for each activity)?

- For the activities not implemented as planned, what are the reasons for poor implementation (resource constraint, decline in interest in the community members assigned with the responsibility, others)?
- Actions taken to cover for unsuccessful key activities.

Participatory Evaluation

The achieved outcomes may or may not be what the community originally planned in their goal setting. The comparison of the outcomes versus the original objectives is an important *self-evaluation* process. For purposes of group motivation and reward, it is important that most of the community (especially the affected groups) participate in the evaluation process so that the lessons learned about what worked and why may be shared throughout the community. The result of the participatory evaluation should be a *new reassessment of the current status* of the community with respect to the problem.

Action Process Matrices Instructions

Assessment of the process of community dialogue and action can be conducted through direct observation, if the evaluator has enough time to spend in the community, or through focus-group discussions and interviews with key leaders. Direct observation should allow for a deeper understanding of the community dynamics regarding dialogue and action. But if the evaluator cannot be present to directly monitor all the dialogue and action process, it is recommended that he/she make notes whenever he/she is present in the community in order to obtain a better documentation of the community dynamics.

Before using the matrices, the evaluator should first carry out a *community profile,* which can be conducted through a series of group interviews in the community during the initial days of fieldwork. As a result of this process the evaluator should have a clear definition of the community, as well as the list of groups, leaders and problems, as defined by the community. Two matrices have been designed – one for

Community Dialogue and another for Collective Action, to record the extent to which the community has undertaken each of the dialogue and collective-action steps. A separate matrix should be filled out for each issue or problem that the community has addressed.

The purpose is to document how far and how well the community has progressed toward resolving all of the problems that it had taken up, during a specified time period. It is important to note that some of the steps may have been skipped or may not have been adequately completed yet. The matrix will provide a single picture of the progress that a community has made on each problem.

Filling the Top of the Matrices

Use a different set of matrices (one for dialogue, another for action) for each problem identified by the community during the "community definition" analysis.

The Dynamics of Social Change

Each cell in the matrix can be treated as a variable for purposes of data analysis. The entry from each cell should be entered into a database under an appropriate variable name. The verbal (as opposed to numerical codes) entries, including the notes in the boxes corresponding to constraints and supports, can be entered as string variables in the same database. The "case" in the data set corresponds to a matrix for a specific community problem or issue. The case number is identical to the problem number listed in the top corner of the matrix. A separate variable should be used to code the name of the community for the study, especially if more than one community is being observed. A community may have several problem "cases" entered under its name.

The dates and sequence of the data for each case (problem/issue) are very important, because one of the main purposes of collecting the data for these matrices is to examine the change over time in the way that communities use dialogue and collective action to solve problems. For example, if a community undertakes dialogue/collective action to resolve three different problems over the course of one year, then the database constructed from the matrix sheets would provide data for three cases (problem cycles) for that community. Each case would have data from all the cells (row/ column).Therefore, for the variable, participants, or number of people who select a course of action, there would be three entries, one for each dialogue/problem cycle, ordered sequentially by time.

The date of each dialogue/problem cycle would also be entered as a variable. This would make it possible to graph the number of participants, by time, over the course of the year covered by the data collection.

The graph would show to what extent the number of participants was increasing, decreasing or staying the same over the course of one year. If a variable is created for each problem type (water supply, AIDS, etc.),then it would be possible, for example, to examine trends in women's participation over time by *type of problem*. Likewise, the percent of women participating could be created for each time period (dialogue/problem cycle) to see the trend in women's participation over time.

If 10 such dialogue/problem cycles are entered over the course of five years then the resulting data set would provide a good description of changes over time *(dynamics)* in the nature of the process of dialogue, decision making, leadership, participation and outcomes *(social change)*.This data and the corresponding graphs can be used in combination with the other information collected about each community to provide a comprehensive description of the communication and social-change process for each community.

SOCIAL CHANGE OUTCOME INDICATORS

Within each outcome, indicators vary by level of difficulty and type of data-collection method. Some are qualitative and others are quantitative measures. As explained before, no one would be expected to use all of the indicators for each outcome.

A variety is included so that each evaluator can choose the one that best fits his/her purpose and resources. For example, leaders who are in touch with members of their community can readily get a sense from talking to people of how satisfied everyone was after the project is completed. They would also know how willing everyone would be to start another project. This constitutes an informal measure of cohesion as groups usually experience it.

However, a change agent might need an indicator that is representative of all members of the community and not just rely upon the opinions of leaders, even though the leaders may be correct. So, change agents may want to collect information on their own in a more systematic manner. The social scientists may want to use one of the numerical scales of cohesion described below in order to get an aggregate measure, such as an average cohesion score. This way they can assess how much cohesion is increasing or decreasing after each process of dialogue and collective action is completed. All three of these methods yield an indication of cohesion but they serve different purposes.

Leadership

Development of sustained and effective leadership, which provides a base for organizing community participation, is an important outcome indicator for social change. Strong and supportive leadership is characterized by a combination of open management, shared vision, team spirit, decentralized control and role clarity. When groups experience leadership that inspires without dominating, members are more likely to get involved, share the vision of the leader(s) (e.g., goals, objectives, indicators of success, values, norms, future orientation),share in the benefits of the program and institutionalize the process of social change. There may be leaders (people or groups, traditional or formal) in the community, but no leaders on the specific issue (e.g., domestic violence, family planning, and adolescent health).Thus, one of the main objectives of a social-change program is to strengthen or develop leadership for that particular problem or program.

Dimensions of Leadership

Operationally, leadership can be defined to have the following six dimensions:

- Extent of leadership,
- Equity and diversity,
- Flexibility,
- Competence in encouraging and securing dialogue and action,
- Vision and innovation, and
- Trustworthiness and popularity.

An overall index of leadership may be developed from these dimensions, and the progress may be measured over time.

DEGREE AND EQUITY OF PARTICIPATION

This dimension measures the range of participation to include the traditionally disenfranchised members of the larger community (e.g., women, lower class, ethnic groups, age, occupation, as related to the issue), as well as the diversity of activities which members get involved, ranging from planning, selection of leaders, decision on services and modes of delivery, resource mobilization and management, to evaluation of program outcomes.

Dimensions of Participation:

- Access to participation, and
- Extent and level of participation.

Information Equity

This refers to the level of awareness and knowledge about an issue, health problem or program that is shared (common wisdom) among different individuals within a group or between different groups in a community. Information equity also refers to the level of access that the community has to the corresponding information sources. Besides assessing the level of information equity at the community level, emphasis may be placed on assessing the corresponding level among specific groups (or most vulnerable groups) related to the issue or program.

High levels of shared information are likely to affect the level of direct or indirect participation in the implementation of the program and other activities related to the issue. Individuals with a good understanding about the issue or program and with access to sources of information will be more likely to participate, and that will reinforce other social-change outcomes such as sense of ownership.

COMMUNICATION FOR SOCIAL CHANGE

If specific knowledge items are identified, an overall knowledge index can be constructed to assess overall community knowledge related to the issue or program. Percentage of community members who are aware of community activities related to the issue or program. A matrix with individually listed program activities can be created to assess specific awareness by different individuals and groups in the community.

Percentage of community members who are aware of community sites or other sources of information related to the issue or program. Percentage of community members who are aware of mechanisms for participation in activities related to the issue/program. Percentage of community members/groups aware of other programs in their community related to issue/program.

Collective efficacy refers to a group's *shared* belief in its *conjoint* capabilities to attain their goals and accomplish desired tasks. It involves the belief or perception that an *effective collective* action is possible to address a social or public health problem. It differs from individual self-efficacy though, of course, is rooted in it. A group of self-doubters cannot be molded into a collectively efficacious group. On the other hand, even if individual members are capable and their self-efficacy beliefs are high, low confidence in the group's capacity for collective action may still inhibit not only collective action but community dialogue as well.

Beliefs of collective efficacy may be a predictor of group performance. Furthermore, collective self-efficacy is not a monolithic group attribute. Individuals who occupy different roles or positions in the same organization may differ in their perceptions of the group's collective efficacy. It is expected that a community's collective efficacy will influence the group's dialogue, goal setting, collective effort and especially their persistence when barriers arise.

There are two different approaches to the measurement and evaluation of collective efficacy:

1. Aggregate appraisals (by members) of their personal capabilities for the functions they perform in the group, and
2. Aggregate appraisals by members of their group's capabilities as a whole. Perceptions of self-efficacy may vary with the tasks at hand and with other contextual factors.

Questions about perceived self-efficacy should be precise and refer to specific circumstances. For example, perceived self-efficacy at negotiating safer sex may depend on the particular context, such as whether one is with one's regular partner, a new partner, somebody one just met, and so forth. Answers to the questions for each of these different contexts, when combined will provide a general measure of self-efficacy for safer sex. The collective efficacy of a community should also be assessed, as far as possible, with regard to a particular task. For example, the community may feel more confident organizing to combat a diarrhea epidemic than an AIDS epidemic.

Dimensions of Collective Self-Efficacy:

- Perceived efficacy to take action as a group.
- Perceived capability of other community members.
- Perceived efficacy to solve problems as a group.

Perceived efficacy to take action as a group refers to the confidence of the community to *work together as a group* and take collective action on an issue confronting the community.

This dimension may be affected by contextual factors in the form of past experiences, a history of factionalism or other conflicts in the community. The following items can be used to assess this dimension. Responses should be coded as, strongly agree, agree, unsure, disagree, strongly disagree (standard Likert- type format). People in this community are always able to discuss problems that affect everyone. If a problem arises that people cannot solve by themselves, the community as a whole will be able to solve it. People in this community usually have trouble dealing with conflict. Whenever our community undertakes a project together, we know that we will all work hard until it is accomplished. Whenever our leaders ask us to work on projects together, almost everyone is willing to join in and to do their share of the work. Whenever a community problem arises, We have very little confidence that we will be able to solve it.

Sense of Ownership

Sense of ownership is defined as the community's feeling/ belief that the problem/issue and/or program belong to them and they have a commitment to the program. How intensively and extensively the people are involved in defining the issue or program, the planning process and the implementation, will affect the sense of ownership.

"Ownership develops when partners play a key role in formulating and implementing a project and understand the benefits of participation. The recognition by each partner that he will be better able to achieve his own goals by collaborating and helping his partners reach their respective goals is the best way to ensure partners are committed for the long haul." Even though an external agent may help determine the needs/ program goals, and guide the implementation process, the community should be heavily involved so that a sense of ownership can develop. The gain of creating a sense of ownership is that it reinforces what people learn and encourages them to integrate the shared learning into related situations. This in turn, feeds back into strengthening other social-change outcomes such as "sense of collective efficacy."

Dimensions of Sense of Ownership

For the purposes of this study, six dimensions of measurement for this outcome can be identified:

- Importance of the issue or program to participants,
- Sense of responsibility for the program,
- Contribution to the program,
- Benefit from the program,
- Participants' sense of ownership of either credit or blame in the program outcome, and
- Personal identification with the program.

Social Cohesion

Social cohesion consists of the forces that act on members of a group or community to remain in, and actively contribute to, the group. In cohesive groups, members want to be part of the group, they generally like one another and get along well, and are loyal and united in the pursuit of group goals. Social cohesion is an important antecedent and consequence of successful collective action. Social cohesion mediates group formation, maintenance, and productivity.

Dimensions of Social Cohesiveness

For the purposes of this study, social cohesion can be divided into at least six related social and cognitive dimensions:

- Sense of belonging,
- Feelings of morale,
- Goal consensus,
- Trust,
- Reciprocity, and
- Network cohesion.

Sense of belonging is the extent to which individual members feel as if they are an important part of the group or community? The group's level of belonging can be measured by means of focus group discussions, in-depth interviews with individual members and sample surveys of community members.

7

Social Movements and the Mass Media

The mass media is a vital resource for most political actors, and it may be even more important for social movements, whose transitional and adversarial nature weakens their ability to secure public legitimacy. Their outsider status, along with their usual resource-poor nature, means that traditional avenues of publicity are not easily accessible and forces them to rely on alternative methods to obtain media access. Traditionally, this involves some form of public spectacle - like a protest - to attract media attention. These activities have become accepted as mechanisms by which social problems are communicated in the public sphere, alongside public opinion polls and elections and they act as vital means by which citizens can signal their discontent.

One of the first detailed examinations of a social movement protest in the media (both press and television) focused on a mass demonstration held against the Vietnam war in Britain. The demonstration involved approximately 60,000 protesters, most of whom marched peacefully through the streets of London (with an insignificant number of protestors involved in violent actions). However, despite the overwhelmingly peaceful nature of the march, the media concentrated most of its coverage on the issue of violence. Although Halloran et al., noted that there were differences between media outlets in their coverage, they were all united by the overall focus on 'the same limited aspect - the issue of violence.' The misrepresentation of this massive political rally, and the totality of the negative coverage across all media outlets led the investigators to conclude that such reporting poses extreme problems for democracy, which may only be remedied by 'some form of institutional rearrangement'.

These are serious charges, and the authors acknowledged that further studies needed to be carried out to determine how systemic these problems were. Since then, many researchers have followed up on this investigation, examining how various social movements interact with media systems. Drawing upon this body of work, this paper will analyse the importance of the role of the mass media for social movements. This will include a review of the literature and recommendations on how such groups may best address their relationships with the mass media. To begin with, a brief discussion of some of the external forces beside the media, which effect the development of social movements and their ensuing relations with the mass media, will be presented.

Foundations of Change

The inherent conflict between corporate driven capitalism and democracy has always caused ruling elites to have their work cut out dissipating the ebb and flow of popular dissent. This contradiction is best exemplified by Crozier et al.'s (1975) classic study, The Crisis of Democracy, which controversially diagnosed the need for 'a greater degree of moderation in democracy.' The first political theorist to accurately document this 'management' dilemma was Antonio Gramsci, who described how elites were able to successfully maintain hegemony over the masses through the use of consensual rather than coercive institutional arrangements. Theobald notes that the 'central importance' of Gramsci's view to radical mass media criticism is 'that current bourgeois control of society, while certainly manifest in material modes of production, is culturally embedded and naturalised in the minds of the people via its hegemony over discourse.'

One vital but overlooked organ of hegemony, that Gramsci was unable to include in his work, are philanthropic foundations, whose rising influence on the contours of civil society only became visible some decades after Gramsci's death. The hegemonic power of foundations, however, is arguably even greater than other hegemonic elements, like the mass media, precisely because their influence has been downplayed (or in many cases simply omitted) by academia. This is especially the case with liberal foundations, which have actively influenced progressive social change by directly co-opting organisations or channelling their activists towards less radical activities. Historically, the work of philanthropic foundations has been most influential in the US, but now similar foundations operate all over the world, and with the resurgence of corporate social responsibility, corporations are also becoming prominent philanthropists. For example, during the 2000 election cycle in the US, 'the corporate outlay on political philanthropy... was probably a minimum of $1-2 billion' dwarfing combined PAC and soft money contributions.

Some academics have begun to address the urgent task of proposing solutions to counteract the anti-democratic nature of such subtle yet pervasive social engineering, because it is clear that manipulation of civil society (by foundations or governments) through selective support of non-governmental organisations raises questions that reach to the heart of all democracies. Furthermore, a growing body of work suggests that similar 'democracy promoting' practices now serve as an integral foreign policy tool to help 'promote polyarchy' over more substantive and participatory forms of democracy. Likewise, other research has begun to examine how selective support of 'independent' media organisations in geo-strategically important countries has helped facilitate revolutions (e.g., the coloured revolutions in Eastern Europe) to further the polyarchal interests of trans-national capitalism.

Referring to the Orange Revolution, Herman (2006) observed 'that the civil society uprising in the Ukraine in 2004-2005, [which was] funded heavily by U.S. government agencies and friendly NGOs, was given much more lavish news treatment than domestic [US] protests, along with editorial support.' Indeed, elite patronage - either by governments or philanthropic foundations - confers a degree of 'legitimacy' upon social activists, which in turn may be accompanied by more favourable media coverage. In the light of these findings, Robinson's (1996) promoting polyarchy thesis predicts that individuals or groups vigorously challenging the status quo and/or transnational capitalist elites would be most likely to be marginalised by the mass media.

THE HOSTILE MEDIA PLAYING

For any social movement to draw beneficial attention to its activities in the mass media, the first barrier it must overcome is the structural constraints of the medium itself. According to Herman and Chomsky's (1988) Propaganda Model, there are five filters through which all news must pass, that actively shape the media's content. These are

- The size, ownership and profit orientation of the media,
- Advertising,
- Sourcing,
- Flak (criticism) and
- Anti-communist ideology, which can be interpreted as keeping the discourse within the boundaries of elite interests. The fact that the Propaganda Model itself is marginalised from most media scholarship is consistent with the model's predictions. Yet there are still a small number of critical scholars who have been able to illustrate the applicability of the Propaganda Model to countries other than the US (where the model was first developed), e.g., in Australia.

In this way, news values filter what appears in the media - and more importantly what doesn't - not in any prescribed way, but more as a result of a sort of tacit professional consensus which usually acts to 'reinforce conventional opinions and established authority'. Meyer suggests that news must also pass through another filter, which he calls 'the rules of stage-managing', which selects news based on its style of presentation and ability to attract an audience's attention. Most protestors are not the focus of regular news beats and so tend to rely on protest events to broadcast their news, however, most of these are ignored in the mainstream media. In addition, social movements have to contend with representative democracy, which leads governments to emphasise that dissent should take place in ballot boxes and not on the streets: a point of view endorsed by the mass media.

In spite of this, the mass media's influence is not monolithic and some social movements and interest groups are able to maintain moderately useful media relations, publicising their activities in a predominantly positive light - something that will be discussed later in more detail. The overall inadequacy, or inequality, of coverage of protestors and social movements compared to other better placed insider groups has caused some authors to lament that the only way for social movements to obtain positive coverage is through the adoption of public relations techniques. This has led to the development of various media handbooks, which explore how social movements may better exploit the mass media. At this stage, it is worth considering that it is not only social movements that complain about adversarial media coverage. Both governments and corporations also convey the same general attitude (to the public at least), regarding their negative treatment by the mythical left wing media.

However, the big difference between insider groups and most social movements is that the former can mobilise huge political and financial resources to publicise their positive activities, and still spend fifty per cent or more of their public relations resources on preventing media attention to their more secretive 'closed door' activities. Arguably the largest, most credentialed and well-resourced social organisation prior to the 1980s was the labour movement, but research has shown that despite these advantages, the British labour movement has been systematically treated with hostility by the media. In 1990, US media watchdog Fairness and Accuracy in Reporting (FAIR) published a report entitled 'Lost in the margins: labor and the media' which concluded that 'the lives of 100 million working people are being routinely ignored, marginalised or inaccurately portrayed in the media'. Current research from the US also shows how the labour movement is still systematically misrepresented in the media, despite its financial strength, application of professional public relations techniques and fundamentally democratic ideals.

Ignoring Campaigners

Other social movements in less influential political positions than the labour movement suffer even more under the strain to publicise their activities, especially when their activities confront the status quo. The US civil rights movement (1954 to 1968) took years of organising and massive public support (and increased militancy) before the media started regularly covering and supporting the protests in the 1960s. Few people know the names of the thousands of heroic leaders and ordinary citizens who gave their lives struggling for freedom. Instead, the media focused their positive coverage on the star like qualities of the movement's more moderate leaders, like Martin Luther King, while demonising and marginalising the more radical elements of the movement.

Two characteristics that strongly influence a social movement's media treatment are the degree to which they are perceived to be 'extreme' (that is, challenging the status quo) and 'militant' (in their tactics); whereby, the more extreme and militant a group, the more critical the media coverage. Thus, although Martin Luther King benefited from his relative moderation in both these regards for most of his life, this changed just prior to his assassination. It is then that he began to link the civil rights movement to basic human rights and economic rights, which subsequently led him to oppose the Vietnam War in 1967 and start building the Poor People's Campaign in the last few months of his life. These events were widely dismissed by the media at the time, and even today few Americans are familiar with them, due to an effective media blackout in media reviews of his life.

This highlights how central the media's representations of social movements are for generating and sustaining public support. In addition, the elevation of movement leaders to the media's centre stage, to the exclusion of ordinary movement participants, may have the effect of discouraging 'normal' citizens from identifying with the movement, which can prevent their active involvement. Tunstall points out how most labour stories during the Thatcher years in the UK focused on the movements leaders, dismissing the grassroots base of ordinary workers. This served to dramatically weaken the labour movement's bargaining position in the media when the Thatcher government decided to phase out much of their communication with the trade union leaders after 1979.

One major difference between earlier popular social movements and the current global justice movement is that the latter tend not to rely on distinct leaders or top-down hierarchal structures to drive their activities. So, in some respects, the media's apparent 'confusion about the protestors' political goals is understandable'. Unfortunately, this equitable trait of the global justice movement has supplied the media with even more ammunition to undermine the protestors' ideals by portraying them as 'lost' and 'leaderless'. However, it should be recognised that the global justice movements' strong emphasis on grassroots participation and consensus decision-making - which admittedly is sometimes messy (or democratic) is their very strength in countering the domineering corporate power structures evident in society today.

Us and Them

Chan and Lee (1984) first described the 'protest paradigm' to illustrate how the mass media tended to focus on limited features of social protests to portray protestors as the 'other'. Characteristics of this reporting paradigm, which separates protestors (them) from non-protesting audiences (us, or some of us), include a reliance on official sources to frame the event, a focus on police confrontation, and an analysis of the protestors' activities (and appearances) rather than their objectives. This somewhat internalised selection process serves to filter which protests are reported, and which are ignored.

The media's exploitation of broad unsubstantiated statements concerning the public's negative opinion of protestors is used to naturalise the status quo, a practice often supported by the utilisation of unfavourable eyewitness comments. Media depictions of hostile bystander reactions act as a powerful form of social control, and serve to undermine the protestors' opinions, as passers-by who are sympathetic to the protestors are often considered to be part of the protest, so tend not to be interviewed. Research has also shown how the media often fail to report the protestors' official opponents, and instead tend to replace them with the police, thus reducing the chance of any meaningful dialogue or debate between the protestors and the targets of their protests.

Another factor that sometimes acts against demonstrators is the media's focus on their social demographics, especially when protests involve high numbers of young adults and students. Under these circumstances, the media may simply dismiss their views as unrepresentative of society, and not worth listening too. In addition, when protest participants are not visibly representative of societal norms, it makes it even easier for the media to label them derogatively as 'outsiders' or 'freaks'. That the media makes systematic use of derogatory stereotypes and negative frames to marginalise outsider groups was born out in Bowie's (1999) examination of the depiction of indigenous American's in three US magazines, *Time, Newsweek and US News & World Report from 1968 to 1979.*

Furthermore, Baylor (1996) undertook a similar assessment of NBC's evening news over the same time period and showed how 'the issue of militancy overshadow[ed] any presentation of the real grievances and issues behind Indian protest' with '98% of the news segments us[ing] either the stereotype or militant frames' (245-246). The US media has made some progress since the nineteenth century - when in 1871 the popular press actually encouraged and justified the massacre of a hundred Indians, mostly women and children - but unfortunately the exact level of progress is still debateable.

Contrary to the needs of democracy - especially any forms of participatory democracy - citizens who hold politicians and/ or corporations directly accountable by protesting in the streets are often labelled by the mass media as 'deviant outsiders' whose activities are directed towards disrupting the status quo for the compliant majority.

Hertog and McLeod's (1995) media coverage of anarchist groups in Minneapolis-St. Paul from 1986 to 1988 demonstrated that by systematically defining protestors as abnormal, the media are able to unfairly prejudice their audience against the issues and ideas raised by protestors. They also showed that, depending on the version of protest coverage audiences watched, people showed big differences in opinion on the way they viewed both the issues raised and the protestors themselves.

Other research has also shown how media coverage of protests can act to increase public hostility towards the protestors' cause. This has important implications for social movements because, if a single report can determine how sympathetic the public is to their goals, consistently antagonistic media treatment is likely to have very negative repercussions regarding public support of protests themselves.

Public empathy towards the activities of social movements changes continuously, but the degree to which society accepts protests may give an indication of the strength of their societies democratic values. This is because protests provide a discernible sign that 'that the marketplace of ideas is free and diverse', providing more possibilities for innovative social change.

Therefore, in societies where even peaceful activists are depicted as deviants - a tactic exploited by President Nixon in 1970, whose election campaign focused on combating 'the 'anarchy' of the anti-war protest' - it is not surprising that the general public often has reservations about the necessity of protest. These worries are compounded by the withdrawal of some of the larger social movements from more 'radical' forms of protest in favour of more 'legitimate' partnerships with corporations and governments: which, in the end, may work to change the boundaries for what the public considers acceptable dissent, strengthening the dividing line between us and them.

Framing Protestors into Obscurity

Analysis of the global justice movements' 2001 May Day protests in London showed how most UK press coverage framed the protests in terms of:

- Law and order, and the problem of policing the protest, fifty nine per cent;
- Economics, and the financial 'cost' of protests to the wider public, nine per cent; or
- Irrationality and spectacle, seven per cent. The remaining coverage (eighteen per cent) identified with the protestors' concerns, but 'with a few notable exceptions, discourses of recognition appeared either in the editorial page columns, leaders, or letters to the editor'. The little positive news that was generated was clearly isolated from the serious hard news sections of the papers, letting the readers know what the media really thought of the protests.

In the same vein, Martin (2004) identified five dominant news frames for how the mass media view labour news in the US: they are:

- 'The consumer is king' - which encourages an individual based (not collective) form of consumer democracy;
- 'The process of production is none of the public's business' - whereby citizen consumers should only busy their minds with making product choices;
- 'The economy is driven by great business leaders and entrepreneurs' - whose efforts can be emulated by anyone with the requisite passion, regardless of background;
- 'The workplace is a meritocracy' - self advancement is

always possible, and the employer bears no responsibility for an individual's problems (of course unions are excluded from this frame); and

- 'Collective economic action is bad'.

Understanding how such frames are continually utilised to negatively categorise social movement issues is crucial to comprehending why subsequent actions taken by activist groups - like protests - are also portrayed in an overwhelmingly bad light. There are frames that are not slanted against protestors, but mainstream media rarely uses them. Instead, the most regularly used frames are those that serve to marginalise protestors, these include the violent crime or property crime story, the carnival frame, the freak show, the Romper Room (or immaturity) frame, the riot frame, the storm watch (warning of potential actions), and lastly the moral decay story.

On May 1st 1973, London witnessed one of the largest trade union protests seen for years, when nearly two million people joined together to oppose the Conservative Party's Industrial Relations Act. In a similar manner to the coverage of the 2001 May Day protest the media downplayed the protest, representing what was 'a sizable manifestation of political class conflict rare in British history' as 'a predicable act of May Day madness'. Typical of the media framing employed surrounding this event, the Daily Telegraph's headline read 'Millions ignore T.U.C. day of protest'.

This narrative was eerily echoed some thirty years later by Newsnight (the BBCs flagship news programme) when political correspondent, David Grossman, 'reporting' on the biggest anti-war march ever seen in Britain said: 'The people have spoken, or have they? What about the millions who didn't march? Was going to the DIY store or watching the football on Saturday a demonstration of support for the government?'

Similarly, in Washington DC (US) on April 25th 2004, what might have been the capital's biggest protest ever took place, when an estimated 500,000 to 1,150,000 people took to the streets to march for womens' reproductive rights.

However, as in the previous examples, this only seemed to encourage the media to 'downplay the size and significance of the event' and 'largely ignore the issues that marchers attempted to bring back into the public discourse'. Likewise, after the September 11th attacks, a study of the New York Times showed that it had consistently 'downplayed and distorted peace rallies and demonstrations against a military response'.

The media messages emitting from the reporting of these protests to the public is unambiguous: don't waste your time with those deviant protestors they're not important! On the other hand, the options for the social movements involved in such demonstrations are not so obvious. Thus, it is of utmost importance that the mass media (and educational systems) should strengthen democratic principles and actively draw social movements into the wider public sphere, not isolate them at its margins.

VIOLENCE IN THE MEDIA AND SOCIAL MOVEMENTS

Violence tends to materialise in either personal or group conflicts, and has long been highlighted as a desirable news value in the mass media. Under normal circumstances, policymaking processes do not lend themselves to this particular media frame, as for the most part they are carried out through consensual decision making. But when individuals do choose to come into conflict verbally (or physically), this form of 'policymaking violence' tends to rate highly in the media. The crucial difference between the media's focus on institutional and protestor violence is that for institutional actors the decision to illustrate their conflict through violence, is for the most part a personal choice, while the same is not usually true for peaceful protestors.

This is because citizens who feel excluded from political processes often participate in mass activities like protests, and so their representation in the media may be tarred by just a few unrepresentative individuals who choose violent methods of expression over peaceful ones. Thus, Winter and Klaehn (2005:

184) describe how press coverage served to discipline protestors at the Organisation of American State meeting in 2000 by depicting 'a "crisis of democracy" in the violent, misguided and indoctrinated embodiment of the protestors, who must be eradicated, so that normalcy: peace, order and "good government" may return.' Likewise, Bennett et al's. study of protests targeting the World Economic Forum (between 2001 and 2003 in the New York Times) concluded that 'the news actively constructed the grassroots globalisation critics as marginal, largely nameless scruffians who threatened civil order with violence, even though actually little disorder actually occurred.'

It is not likely that protestor violence will endear its participants (and their associated social movements) to the public, especially when this becomes (as it nearly always does) the focal point for media coverage. In fact, it seems most likely that media attention obtained through violence will lead to social isolation. However, disturbingly (for democracy), some suggest that the practice of 'engaging in what is seen as spectacular, irrational, coercive, violent, and antisocial behaviour is the most reliable way to introduce [into the media] new rationalities that may have transformative consequences'. The use of violence is clearly a contestable, and in many people's view, an undesirable solution to resolving the problem of the nexus between social movements' and the media, but it proves how desperately outsider groups fight to get their message heard. Indeed, in some regards, the media encourages such behaviour, because if there are few differences between two protest groups, it is the more conflictual or violent event that obtains the most media coverage.

Fortunately, though, most people still believe in the power of non-violent protests (as evidenced by the majority of peaceful activists present at most mass protests) even if, as is often the case, their peaceful pleas remain unheard in the mass media. Another problem of the media's fixation on protestor violence is that it often means that the media overlook the role of police violence. For example, environmental protestors had occupied US Congressional Republican Representative Frank

Riggs office in California October 1997 and were confronted by police who used pepper spray to restrain them.

Throughout this confrontation - which was filmed - one of the protestors managed to calmly articulate her group's reasons for protesting; however, that segment was edited out from the television news report. As well as demonstrating how activists can be silenced in the media (or have their agendas distorted), this type of reporting serves to normalise police violence against protestors, which is dangerous for all involved in peaceful protest.

SPLAYING THE MEDIA GAME

Despite the extremely negative picture painted in the previous section, there are still some winners in the 'media game'. So while losers, like the largest protest ever held in Washington, DC received just a single story on page three in USA Today the day after the march, and a 'handful of march-related stories over a few days' in the New York Times and The Washington Post, 'others ignored the event almost completely'. A 1997 march organised by the Promise Keepers 'an evangelical men's organization with an anti-feminist and anti-gay theology' end up as winners of the media game.

Again, the Promise Keepers march took place in Washington DC and although it was approximately half the size of the women's march (estimated attendance of 480,000-750,000 demonstrators) it received far more media coverage. USA Today ran four stories before the event and four afterwards, while the broadcast networks (ABC, CBS and NBC) ran 'more than three times the coverage the networks devoted to the women's march'. Furthermore, the only study examining media coverage of the Promise Keepers in US newspapers - from 1991 (their founding year) through to April 1996 - concluded that their coverage was 'overwhelmingly positive', making the Promise Keepers true winners of the media game.

Another 'winner' was a brand new social movement (formed in Belgium in the wake of the controversy surrounding the arrest of murderer Marc Dutroux in 1996), which mobilised Belgium's largest ever demonstration - the White March. A study examining the media coverage surrounding this protest determined that the primary reason for its overwhelming success was because the media 'undertook large-scale and unconcealed motivational framing efforts' to mobilise the public in support of the protest.

This is a perfect example of a social movement that is an impressive winner of the media game, and a crucial question to ask is why was this the case? Walgrave and Manssens outlined a number of specific contextual factors that might have encouraged the media to support the protest. Sadly, many of these factors were met when Howard Sattler, the host of a popular Australian talkback radio program, stirred up racist sentiments amongst his listeners, promoting a 'Rally for Justice' which drew thirty thousand angry protestors on to the streets. The protests were even able to pressure the government to introduce racist laws that contravened international human rights legislation.

Even when progressive activist groups 'win' in the media game, obtaining positive media coverage supportive of their objectives; they may still be losing in other respects, as the following discussion of the (US) anti-sweatshop movement illustrates. After a long history of labour abuse in sweatshops worldwide, it was only in the mid 1990s that the issue started receiving serious attention in the US mass media (coinciding with a couple of high profile sweatshop investigations).

Contrary to 'normal' social movement coverage, analysis of this coverage showed that sweatshop activists actually 'achieved a position of definitional prominence' over corporate interests, a position typically reserved for powerful institutional actors. This was a remarkable achievement, however, this success was undermined by the media's dominant focus on micro-level issues, such as individual sweatshops, and their aversion to the discussion of the systemic structural inequalities supporting the use of sweatshops. Media coverage also located the root of the problem in western consumer shopping activities, not at the doorstep of the businesses profiting from the use of sweatshops, which served to cloud the issue of responsibility.

Therefore, although the anti-sweatshop movement may have successfully campaigned for limited labour reforms - some of which have now become institutionalised - paradoxically, this success may render their long-term goal of eradicating sweatshops inoperable. Businesses successfully avoided regulation by promoting self-regulation, and even though the use of sweatshops is still common practice, media coverage of sweatshops has been far less visible since 2000, reducing the anti-sweatshop movement's ability to maintain public support and awareness for their campaigns. Furthermore, current estimates suggest that there are still about 250,000 sweatshop workers employed in the US alone.

Some social movements obtain their desired media coverage by adopting tactics that focus on mobilising short-term public support. One commonly used tactic - that may work against longer-term mobilisation of social movement supporters - is emotional management. Such tactics, rely upon manipulating audiences by pushing emotional hot buttons, stimulating reactive responses from targets, but not necessarily well thought out responses that might lead on to long term commitments. The use of emotive images in the media to generate support for the victims of the famine in Niger 2005 is a good example of this type of campaigning.

The politics of symbols and their manipulation may be successful in the short term, but social movements engaged in such practices need to consider whether they are weakening the ability of other progressive social movements to recruit people committed to long term social change. Lasting commitments to social movements are built on the basis of trusting relationships, which are most effectively developed through one on one communications, not through the media. Social movements need to encourage their participants to be critical of manipulative practices because it is the results of activities that discourage activism in the first place.

Competing for Coverage

Taking a historical approach to understanding differences in movement-media relations, Rucht suggests that new social movements in the 1970s and 1980s gradually moved away from more confrontational approaches to the mass media, and increasingly utilised 'adaptation strategies'. This in turn, has led social movements to a greater reliance on the mainstream media, with less emphasis on maintaining their inwardly focused alternative media. The rise of transnational social movements in the 1990s saw this trend extend, and increasingly, social movements have adopted professionalised public relations techniques to market their causes.

Davis (2002) recognised that various UK campaigning groups have been able to acquire positive media profiles by relying on professional public relations techniques, rather than the creation of dramatic mediagenic images. This seems to have enabled increasing numbers of outsider interest groups greater opportunities to obtain positive media coverage. However, in order to gain a ticket to this exclusive media club, there is an unwritten price that must be paid because as Gamson pointed out 'the media may offer occasional models of collective action that make a difference, but they are highly selective ones.' Reformist movements are far more likely to survive the ravages of media distortion than more revolutionary ones, whose public relations messages can be overwhelmed by disparaging media frames.

Gitlin (1980: 284) describes how more reformist campaigns, like those led by Ralph Nader in the 1960s (which fought for consumer rights), were rewarded with acceptance by the mainstream media and promoted to the status of 'regular news makers.' This is particularly important, as one study comparing press and television coverage of protests in Washington DC (between 1982 and 1991), showed that overall coverage had decreased while the number of protests had increased massively. Furthermore, the ongoing corporatisation of social movements encourages the larger non-governmental organisations to view their success through an economic lens, which leads them to focus predominantly on maintaining and expanding membership/funding.

The rational result of this economic orientation, is that they often 'deliberately design their actions and broader campaigns to attract media attention and positive coverage'. Therefore, social movements may water down their demands - to appear less challenging to the status quo - leaving them more vulnerable to cooption by political and economic elites. In such cases, social movement may even start to consider the development of positive relationships with the media as more important than mobilising activists or influencing policy decisions.

Playing by Corporate Rules

The general mainstreaming of media tactics has also been accompanied by the general dilution of radical media critiques (to 'safer' moderate criticisms) which only superficially confront the status quo: arguably strengthening media organisations hegemonic position in society. The future may appear to look rosy for some social movements, but if they just sit by and watch the more radical (media compromised) groups fall by the wayside, how long will it take before they themselves rank among the most 'radical' groups. Maybe then, such groups will have to re-evaluate their media-centric tactics in the light of their newfound 'radical' status.

Unions are a good example of a group that through access to significant financial resources, have been able to adapt their tactics to become more media friendly. This can be seen by their tactical focus on 'the needs of 'the public' and/or attack[s on] 'greedy' and 'incompetent' corporate and government elites'. However, in utilising such strategies unions are now 'less likely to argue about jobs and money' and have 'dilut[ed] some of their long-term political objectives'. Their media-centric approach, serves to fragment and isolate their successful actions from one another, encouraging media coverage in an episodic, instead of thematic manner.

Similarly, in the 1960s and 1970s the National Organization

for Women, adopted a position of media pragmatism, and although they succeeded in becoming a key feminist source for the media in the US, their 'leader[s] were very sensitive to questions and debate on sexuality...opt[ing] out of an important part of the domain of personal politics that ha[d] been the hallmark of the feminist movement'. As Tuchman concluded: 'Ironically, yet logically, the successful institutionalization of the women's movement limited its ability to carry forth radical issues.' Social movements may improve their media visibility, but paradoxically by making tactical concessions to obtain media coverage, they may render their longer-term objectives invisible to their audience.

McCarthy et al. (1998) studied which factors contributed towards media coverage of demonstrations in Washington DC and concluded that other than the estimated size of the protest, one of the best predictors of coverage is it's conformity with current media issue attention cycles. Other research has also shown that if protests are not tied to legislative issues, they have a much harder time achieving media coverage, especially if they occurred in a '31-day period in which many other local public message events were also occurring'.

These findings portend dire consequences for recruitment of future activists through the media, and for sustainable activism in general, as they place severe limitations on a movement's ability to receive thematic coverage of their protest activities. This is because: 'If media issue attention cycles come to play a more significant role than do the form, context, substance, or size of citizen protests in determining which demonstrations are selected for media coverage, then protest in modern democracies will have become mediated to a greater extent' than ever supposed.

Research in the US has shown that protests or social movements that challenge the legitimacy of the governments foreign policies, are less likely to be covered by the mass media or more likely to be heavily 'denigrated and delegitimised'. A prominent example of this was the discussions surrounding the North American Free Trade Agreement (NAFTA). Goss

(2001) examined the New York Times' coverage of NAFTA and found that it served as an effective mouthpiece for the government and corporate interests, downplaying the significance of the agreement and limiting the terms of the debate to elite interests.

In this way, the labour movement, who totally opposed the terms of the agreement, were almost completely ignored in the media coverage. In direct response to the disastrous consequences of NAFTA, thousands of people came together in Seattle in 1999 to campaign for more equitable global trade rules. Previously, the mass media were able to easily bury the activist case, but in Seattle this was not so simple due to the physical presence of 50,000 concerned citizens. This placed the media in a fix, because if they were to honestly discuss the issues being raised by the protest they would have had to question the validity of the entire economic system. So instead, the media made full use of the adversarial tactics and frames (outlined previously) to systematically misrepresent and delegitimise the protestors' opinions.

The same principle of marginalisation normally holds true for groups challenging domestic policy making issues where there is elite consensus. The US anti-nuclear energy movement is a good example, and their actions were rendered next-to-invisible by the media. In spite of this, through determined grassroots education and organising, the anti-nuclear energy movement slowly grew, until public opinion polls in 1975 showed that between twenty to thirty per cent of the public opposed nuclear energy.

However, even with increasing public support, the mass arrest of 177 demonstrators the following year went unreported in the Washington Post and the Los Angeles Times, while receiving just two paragraphs on page 32 of the New York Times. This illustrates the enormity of the media barriers facing social movements, as this occurred to a movement that had a sizable proportion of public support. Not surprisingly, the movement against nuclear weapons was treated with even more disdain by the media, so that 'during the biggest demonstrations, in late April and early May 1978, the New York Times ran a small notice on page 14' and the 'Washington Post and the Los Angeles Times ran nothing'.

Similarly, the environmental movement has also found itself regularly marginalised from the media. Smaller social movements, targeting local issues, will be more likely to receive positive coverage than larger groups calling for more systemic and challenging reforms: as it tends to be the social movements that are most vigorously pushing the boundaries for dissent in society that are most marginalised from the mainstream media. This may be true, but that does not necessarily mean that reformist groups will obtain glowing media coverage. In fact, a recent survey of newspaper coverage of social protest in Wisconsin, US, from 1960 to 1999 concluded that even moderate reform groups tend to receive marginalising media coverage, and only 'protest groups seeking to support the status quo can expect more favourable treatment'.

All the examples in this section have shown how social movements are routinely marginalised or disappeared by the mainstream media. This may set in motion (or perpetuate) a 'spiral of silence', as media audiences sympathetic to social movement ideas, may feel less likely to speak out if they perceive the activists to be part of an small (invisible) minority in society, an idea forcefully communicated by the media. This of course has knock-on effects for a social movement's recruitment and long-term viability. Unfortunately, despite receiving consistently negative coverage some social movements still struggle to obtain further poor coverage: so is bad publicity actually worse than no publicity?

This is not an easy question to answer, as poor publicity may still result in the recruitment of new members. However, maybe the question need not even be asked, as surely good publicity is better than either poor publicity or none at all. Instead, perhaps social movements should be questioning the mass media's portrayal of 'reality' not just their own promotional activities - with a view to changing and reforming the mass media itself.

Necessary Reforms for Social Justice

Cromwell argues 'that campaigners are often unwilling to contemplate the notion that there is an inherent media resistance to their message.' Furthermore, he suggests that even activists who are familiar with radical mass media critiques, like Herman and Chomsky's (1988) propaganda model, often hold the 'false impression that "big companies try to control the news in their favour"' which 'is the "conspiracy" charge that Herman and Chomsky cogently refuted from day one'. Therefore, listening to activists, and working out how they relate to the media, should be the first step for any activists working towards developing the case for media reform.

Social movements have a limited number of outlets for their stories: internally distributed news, which typically reaches few people (especially those outside of the social movements immediate activities), and externally distributed news whose distribution relies on the mainstream media. Rising use of the internet has strengthened many social movements ability to distribute their news more widely via alternative media, but most progress has been made in developing effective internal communications.

Unfortunately, most people lie outside of activist communication networks, and the wealth of information produced by social movements passes them by unnoticed. A single daily newspaper already provides a vast amount of information to digest. So considering that most people do not read newspapers cover to cover, it may be reasonable to suggest that few people feel the need to actively search for additional information to supplement their daily news intake.

Social movements who wish to reach out to a mass audience must (at present) primarily rely on the mass media to publicise their cause. However, the relationship between the two is fundamentally asymmetrical, which leaves social movements vulnerable to the media's beck and call - placing social movements in a catch-22 situation. Should they make the best of their media-given lot, good or bad? Or should they attempt to reform the media, and risk biting (or at least nibbling) the hand that feeds them?

With the advent of transnational social movements and improved international communications, new doors have opened, which may help make such questions a little easier to answer. In recent years, in minority countries, participation in social movements has risen substantially, but it is in the majority countries where growth in social movements has advanced most rapidly.

This is despite the fact that protesting is a genuinely dangerous form of political expression in countries where governments routinely utilise repressive forms of social control to clamp down on dissidents. In the face of this oppression, millions of people from the majority world are joining together to protest against the multitude of exploitative economic reforms being imposed on them by corporate driven globalisation.

However, '[i]ronically... the era of globalisation has coincided with an increasingly parochial focus by the Western media... Meanwhile coverage of the South, where it existed at all, has diminished, allowing a limited and distorted view of the developing world'. In minority countries, global justice movements are working hard to expose the gross bankruptcy of the current form of globalisation, and are sometimes able to permeate the public's consciousness through the mass media. However, while they struggle to be heard, there are already signs in majority countries of massive mobilisations of citizens who oppose corporate hegemony.

Yet, these millions of protestors remain hidden away from most Western eyes, by the very same media that social movements in the minority countries cooperate with. Western media portray the global justice movement at home as either 'violent troublemakers' or 'middle-class do-gooders' and marginalise the bulk of protestors in majority countries who are campaigning against the same neo-liberalism by simply not reporting their activities. To compound this problem, on the rare occasion when the media does delve into majority world issues, audiences were misinformed, due to the low level of explanations and context given, and generally hold majority world citizens in low regard (although it has been shown that such opinions could be radically changed by the quality of information received).

What then would happen if the media covered these popular uprisings in the majority world in a sympathetic way? Obviously, a lot - however, it is unlikely that this will happen in the near future, as the media do not even report positively on the global justice movement in their own countries. Instead, it might be more interesting for activists to consider which of the two they should be allying themselves with: media institutions or the majority of the global citizenry? Choosing the latter does not mean neglecting all media outlets in favour of interpersonal communication. Far from it: by choosing to side wholeheartedly with the public, social movements would need to make substantial investments in alternative media (in minority and majority countries alike) to publicise their activities globally, while also concentrating on the urgent task of publicising the need for media reform. The global justice movement might then be able to stop wasting precious resources in their uphill struggle to coax the mass media to support them, which counts upon the media acting against its own - profit orientated - interests.

If the media continues to encourage apathy through the use of 'neutral frames', non-coverage, or over-coverage with limited solutions, social movements need to consider how beneficial it is to seek such disempowering media coverage. Furthermore, there is the possibility that even positive coverage may ultimately work to undermine their (or other movements) long-term objectives (that is to strengthen democratic processes). Most people are aware that numerous catastrophic problems are challenging human existence, but if they learn about these issues in an episodic manner that leaves them feeling helpless, where the only consistent solution offered by the media is changing their personal consumption patterns, can social movements really expect to build a mass movement for global justice in the minority world?

The media systems we currently have are not up to this task, so social movement activists need to begin seriously thinking about how they might change the mass media. To a limited extent some social movements (especially in the US) are already undertaking some actions to create a more democratic media environment, but more needs to be done to build these actions into a truly global project, to counter the global reach of media corporations. However, to date, progressive social movements have generally rejected media democratisation as a political issue. The rationale for this un-decision may be numerous, but ultimately, the desertion of media democratisation has worked against many progressive social movements, who continue to suffer within the confines of the increasingly conservative mass media.

Key to any social movement's eventual success in reforming the current world order is its ability to garner majority support, which is severely restricted by the mass media. Global justice movements profess to want to mobilise entire communities worldwide to enable truly participative decision-making. However, if this is really the case, they need to consider whether the same media system that serves to naturalise and legitimise elite decision-making, can really encourage its antithesis, collective grassroots decision-making. It seems an anathema to even consider that by working on the terms set by the mass media, social movements are actually legitimising and tightening its hegemonic power over society, even while it simultaneously acts to de-legitimise or ignore the global justice movement.

Therefore, it is time for social movements to take collective action. To start with 'democratic media reform needs to be recast as an end in itself - a public good - not simply a means by which each movement can get its message out'. In this way, a media reform project can be linked to the wider array of social movements calling for a more equitable and participatory democracy.

8

Mass Media in Community Development

In recent years, mass media has become a powerful tool for bringing about social change. "The same techniques which were developed in industry for promoting commercial goods and services are now being applied to community development," explains marketing consultant Dr. Graham Jackson, principal lecturer at the first course on Use of Mass Media in Community Development to have been held at the Golda Meir Mt. Carmel International Training Centre (MCTC) in Haifa, within the framework of MASHAV. The goal of this course, which took place in November and December 1995, was to analyze community problems and techniques used in community development, with emphasis on the use of media as a strategy for governmental and non-governmental organizations in creating social change. Participants included 29 media people and community development workers from 19 countries of Asia, Africa, Eastern Europe, the Caribbean and Oceania.

The course was held in cooperation with the Rutenberg Institute in Haifa which holds training sessions for youth from all over the world. "Our goal," says Director General Michael J. Hanan, "is to provide the participants with practical tools they can take home and immediately translate into action in their countries." In the radio studio at the Rutenberg Institute, the participants recorded jingles, in the television studio they filmed and edited videos, and in the computer room they created colourful brochures and posters, using graphics and word processing software. In the computer laboratory at MCTC, students were familiarized with word processing, graphics, spreadsheet and multimedia software.

A study visit was made to Kibbutz Ramat Yohanan (pop. 800), northeast of Haifa, where journalist David Davidovich runs a closed circuit cable community television channel. He showed the participants around the studio and described the various programs broadcast to members of the kibbutz. Meetings are broadcast, for the benefit of those who can't attend, and there is an educational game show where the children compete, answering questions on subjects such as religious holidays and famous authors. Holiday celebrations are also filmed and members are interviewed regarding current issues. In addition, whenever significant changes are to be made in the kibbutz way of life, there are televised debates. During the primaries for the upcoming Israeli elections, visits of political figures were broadcast.

MEDIA AS PARTNER IN SOCIAL PROCESS

By working as a partner in the process of social change, the media can bring about positive results in society. Dr. Hanita Zimrin, Chairperson of the Israel Association for Child Protection, gave a lecture on this theme, sharing her research on the way child abuse has been depicted in the Israeli media. From a state of almost total denial until 1979, when there were only four articles on this subject, over the years the Israeli media began to shed light on this problem, warning the public what signs to watch for and notifying the abused where they could turn for help. In 1993 there were 1,956 articles on child abuse. "At that time, a lot of creativity went into the headlines," said Dr. Zimrin. "For example 'The house with closed shutters.' But due to intense competition, newspapers began vying for our attention, producing headlines aimed at increasing our adrenaline level, such as 'Fifteen- year- old girl: Daddy abused me sexually.' Due to overexposure, the coverage lost its effectiveness and, by 1995, the number of articles on this subject had fallen to 840.

Participants were also provided with a sound basis on the subject of advertising by Dr. Jackson, who uses a "customer-oriented" approach, defining social marketing as "the design, implementation and control of programs seeking to increase the acceptability of a social idea, cause or practice in a target group." Community development, he says, can be promoted by passing laws, developing appropriate technology, making undesirable behaviour very costly or providing relevant information. Social marketing attempts to encourage desired attitudes and behaviour through a comprehensive, integrated marketing communication and selling campaign.

"Advertising," he continues, "first consists of defining the target audience, its reasons for buying or using a specific product, how to overcome customer resistance, and the identification of specific customer groups in which purchasing motivations, consumer behaviour and media habits are similar. A marketing mix can then be developed, which matches the needs of the specific target audience. "The social marketing planning process consists of defining the objectives of the social change, identifying all possible target audiences, identifying available mass media, considering alternative marketing approaches, developing a marketing plan, obtaining funding and backing, then building an appropriate marketing organization to implement this plan, and finally evaluating the results."

The class was divided into groups, each choosing a subject for its advertising and public relations campaign, to be presented to the class at the end of the course. "The Elimination of Stereotypes of Women in the Mass Media" was the subject chosen by three women from Eastern Europe - Irina Lushina, a journalist from Kazakhstan, Iveta Hankova, a journalist from Slovakia, and Liliana Pagu, president of a Romanian Women's Association. Their project focused on the planning of an international women's conference to be held in Bucharest in May, 1996. "The goal of this proposed conference," says Liliana Pagu, "is to fight for women's rights. In the post-Beijing conference area, we have to transform words into action. Our aim is the elimination of stereotypes of women in the mass media. This is a problem for women all over the world, but especially so in Eastern and Central Europe since the revolution, where women are depicted as housewives and as sex objects. In addition to our conference, we are planning a multi-media exhibition as well as a European Feminist Book Fair, where the central theme will be Women as Producers, Transmitters and Consumers of Culture."

An AIDS campaign produced by Vincent Seutloali of Lesotho, Richard Wafula of Kenya and Keziah Elizabeth Nash of St. Vincent, the aim of which was to prevent the transmission of HIV through health education, used the slogan "STOP AIDS - ACT NOW!" with condoms in the Os. The group utilized radio jingles and proposed a weekly radio drama called "Death is Knocking at the Door," a traveling theatre group and musical performances. They produced informational brochures and fact sheets on AIDS, to be supplemented by public meetings in village communities, in cooperation with the Planned Parenthood Association.

Another group (Georgios Damianos of Cyprus, Jocelyn Villacorte and May de Guzman both of the Philippines, Worapot Phuamgsuwon of Thailand and Vernon Worrell of Barbados) planned a campaign to promote the management of household garbage in low-income, urban communities. Its main target audience was families, in the belief that in low-income communities in developing countries, people's view of life is very temporal and thus they tend to be indifferent to their environment.

The goals of the campaign included creating awareness of proper methods of disposal of household garbage and educating the target audience about recycling. Ways of reaching these goals included a "Cleanest Street in the Block" contest. Their posters were humorous and their radio commercials stressed the group's slogan: "CLEAN UP! Reduce, re-use and recycle your garbage." A five-minute video was produced, in order to educate community members about the amount of garbage to be disposed of and the importance of community support in the project. Upon her return home,

May de Guzman, a public relations officer, plans to propose this same media campaign to her employer, the Philippines Department of Health.

Says Vernon P. Worrell, a community social worker from Barbados: "I was the one who suggested including children as part of the target audience in the garbage disposal campaign, in order to get them involved in cleaning up the community during the summer holidays. This would provide them with meaningful activity and, at the same time, they could assist and influence their parents. In order to prevent future problems, it is best to start with young children and have them integrated into the community and taking responsibility for their actions from an early age. We chose this topic because garbage disposal is a universal problem which applies to every city in every country."

Worapot Phuangsuwon, a media producer from Thailand, explained, "At home, we generally use the public relations approach to community development, that is, we let people know that something is good and that they should try it. Here in this course I learned about the advertising approach, which is new to me. We try to create a demand, so people will want to use a certain product.

"One highly successful example we were shown was a public service advertisement from Israeli television. Children in Israel must wear helmets when riding bicycles, but this is not always the case. In order to show a child what can happen to him if he falls off a bicycle, the ad begins with a watermelon falling and breaking, splat! in half. It then shows a second watermelon, with a helmet strapped onto it, which falls, rolls over and remains intact. Thus, with no use of force, this simple, direct ad has influenced a lot of Israeli children to use helmets when riding bicycles." Dr. Jackson was delighted with the presentations. "Not only have the students integrated everything they were taught, but their creative touches show how much can be done in a media program, even with a modest budget. The presentations showed a high level of creativity and professionalism."

Course Director Ms. Hava Karrie points out that the unique aspect of this course was that media people, community social workers and heads of women's organizations had the opportunity to learn about each other's perspectives. "Media people got a close look at various social services," she says, "and by understanding their complexity discovered how they could contribute to increasing awareness about social problems. Those working in the helping professions understood how they can 'use' the media for raising social issues in the general public." MCTC intends to repeat this course in 1997.

It is said that big minds discuss issues but small or swallow minds discuss/attack persons. The significance of communication for human life cannot be overestimated. This is true because beyond the physical requirements of food and shelter man needs to communicate with his/her fellow human beings. This urge for communication is a primal one and in our contemporary civilization a necessity for survival. That is to say without communication no society can exist, much less develop and survive. For the existence as well as the organization of every society communication is a fundamental and vital process.

MASS COMMUNICATION AND THE MASS MEDIA

Among the four identified forms of communication is mass communication, which deals with messages addressed from one to many persons mediated by elements in mass media such as radio, television, film, newspaper, magazine, book etc.

Mass communication is the technological means of sending information, ideas and opinions from a mass communicator to a complex audience. It is also defined as comprising the institutions and techniques by which specialized groups such as broadcasters, film producers and publishers employ technological devices to disseminate symbolic content to large heterogeneous and widely disperse audience. Mass communicators are impersonal. They are part of the institutions they work for and should not be blamed personally for what comes from the institutions. The credibility of the message is not for the individual communicator, but for the institution or the organization that sends it. Thus, mass communication deals with collective sender. For example, a newspaper is not produced by only one person. The newspaper is the end results of collective efforts of reporters, editors, type-setters, proofreaders, designers and printers. These must be well-trained persons.

It is, however, sad to admit that the mass media have been infiltrated by some unqualified persons as well as some unscrupulous individuals with their own political agendas other than to serve the communities they are supposed to educate, inform, entertain and mobilize for development. Hence, the establishment of media commissions in most democratic and civilized communities! Institutions and organizations engaged in mass communication anywhere must be weary of such persons. The other important area of notice is that mass communication deals with the concept of mass audience. Here, there is no common motivation. Audience do not act together. They belong to different classes-different education and socio-economic status.

The message communicated in the mass media is open to the public and everyone has access to it provided she/he has the mass communication technological device as well as understands the language in which the message is sent. Mass communication has a specific method of feed-back which could be in the form of letters to the editor, rejoinders, reviews and articles. This method takes time to go through and it is often volunteered. Not everybody would have the capability to do it. Many people also feel lazy to write. If this is how mass communication works then what are the specific functions of the mass media in society?

Function of the Mass Media

Though there are two main functions of mass communication, which are overt and latent functions of communication, six specific functions of the mass media could be identified here.

These are:

1. *Surveiance of the environment:* This is the collection and distribution of information within and outside a particular environment. The information flow is necessary for unity and coherence if we live in the society of collectivity;
2. *Correlation of parts of the society:* This includes the interpretation of the information, the prescription of conduct and, the comment on social value;
3. *Transmission of social heritage:* By communicating information through the mass media we are transmitting social and cultural values, which aim at sustaining the society;
4. *Educating the masses:* Education on the policies of governments and on the rights and responsibilities could be carried out through the mass media.
5. *Entertainment function:* The mass media also entertain the public by providing emotional relaxation, intrinsic and cultural enjoyment (i.e. provision of momentary escape from problems) and killing boredom; and
6. *Mobilisation function:* This function of the mass media is very important to developing communities everywhere. It seeks to bring the people together and helps to advance national development.

It could be seen from the foregoing functions that the mass media provide information and education, personal identity, entertainment and most importantly integration and social interaction by giving insight into the circumstances of others as well as by helping with the development of social empathy.

The advent of press freedom has given rise to unprecedented abuse of the mass media by unscrupulous mass communicators and authoritarian leaders in society. There is proliferation of community newspapers and FM radio stations in Ghana and the Ghanaian communities around the world. There is also access to internet and the SIL forum on the popular ghanaweb site which bring Ghanaians together everyday by the magic of the electronic media.

While this development should be welcomed and appreciated in the light of healthy competition among ethnic media practitioners there is also the inherent danger of dividing and destroying the very communities these mass communicators seek to help develop! The path of sycophancy, bootlicking, blackmailing of individuals and arrogance of political affiliation lies close to the good functions of the mass media discussed above and must be avoided if the role of the media in our community development is to be made meaningful. The mass media must serve essential functions in the society by accepting and fulfilling certain obligations to the society.

These obligations are mainly to be met by setting high professional standards of informativeness, truth, accuracy, objectivity and balance. In accepting and applying these obligations the elements of the mass media should be self-regulating within the framework of law and established institutions. They should therefore avoid whatever might lead to crime, violence or civil disorder or give offence to any group of people in the society because of their faith or ethnicity. The media as a whole should be pluralistic and reflect the diversity of their society by giving access to various points of views and to rights of reply.

It is therefore incumbent upon our ethnic press (community newspapers and local FM radio stations) to keep our communities connected to the past by communicating the stories and traditions we hold dear. And at the same time connect our communities to the present and to the future by delivering images and news of our people around the world and forming the foundation and values for our children to continue. Instead of undermining each other, the many Ghanaian newspapers and FM radio stations home and abroad should give our communities a strong voice that is not always represented in the mainstream media in the developed countries. Lets help keep our communities around the world united and strong. Together we stand, divided we fall.

MASS MEDIA IN COMMUNITY EDUCATION AND CHILD ABUDE PREVENTION STRATTEGIES

A previous Issues Paper focusing on the prevention of child maltreatment noted that 'the African proverb, "It takes a village to raise a child", epitomises the importance of the role of the wider community in raising children and young people'. Increasingly, responsibility for children is not entrusted solely to parents or guardians but to whole communities. Strategies that aim to optimise the experiences of children and young people, and to prevent child abuse and neglect, are therefore required to ascertain, and perhaps confront, commonly held community attitudes and responses to all children and young people, and to increase community awareness of issues that may affect children and young people.

According to the National Child Protection Council: 'Prevention of abuse involves changing those individual and community attitudes, beliefs and circumstances which allow the abuse to occur.'

The media play a significant role in forming and influencing people's attitudes and behaviour. Issues Paper 14, Child abuse and the media, drew attention to the essential role of the media in increasing society's awareness of, and response to, child abuse and neglect. Of particular note was the part played by news and features that reported on specific child abuse cases, research and intervention strategies. Such media attention to child abuse has, at times, positively influenced public, professional and political responses to the circumstances in which children and young people find themselves. Understanding media influences, and how to use the media constructively, may thus be an essential tool for those who advocate for children, young people, and their families.

In addition to news stories, feature articles, and investigative journalism, sporadic mass media education and prevention campaigns are launched. These campaigns usually endeavour to broaden community knowledge of child abuse and neglect, to influence people's attitudes towards children and young people, and to change behaviours that contribute to, or precipitate, the problem of child abuse and neglect in our communities.

For several reasons, however, the effectiveness of these campaigns remains contentious. Primarily, the effectiveness of mass media in the prevention of child abuse and neglect is debatable. For example, Rayner (1996) argues that 'media campaigns are bloody expensive' and their impact is difficult to determine. Expensive media campaigns may be hard to justify in a political climate where limited funds and resources are provided to address children's needs. Further, McDevitt (1996: 270) cites O'Keefe and Reed (1990: 215) to note that: 'At best, the media are "effective at building citizen awareness of an issue" but more complex attitudinal or behavioural change requires "more direct forms of citizen contact and intervention".'

Others argue, however, that mass media campaigns and media coverage of the abuse and neglect of children perform an important and significant role in placing issues such as child abuse on the public and political agenda. Lindsey (1994: 163) maintains that: 'Media has a central role in mediating information and forming public opinion. The media casts an eye on events that few of us directly experience and renders remote happenings observable and meaningful.'

As Wurtele and Miller-Perrin (1993) have observed, media coverage of child sexual assault has contributed to demystifying and reducing the secrecy that has characteristically surrounded its occurrence. Similarly, a review of the literature on mass media campaigns reveals many examples of campaigns impacting on public knowledge about issues such as work safety, drug and alcohol use, drink-driving, speeding, cigarette smoking, obesity, AIDS, and domestic violence. Attitudinal and/or behavioural change may also occur during campaigns, although this result may be short-lived, lapsing when campaigns end.

Mass media present the opportunity to communicate to

large numbers of people and to target particular groups of people. As observed by Gamble and Gamble, mass communication is significantly different from other forms of communication. They note that mass communication has the capacity to reach 'simultaneously' many thousands of people who are not related to the sender. It depends on 'technical devices' or 'machines' to quickly distribute messages to diverse audiences often unknown to each other. It is accessible to many people, but may be avoided. It is orchestrated by specialists whose intent is to persuade potential audiences of the benefits of their attention. It is 'controlled by gatekeepers' who censor the content of messages. And finally, unlike one-to-one communication, it produces only minimal, delayed feedback to its senders.

However, mass communication simultaneously presents opportunities and limitations, both of which require consideration when planning mass media assisted eradication of social problems such as child abuse and neglect. According to Wellings and Macdowall, drawing on Tones et al. (1990): 'The strength of the mass media . . . lies in helping to put issues on the public agenda, in reinforcing local efforts, in raising consciousness about . . . issues and in conveying simple information . . . The limitations of the mass media are that they are less effective in conveying complex information, in teaching skills, in shifting attitudes and beliefs, and in changing behaviour in the absence of other enabling factors.'

Campaigns, and other forms of media education and entertainment (such as television programs, film and live productions), may be targeted at all families with a view to encouraging positive attitudes toward children and stopping abuse before it starts or is even considered (primary prevention). Groups of people identified as particularly susceptible to abusive behaviour may be targeted (secondary prevention). Further, a campaign or program may target families in which abuse has already occurred with the intention of preventing recurrence of the abuse (tertiary prevention). Thus, a well-focused mass media campaign, educational program or live-theatre production has the potential to contribute successfully to community education and the prevention of child abuse and neglect.

However, as will be emphasised throughout this Issues Paper, campaign strategies may only be successful to the degree that they are backed by community education and support programs:

'A media campaign can be effective, but it means nothing unless the campaign is integrated into an overall approach dealing with the various aspects of the problem being addressed.'

'Whatever happens at the mass level must be complemented and supported at a grass roots level for any long-term behavioural change to occur.'

A report on a recent Western Australian mass mediabased campaign, 'Freedom from Fear', which targeted male perpetrators of domestic violence, identified 'five potential message strategies' for mass media prevention campaigns:

- Criminal sanctions: a traditional emphasis on legal threats;
- Community intervention: an approach encouraging friends and neighbours to report domestic violence or intervene with the perpetrator or victim;
- Social disapproval: a theme emphasising shame and embarrassment (that is, 'real men don't hit women');
- Consequences: a theme based on the impact of the violence on their partner or children; and
- Help is available: emphasising that help is available if the man desires to change.

These strategies grew out of a review of the literature and interviews with domestic violence workers. Each of these five strategies has strengths and weaknesses that warrant consideration in the formation of media messages for education and prevention campaigns. This Issues Paper describes some recent and past mass media education and prevention campaigns, television programs, films, and live theatre productions.

Their raison d'étre, their justification in the current economic and political environment, and their impact are discussed. Information gained from evaluations is highlighted and recommendations for future media campaigns and initiatives are made. The primary focus of this paper is the media-assisted prevention of all forms of child abuse and neglect. However, examples of mass media-based prevention in other areas such as health and safety are drawn upon, and each of the message strategies noted above will become apparent in the context of current or past campaigns and media approaches to prevention.

Community Education and Prevention Campaigns

In the year 1990-1991 reports of child abuse and neglect to Australian child protection authorities numbered 49,721. According to the Australian Institute of Health and Welfare, in 2000-2001 reports had increased to 115,471; following investigation, 27,367 cases were confirmed or substantiated as involving child abuse and/or neglect. The physical abuse, sexual abuse, emotional abuse, and neglect of children have a long recorded history. In the mid to late 1800s, Toulmouche, Tardieu, Bernard and Lacassagne reported that children were often sexually assaulted, that children reported honestly about their abuse, and that the perpetrators of abuse were often the children's fathers and brothers.

Corby (1993) notes that Kempe's 'discovery' of the battered child syndrome in 1962, and the 'discovery' of child sexual abuse in Britain in the 1980s were in fact 're-discoveries'. According to Corby (1993: 16): 'Child abuse is not a new phenomenon, nor is public or state concern about it. Nevertheless fresh attempts to tackle child mistreatment are usually accompanied by the declaration that it is a new and as yet undiscovered problem. This 'newness' is seen as an important part of the process of establishing it as an issue requiring resources to tackle it.'

Historically, children have been accorded little, if any, status in society. Deprived of rights and perceived as the property of their parents or guardians, children could be treated any way their 'owners' saw fit. In this context, community awareness and acceptance of the reality of child abuse, particularly child abuse perpetrated by family members, has been slow. 'Stranger danger', beliefs that children's stories are untrustworthy, and beliefs that parents always act in the best interests of their children, appear to be easier for communities to accept. Such beliefs may present people with a means of turning a blind eye to the reality that child abuse is often perpetrated by adults well known to children, in children's own homes, and in other trusted environments.

In relation to child sexual abuse, for example, Kitzinger and Skidmore (1995: 53) quote one interviewee from Kidscape in the United Kingdom: 'People don't want to be associated with child abuse as incest . . . it's a message we try to get across to the press but they're very wary . . . it's easier and safer to concentrate on strangers and bullying.' Olafsen, Corwin and Summit (1993) have argued that cycles of awareness followed by suppression have typified society's response to child sexual abuse. Arguably, this has been society's response to all forms of child abuse and neglect of children. Mass media education and prevention campaigns present one means of breaking cycles of suppression and denial. The media have played a key role in periodically placing the issue of child abuse on the public agenda.

Conceptualisation of Childhood and Adolescence

This section discusses: images of children and young people in society and in the media; media influences on children and children's rights; and the impact of media campaigns on the victims of child abuse.

Journalists willing to advocate for children and young people face the challenge of counterbalancing negative images or 'demonisation' (Franklin and Horwath 1996) of children and, particularly, of adolescents, in print, television and film. Starkly contrasting with once popular views of childhood as a time of innocence, less than positive images of children and young people in the media may place obstacles in the path of attempts to prevent their abuse and neglect.

It is notable that child abuse media prevention campaigns rarely, if ever, focus on the maltreatment of adolescents rather attention is given to societal problems, perhaps stemming from child abuse, such as drug use, youth suicide and chroming. Similarly, as observed by Mendes (2000: 50), drawing on Vinson (1987), Aldridge (1994) and Wilczynski and Sinclair (1999): 'Structural disadvantages contributing to child abuse and neglect such as poverty, unemployment, and gender or race-based discrimination are rendered invisible [in the media].'

A comparison of the media coverage of three child murder cases - two in the United Kingdom and one in Australia - highlights significantly different images of children created, or reinforced, by media comment. Alder and Polk (2001) observe the language used and attitudes portrayed in the media coverage. In 1968, 11-year old Mary Bell murdered two boys, aged three and four in the UK. Twenty-five years later, in 1993, two ten-year-old boys murdered two-year-old Jamie Bulger in the UK, and in Australia in 1998, a ten-year-old boy was charged with drowning a six-year-old playmate.

According to Alder and Polk (2001), while media commentary in the Mary Bell case expressed 'concern for the offender' who was perceived by many as the 'surviving child of this tragedy', the latter two cases predominantly yielded media commentary that described the child offenders as 'evil', callous and reckless. Alder and Polk (2001: 134) contend that: 'What may have changed in the years since the Bell case is the gradual evolution of an internationalised media, capable of the instantaneous transfer of 'infotainment' around the globe . . . these outlets have a special appetite for the bizarre and unusual.'

Franklin and Horwath (1996) further observe a concerning change in society's perception of children which, as Tomison (1997) has noted, extends to adolescents. Less often perceived as 'innocent' and 'innately good', it seems a child or young person may now be portrayed as a 'powerful, destructive human being'. The cases described above are distressing and uncommon. Negative images of children (perhaps stemming from such cases), and media reinforcement of feelings that children and young people are a burden on families and on society, do not assist in the prevention of child abuse and neglect. Further exploration of the lives experienced by young offenders, while not detracting from the horror of events that occur, almost invariably reveals their own victimisation as children or as adolescents.3

Moreover, as Tomison (1997: 22) claims, perceiving children as 'powerful' and 'evil' beings may 'dehumanise' children and serve to justify child abuse. He further contends that the negative portrayal of children in the media may result in victims of abuse blaming themselves for their abuse. Victims may be led to believe that they deserved the assaults perpetrated against them, and thus accept their abuse as justified. Further, Tomison (1997) cites Winn (1993) and Garbarino (1992) to note that these negative images of children may indeed be magnified once the child becomes an adolescent. Negative stereotypes of young people, he contends, may contribute to the incidence of adolescent maltreatment, exacerbating 'the problems of troubled youth in troubled families, providing a justification for unresponsive parenting and increasing the probability of serious family conflict'.

By putting pressure on governments to increase community supports for children and families, and by presenting positive, empathetic images of children and young people, the media may have a powerful influence in preventing, rather than perhaps indirectly promoting, child maltreatment. As Walby argues: 'Children and childhood need to be better appreciated; families with children need a more supportive environment; issues affecting children need more sophisticated debate; and services for children and the people who work for them need more support from the public.'

The impact of media advertising on children and adolescents is well documented, as is concern about some aspects of the media's powerful influence on children's attitudes and behaviours. Television may be 'a more powerful socialisation agent than peers and teachers'. As acknowledged in a major New Zealand newspaper, it is notable that: 'The media promote violence as an effective way of dealing with conflict through television, films, videos, and interactive video games'.

In evidence given to the Victorian Government Inquiry into the Effects of Television and Multimedia on Children and Families in Victoria, Michael Carr-Gregg (2000: 68) further endorses this view: 'Contrary to some claims, many people in the medical, public health, and scientific communities are in agreement that the relationship between television violence and aggression and violence in young people does exist. Exhaustive reviews of the evidence accumulated over 40 years - and we are talking about 3000 different studies - have led researchers to conclude unequivocally that mass media significantly contributes to the aggressive behaviour and attitudes of many children, adolescents, and, of course, adults.'

However, this power of the media to negatively influence children's attitudes and behaviours may be used to impact positively on the lives of children and adolescents. According to the Inquiry into the Effects of Television and Multimedia on Children and Families in Victoria (2000: 35): 'Qualitative evidence suggests that quality children's television can enhance child development by providing positive role models of cooperation and collaboration as a responsible way of acting in the world.' Indeed, the constructive use of mass media can assist in teaching children and young people socially desirable ways of dealing with conflict, knowledge of their rights to integrity and protection from harm, healthy eating habits and lifestyles, and ways to assert themselves and their rights in a positive, acceptable manner.

As noted in the Inquiry into the Effects of Television and Multimedia on Children and Families in Victoria (2000: 37), evaluations of educational television programmes, designed either for pre-schoolers or for older children, have suggested their effectiveness in 'heightening a range of social behaviours', diminishing 'the effects of stereotyping', increasing 'preparedness for adolescence', and stimulating the discussion of 'solutions to general social issues'. Research suggests that, at least in the short term, television viewing of such programs may increase children's and young people's knowledge and positively change attitudes and behaviours. Unfortunately, longitudinal studies exploring sustained effects are rare and thus inconclusive.

The Inquiry into the Effects of Television and Multimedia on Children and Families in Victoria (2000: 33) further notes that television 'is one of the most popular forms of mass communication and entertainment in Australia [and] has been under-utilised as an educative tool', and suggests that perhaps narrow vision has meant that the deliberate use of television simultaneously to entertain and educate has not been fully recognised. Despite this, Postman (1994) has argued that television is rapidly becoming 'the first curriculum', with educational institutions such as schools following behind.

According to the Inquiry into the Effects of Television and Multimedia on Children and Families in Victoria (2000: 1): 'The one thing on which the critics and the defenders of television agree is that it is a central and pervasive part of modern life. Children can spend more time watching television than any other activity except sleep . . . it is a major socialising force in children's lives.' Mass media education and prevention campaigns may be designed to target children and young people, providing them with useful information and alerting them to avenues for further information, help and support.

Campaigns can also use regular television programs for children. Drawing on the research of Baran, Chase and Courtright (1979) and Forge and Phemister (1987), the Inquiry into the Effects of Television and Multimedia on Children and Families in Victoria (2000: 15) states: 'Children . . . have shown cooperative behaviour following one observation of just one episode of positive social behaviour in a commercial television drama . . . and cartoons with a positive social message have produced positive behaviours in pre-schoolers . . . Discussions of complex issues and approaches to conflict resolution have also been successfully utilised in Australian drama.'

Campaign organisers can approach producers of popular children's television requesting that they incorporate messages, such as a child's right to physical integrity and to protection from harm, and depict desired protective behaviours, such as seeking help if a child feels threatened or unsafe. Further, campaigns may be designed to give children and young people an opportunity to express their views on issues that affect them, specifically targeting adult audiences that habitually ignore the views and experiences of children and young people. Research on the physical punishment of children (Saunders, in progress) suggests, for example, that adults may be interested to hear children's views on the issue of physical discipline, and children interviewed in the research were keen for adults to hear their views. To date, however, the media rarely, if ever, consults children and takes their views into account before reporting on the physical punishment of children. Indeed, the media often trivialises the issue of physical punishment.

Tomison (1996: 77) has noted that, The United Kingdom Commission of Inquiry into the Prevention of Child Abuse made a recommendation that the media 'take a more balanced and sympathetic view of children'. Tomison (1997: 25) highlights that: 'In line with a belief in the importance of 'listening to children', the Commission felt that the media should take the views of children into account when presenting on an issue in which children have some interest. The Commission (1996) recommended that the media should have an obligation to consider a child's best interest in stories in which children feature, and that the failure to do so would constitute grounds for a complaint to a relevant authority.'

Impact on Victims of Child Abuse

The impact of media campaigns on the lives of victims is sometimes reported in print media stories about them. Writing about Annie, a victim of sexual assault by her stepfather, Dixon (1993: 1) reported how Annie remembered her reaction as a child to an advertisement about sexual abuse: 'Her grandmother caught the fleeting look of despair and pain in her face. Her grandmother [who had previously had unconfirmed suspicions] asked [Annie] again about her stepfather. Annie says she burst into tears.'

In the same year, the Sydney Morning Herald published a piece about another victim of sexual abuse, assaulted by her stepfather. It was reported that shortly before driving over him with her car, causing long-term injuries, the victim saw 'a televised community announcement about standing up against child abuse'. As in many cases of incest, the victim's stepfather had been released from prison after serving a sentence which was perceived by his victim as not fitting the crime she had suffered.

In The Age in 1998 Kissane wrote about Cathy Freeman and other celebrities who, through the media, have revealed their sexual abuse as children. She also reported on the experience of Karen Hogan who heads the Melbourne Royal Children's Hospital's Gatehouse Centre for abused children: 'For one little girl, this week, something has changed. Her mother recently rang Hogan . . . for advice. The family suspected that the girl had suffered sexual abuse some time ago, but had been unable to confirm it. This week the girl told her mother, "Mum, you know what happened to Cathy Freeman? That happened to me".'

Cathy Freeman, Derryn Hinch, Angry Anderson, Debra Byrne, Oprah Winfrey, Roseanne Barr and Roger Moore are a few of the celebrities who have exposed their own experiences of child sexual abuse through the media. Kissane quoted Joe Tucci, Executive Director of Australians Against Child Abuse, an agency that offers counselling to abused children, who commented on the possible effect of celebrity disclosures through the media: 'The most important result of someone like Cathy Freeman speaking out is that it helps lessen the shame for people who come after her . . . It hooks into exactly what the kids are struggling with. They say, 'Look at the courage it took them to come out and talk about it; I'm courageous, I did a similar thing to Cathy Freeman and Angry Anderson.' It gives them hope about success, that they, too, will recover from the abuse.'

The impact of a media campaign may be dramatic and farreaching as it is occurring, and perhaps for a short time afterwards. However, campaigns drawing attention to child abuse will be more effective if they are ongoing. Mass media campaigns have the potential to confront society with the horrific nature of much child abuse. Such campaigns can also educate the public about the many, often co-existing, forms of abuse suffered by children. They can also draw attention to the status of children in society, highlighting children's dependency and vulnerability to abuse and neglect.

According to Hall and Stannard: 'The physical and emotional impacts of child abuse are very clear. However, the long-term loss of productivity through lower achievement levels, unemployment and family dislocation are less apparent. Research shows that the child abuse can also lead to criminal behaviour among young people. These costs must be met by the taxpayer for years to come through increasing [financial] claims as well as health, counselling, welfare, police and prison services.'

Mass media education and prevention campaigns present a viable means for governments to be seen to be doing something in relation to the problem of child abuse and neglect. Campaigns may assist not only in the prevention of immediate harm to children and young people but also in allaying the long-term social and economic consequences of child maltreatment. Campaigns must, of course, be backed by supportive services for children, young people and their families.

MASS MEDIA EDUCATION AND PREVENTION

Drawing on the research of Nielson (1998) and the Federation of Australian Commercial Television Stations (1995), Sanders, Montgomery and Brechman-Toussaint (2000: 939-940) note that: Australian adults spend about three hours per day watching television; 61 per cent of Australian adults choose television viewing to stay informed and to access news; and 79.65 per cent of Australian adults consider themselves to be most influenced by television advertising.

An article in *The Age* in 1993 demonstrated the potentially powerful influence of the media on people's attitudes.

Milburn (1993: 5) reported on the cancellation, after five days sitting, of a trial against a foster parent charged with the sexual penetration and sexual abuse of an 11-year-old boy in his care. Concerns were raised by the accused's defence lawyer about an Age article describing a television mini-series to be screened on Channel 10. In reply, the judge ordered that the trial be cancelled: '. . . the boy's lawyer said the article was unlikely to prejudice the jury... [The article] focused on the Catholic Church and priests in a Canadian orphanage, whereas the charged foster parent was not a priest, had no particular religious affiliation, and the sexual abuse was alleged to have occurred in his private home.' Nevertheless, the trial was cancelled, causing great distress to the child victim and others.

Clearly, the perceived power of the media, as exemplified in this case, may be used in child abuse prevention campaigns. Krugman (1996: 259) notes that in 1990, faced with what they perceived to be a national emergency, the United States Advisory Board on Child Abuse and Neglect '. . . called on the media to avoid raising public awareness that child abuse exists, and rather help the public understand the complexity of the problem and how it could be prevented'.

This view appears to be turning a blind eye to the reality of child abuse and neglect. Importantly, the literature documenting past and present media campaigns consistently stresses a dual role for the media - to portray the existence of child abuse and to present ways of addressing and preventing it: 'Media prevention needs to provide information about both the problem behaviour and how to deal with it effectively'.

As noted above, the success of a child abuse education and prevention campaign will be influenced by available funding, existing support services, and other educational activities, such as prevention programs in schools. Writing about the impact of a media campaign in the United States designed to increase public action to help maltreated children in addictive families, Andrews, McLeese and Currant made the following recommendations:

'Public awareness about effective ways to help is likely to lead to citizen action. Too often, media messages focus on the nature and extent of the problem without suggesting what can be done to change it . . .

The services system needs to be prepared for the public's response to a media message. Increasing public awareness raises demands for assistance and information.

Increased efforts are needed to promote personal ways of helping, without formal system intervention . . . many people believe in their own capacity to help. This is consistent with the 'neighbors helping neighbors' approach recommended by the US Advisory Board on Child Abuse and Neglect (1993). With encouragement and information more people might act on their beliefs.'

CHARACTERISTICS OF SOME MEDIA CAMPAIGNS

Susan Wilson has observed: 'For advocates, the press is a grand piano waiting for a player. Strike the chords through a news story, a guest column, or an editorial, and thousands will hear. Working in concert, unbiased reporters and smart advocates can make music together.' Press releases are one of the most important primary sources of media news stories. Journalists spend much of their time 'rewriting' press releases and creating stories from written information provided to them by individuals, groups, and organisations.

Many news stories are derived from 'facts created for journalists by individuals and bureaucracies'. Thus, information provided to media outlets that sheds light on an issue such as child abuse, may occur either in an organised manner through well-researched and planned mass media education and prevention campaigns, or through press releases, opinion pieces, and letters to newspapers focussing on current cases or significant issues or events.

As states: 'There are abundant opportunities to engage in valuable public information, community education and prevention activities through the print and broadcast media.'

'Advocacy journalists' can be a powerful ally. The media 'can sway hearts and minds . . . define center stage'. The media can bring pressure to bear on governments. Media coverage of a particular issue may assist in initiating or consolidating attitudinal and behavioural change. As noted in Issues Paper no. 15, 'mere coverage of issues affecting children places journalists in the role of advocate'. A recent example of media-driven action in response to child abuse occurred as a result of a letter sent to a major newspaper. The headline TRAPPED BYALETTER, in the South Australian newspaper, The Advertiser, preceded the paper's 'top story' released by reporter Sam Weir:

'An anonymous letter sent to The Advertiser more than two years ago triggered a chain of events which ended in former magistrate Peter Michael Liddy's conviction on child sex abuse charges. The two-page letter - handed to police five months before Liddy's arrest . . . alleged that he had been molesting children and using the Surf Life Saving Club for "his supply of victims". Sent to the Family Forum section, the letter was referred to the Police Exploitation Investigation Section.'

Written anonymously, the author of this letter correctly anticipated the power of the media to advocate on behalf of the victimised children. The actual letter could not be printed in the paper prior to the conviction. Nevertheless, the story (two years later) emanating from the fact that the letter had been sent to, and acted upon, by the newspaper reveals the sense of achievement the newspaper employees gained from being able to assist in bringing this man to justice. It also demonstrates the important role of the media as an instigator of political, social or legal action when other avenues may have proven unproductive.

A Cirrent Mass Media Campaign

In Victoria in May 2000, Australians Against Child Abuse launched a child abuse prevention campaign ' Every Child is Important'. This primary prevention campaign used a 'comforting' approach and incorporated a significant mass media component. As outlined in 'More action - less talk! Community responses to child abuse prevention', the campaign sought to elicit a commitment from adults to adults to develop safe and non-abusive relationships with children; persuade adults to stop behaving in ways which are harmful to children; educate adults about the important needs of children; and better inform adults about the causes and consequences of child abuse.

The campaign encouraged all adults to think and view children as a source of hope; understand the developmental variables of children; respect the meaning children give to their experiences; engage positively with the principles of children's rights; and appreciate more fully the capacities and contribution of children to the cultural and emotional life of families and communities. The campaign also addressed: the commonly held belief that children are a cost to society; the perceived suspicion that any application of the notion of children's rights will mean an erosion of parent's rights; and the public's lack of understanding about the extent and nature of child abuse in Australia.

The campaign continued until the end of 2001. Asong, written by Van Morrison and performed by Rod Stewart, 'Have I Told You Lately That I Love You', was the focus of a television advertising campaign that aimed to stimulate people's thoughts about the importance and value of children and how this is communicated to them. Television commercials were backed up by press and radio advertisements. In addition to advertising, the campaign sought media attention by involving Tracy Bartram, FOX FM radio personality, as an ambassador for the campaign. Media attention was drawn to the campaign's launch. A free information kit for parents was made available, parent's seminar sessions, featuring Michael Grose, were conducted, and a website made readily available to the public. The campaign did not receive state or federal funding but relied heavily on in-kind support from individuals and Victorian businesses.

Quantum Market Research monitored the effectiveness of the campaign. In May 2000 and October 2000 telephone interviews were conducted with a representative sample of 301 adults. Public dissemination of research outcomes formed part of the campaign strategy. Tucci et al. (2001: 20-21) report that the initial research findings, five months into the campaign, revealed that: 'Child abuse is as serious social problem that is poorly understood by the Victorian public . . . While 51per cent of respondents believed the community recognised child abuse as a serious social problem and another 21 per cent believed they accurately understood the extent and nature of child abuse in Australia, this is clearly not the case . . . 59 per cent were unable even to guess the number of reports of child abuse received annually . . . only 4 per cent of respondents accurately estimated the size of the problem. Twenty-nine per cent of respondents underestimated the problem by at least 90,000 reports. The idea that adults can hurt children is disturbing and likely underpins the belief by 51 per cent of respondents that the community treats this issue seriously, but when asked to account for the extent to which children are being abused by adults, community awareness is sadly lacking.'

Eighty per cent of respondents strongly supported the need for a campaign against child abuse. Australians Against Child Abuse thus feels confident that the 'Every Child is Important' campaign will significantly influence public attitudes and responses to children and to child abuse. Ongoing research into the impact of the campaign will in itself be valuable in contributing to the debate about the educative and cost effectiveness of mass media campaigns aimed at preventing child abuse and neglect.

Primary Prevention

The NSPCC Full Stop Campaign, launched in the United

Kingdom in May 1999, has the ambitious aim of ending cruelty to children within 20 years. Costing three million pounds, it proposes to change attitudes and behaviour towards children, to make it everybody's business to protect children, and to launch new services and approaches. The campaign is supported by Prince Andrew, popular personalities such as the Spice Girls, the English football star Alan Shearer, and companies such as British Telecom and Microsoft.

As Rudaizky (quoted in Hall 1999) explains, a pictorial theme of the campaign is people covering their eyes: 'The theme of the eyes being covered is about people not facing up to the reality of what is happening. Our intention was not to shock but to move people into doing something about it. Child abuse is not nice to talk about.

It is an upsetting subject but unless we talk about it, we will not end it.' This objective highlights the suppression/ awareness phenomenon mentioned above, and draws attention again to the need for ongoing rather than intermittent prevention campaigns.

Gaps in knowledge and misconceptions about child sexual abuse appear to persist despite media campaigns such as those conducted in Victoria and New South Wales. In spite of this, both campaigns were evaluated and deemed for the most part to have been successful. The Victorian (1992) and New South Wales (1986-1988) mass media campaigns sought to draw the public's attention to the sexual assault of children. With prompting, people may remember the slogans used for the campaigns: 'Child Sexual Assault, It's Often Closer to Home than You Think'; 'Child Sexual Assault Offenders. No Excuses Never Ever'; 'Child Sexual Assault is a Crime'; and 'Stand Up Victoria: Stand Up Against Child Sexual Abuse'.

The Victorian and New South Wales media campaigns comprised television commercials and community service announcements, press advertisements, information booklets, stickers, posters and telephone hotlines.

In Victoria, the criteria used to evaluate the success of the campaign included:

- An increased acceptance of the seriousness of child sexual assault;
- A higher perception of the prevalence of child sexual assault;
- A higher awareness of the potential for sexual abuse to be perpetrated by adults known to the child;
- An increase in awareness of the types of organisations who could be approached for help;
- An increasingly strong belief that there is a need to take action to address child sexual assault; and
- An increase in the belief that a child is best out of the home if child sexual assault is occurring. (Wallis Consulting Group 1992)

Apparently, removing the perpetrator rather than the child from the home was not considered either at this time or in this campaign. Issues documented as needing to be addressed following the Victorian campaign included:

- There was little acknowledgment of the existence of female offenders;
- A number of mothers believed that the child victim of sexual assault might be to blame, and a number of males blamed the female in the home for the occurrence of child sexual assault;
- There was resistance to reporting child sexual assault to doctors, the police or to Community Services Victoria (as the Department of Human Services was then known); and
- There was a retention of the misconception that children provoke men who sexually assault them.

The campaign in New South Wales was conducted over three years and involved three stages. The first stage lasted seven weeks and began in October 1986. The second stage lasted eight weeks and began in May 1987. The third stage, which replayed the radio and television advertisements of the first two campaigns, began in June 1988. The campaign was deemed to have been successful 'to the extent that it achieved improved knowledge about child sexual assault . . . [the campaign] broke the taboo'.

One of the main messages the campaign set out to communicate to the community was that children are at a greater risk of sexual abuse by relatives and family friends than by strangers, and child sexual offenders ought to take responsibility for their actions. The campaign aimed to promote community awareness of why perpetrators of child sexual assault commit this crime, how attitudes in society influence their behaviour; and how these attitudes arise in the first place.

Concerns documented following the evaluation of the media campaign included:

- An increase in the number of people who would talk to the offender as a means of addressing the issue, perhaps further endangering the child;
- that by concentrating on one form of abuse important connections with other forms of abuse may not have been made; and
- that the campaigns could have been even more multilingual and culturally specific.

Calvert also stressed that: 'Mass media campaigns will only have an impact on attitudes and behaviour if they are run over a long period of time . . . supported by a range of other activities . . . prevention strategies obviously require a sustained effort and commitment to resources if they are to be successful . . . additional and adequate funding must be provided. Unless these things are achieved, the prevention campaigns will be like pouring water on sand: gone as soon as it is poured.'

Depending on their content, the messages of the Victorian and the New South Wales campaigns were targeted at adolescents, men and/or families. Consideration was given to viewing times and programs, favoured by males, such as sports programmes. The important messages that these campaigns set out to convey are unlikely to be retained by communities that characteristically change in nature and composition, unless they are conveyed to people continually rather than in short bursts over a relatively short period of time.

CONFRONTING CAMPAIGNS

In New Zealand, Roberts (1998) has written about a recent confronting Rape Crisis awareness campaign focusing on incest. The campaign was called It's okay to talk about incest. Its aim was to break the silence, 'to drive home the message that incest exists and everyone needs to talk about and challenge it'. The campaign's media advertisements carried the personal messages of five incest survivors. One survivor of sexual abuse by her father revealed in an advertisement: 'Nobody forced him to come into my bedroom two or three times a week from when I was four. Nobody held a knife to his throat to make him lie on top of me. There was no-one blackmailing him to pinch what weren't even nipples yet'. Graphic detail in the survivors true stories was followed by evidence of the emotional suffering of victims of incest:

'I haven't been able to get close to people, to trust anyone. I feel that time's running out for me to have a really close, fulfilling relationship with someone I can trust.'

The success of this media campaign in terms of public exposure to the problem of incest and government recognition of the effects of incest was considerable. Unfortunately, the campaign ran only for one week. In the United Kingdom, a recent Barnardo's advertisement attracted censorship because of its confronting nature.

The Committee of Advertising Practice discouraged newspapers from publishing a digitally altered advertisement depicting:

'A 10-month-old boy sitting on a dirty floor wearing only a nappy, clutching a syringe and gripping a tourniquet in his teeth. The text reads: ' John Donaldson. Age 23. Battered as a child, it was always possible that John would turn to drugs. With Barnardo's help, child abuse need not lead to an empty future.'

The advertisement was the fifth in a confronting Barnardo's campaign intending to demonstrate what can happen to abused or disadvantaged children who do not receive the help they need when they are young. In retaliation against the censorship, Barnardo's director of marketing and communication argued: 'They're not making due allowance for a charity talking about its work. If this was a supermarket trying to use shock tactics just to sell products from its shelves one might agree with the committee.'

It appears that the reality of child abuse and its impact may be too confronting for some members of the community to absorb and to address. Other mass media campaigns in England have run without censure. Two recent examples include the NSPCC Full Stop Campaign and another NSPCC campaign.

The NSPCC 'Campaign Against Baby Battering', costing 1.7 million pounds, was launched in April 2000. It was prompted by the fact that: 'At least one baby is killed every fortnight in domestic violence in England and Wales', and recent British research revealed that, in a period of 12 months, 92 babies suffered serious brain injuries caused by shaking. The campaign's message, aimed at parents overly stressed by crying infants, was: 'Before you cross that line, stop.' Posters showed happy images of parents cuddling babies. Captions underneath read: 'By bedtime she wanted to shake him like a rag doll', and 'That night he felt like slamming her against the cot'. For three weeks advertisements were shown on prime time television, supported by 7500 billboards and the distribution of one million leaflets.

A Campaign Targeting Businessmen

A notable example of how a mass media campaign can target a particular group of people was run in the United States in 1994. Brown (1994) reported on a campaign, 'Children: An investment that's guaranteed to grow', that targeted businessmen: 'This spring's major ad campaign to prevent child abuse won't picture a bruised toddler or an out-of- control parent. It will show a stack of books on business.

And it won't move you to tears. Instead it will suggest you see children much as you might view a stock portfolio - an investment, as one of the ads says, "that's guaranteed to grow".' The advertisements for this campaign were displayed on television during baseball games, in Money Magazine, Fortune and Newsweek, and on public transport. This 'investment' campaign followed a previous campaign that encouraged parents to turn to family, friends or a help line for support before they hurt their child:

'In a TV spot, a parent yells in the background, "Can't you do anything right?" and "How'd you like a reason to cry?", while the announcer urges parents to seek help . . . "This is one time a few words can't hurt".'

This campaign was found to be successful in getting the message across to many women. Surveys revealed, however, that richer and well-educated men believed that 'what happened in their families was nobody's business but their own'. The follow-up campaign was thus designed to reach businessmen.

Godenzi and De Puy (2001) describe a campaign launched by the Canadian Association of Broadcasters working cooperatively with Canadian Government Departments of Health, Justice and Defence. Focusing on violence against women and children, the campaign included radio and television commercials, information leaflets outlining both facts about violence and tips on how to deal with it. Tips addressed 'managing anger, helping abused persons, devising safety plans, coping with family violence, and getting help'.

The campaign also raised and addressed the issue of media violence. It further specifically targeted potential or current abusers by asking questions such as: 'Do you always have to be the one in charge? Do you blame your partner for everything that goes wrong?' These questions were followed with strategies that help to control one's feelings and information on ways to access professional assistance.

The Freedom from Fear campaign in Western Australia targeted male perpetrators of domestic violence. As noted in the introduction to this paper, five media strategies used in mass media prevention campaigns were identified prior to the campaign's implementation. They are 'criminal sanctions'; 'community intervention'; 'social disapproval'; 'consequences'; and 'help available'. Through formative research which involved interviewing domestic violence workers, the organisers of this campaign found strategies four and five to be the most effective for their campaign. Perpetrators were concerned about the impact of their violence on their children, and they were interested to know how to seek help.

ParentLink, a collective of Missouri agencies in the United States, similarly uses these strategies in their media campaign When You're Under the Influence, They're Under Yours: 'When he gets to work, he sees a poster with this same caption. He begins to wonder about his drinking and its impact on his children.

For more information, he calls ParentLinks's Warmline . . . he has an opportunity to problem solve over the phone, and learns more about his substance abuse and its impact on his family. He obtains materials to read and information about substance abuse counselling programs in his community.'

King et al. (1999) report on a New South Wales campaign, 'First aid for Scalds', primarily involving advertisements on ethnic radio and ethnic newspapers, designed to reach people from non-English speaking backgrounds, specifically Vietnamese, Chinese and Arabic. While similar campaigns have been successful in educating the English-speaking community about prevention and treatment of scald injuries to children, clearly there is also a need in a multi-cultural society such as Australia to ensure that everyone gets exposure to campaign messages that are culturally and linguistically appropriate. King et al. (1999: 105), drawing on Meiser and Gurr (1996), suggest that: 'Multicultural radio (community and government sponsored), television, multicultural print, translated materials, community networks, and family and friends have all been identified as significant information pathways for people from non-English speaking backgrounds.'

Evaluation of the campaign, through before and after telephone surveys, revealed that the campaign was successful. The knowledge of all three groups had increased, though there were differences in absorption of the campaign material by the three targeted groups. Greater exposure to campaign material appears to have resulted in greater campaign effectiveness in the Vietnamese community. King et al. conclude that: 'This initiative provides a model of how community based injury prevention can target several language groups, with adjustments in messages and media according to cultural differences. It illustrates the success of this approach, as well as the significant variability between groups.'

IMPACT OF OTHER MEDIA ON PERCEPTIOND OF CHILD

Child abuse is now increasingly the subject of television dramas, documentaries, films, and live theatre productions. Some of them, characteristically controversial, have attracted comment in the literature and have been reviewed in the print media. Television programs are often followed by information about where victims and offenders/potential offenders can seek help, and phone numbers to ring (helplines) are often displayed. Discussion about the impact of these types of media on the public's perception of child abuse and on efforts to combat the abuse of children presents both positive and negative comment. The following discussion presents some examples and commentary.

Sanders et al. (2000) at the University of Queensland, evaluated Families - a 12-part prevention-focused television series 'designed to provide empirically validated parenting information in an interesting and entertaining format' (2000: 940). The series presented a parenting model, suggesting strategies parents could use with their children. It aimed to reassure parents that it is normal for parenting to be challenging, and it hoped to increase parents' confidence that positive changes in children's behaviour were achievable. The series also aimed to increase awareness in the community of the importance of 'positive family relationships' to the positive development of young people.

This 'media-based television series' was considered to be successful, specifically in relation to its impact on increasing the parenting confidence of mothers. However, Sanders et al. (2000: 945) concluded that the impact of the series could have been increased: 'by the strategic provision of service support systems, such as telephone information contact lines or parenting resource centres, which could be advertised as part of a coordinated media strategy planned to coincide with the airing of the television program. These services could provide information and back-up resources, such as parenting tip sheets, to parents seeking further advice after viewing the program. Staff at these centres could also identify and refer families who may need more intensive help.

Edutainment

Donovan (1992) insists that 'edutainment' incorporating educational messages in television soap-operas and drama requires very close liaison between writers, producers and experts in the field, such as child sexual abuse counsellors. Moreover, according to Donovan (1992: 30): 'Documentaries and feature articles should not relate solely to child abuse but should deal also with family and child welfare issues. They should include positive modelling behaviours as well as highlighting unacceptable practices and the consequences of these unacceptable practices.'

Cooper, Roter and Langlieb (2000) report on an initiative on United States television called Following ER. Designed to provide factual follow-up information on medical and social issues dramatised on ER, the popular television program, Following ER forms part of the evening news. Cooper et al. state: 'The prime time link is maximised by prefacing the segments with a brief rendition of ER's distinctive theme music and a relevant video clip from the show . . . Following ER borrows some of the intensity and action of ER to build a context for prevention news stories.' Links of this nature may make some prevention information more appealing thus maintaining audience attention to, and retention of, messages.

It has been suggested that sometimes 'drama reaches the parts the documentary cannot'. Writing about Testimony of a Child, a BBC screenplay that presents 'the other side of the Cleveland child sexual abuse saga - the story of an abused child going home to [the] abuser', Campbell argues that sexual assault 'presents television with terrible problems. Television is about seeing. But it censors what we need to see if we are to understand because it bows to propriety and thus contains what is knowable . . .'

Despite this, Campbell (1989: 45) notes the power of fictitious drama based on fact to: ' invite you to think: what would you do if faced with that child's face, his fantasies full of terror and death, his starvation, his stubborn silences, his sore bum. And what would you do if those riddles were amplified by his little sister showing you a sexual relationship with a daddy dolly?'

A documentary screened in the United Kingdom in 1992 entitled Beyond Belief claimed to show new evidence of satanic/ritual abuse in Britain. Following the program, helplines were overloaded with calls from people who had experienced sexual or ritual abuse. Counsellors noted that: 'The program appeared to have given callers permission to speak of their experiences and their gratitude that someone, somewhere took what they said seriously.' Henderson, a fellow at Glasgow University's mass media unit, as quoted by Hellen (1998) commented that: 'A lot of people who have suffered child abuse quite simply lack the vocabulary, because of shame or fear, to come to terms with what has happened. Provided a drama does not place blame on the child, it can be very helpful.'

Some writers promote film as being helpful in education about child abuse. In her review of 17 films for child sexual abuse prevention and treatment, Byers (1986: 545) argues that: 'Filmmakers have provided a vehicle that in some ways surpasses any other in the ongoing endeavour to educate children and adults in the prevention of child abuse.' Film presents the opportunity for various issues, such as children's stories not being believed, perpetrators not being punished, and painful experiences of child sexual abuse being remembered, to be brought to life.

The impact of these issues on the people involved may be powerfully explored. However, some writers express concern that with the increasing numbers of dramas and books concentrating on child sexual abuse and paedophilia there are 'dangers either that we become comfortable about the crime and start to regard it as acceptable, which it must never be, or that we become hysterical'.

Live Theatre Productions

In 1993, two plays opened in New South Wales within a month of each other. Reporting on a controversial play entitled Cold Hands, Armstrong (1993: 11) argued that the play: ' ...portrays a week in the life of a 12 year-old girl . . . sexually assaulted by her father and . . . pregnant. The play's focus allows the audience to gain an insight into the child's fear and trauma, the father's feeble rationalisation and defence, and the mother's fear of confronting the truth.

Armstrong noted that the New South Wales Child Protection Council showed professional interest in the play and that plays have been used as part of child abuse awareness campaigns. The play's director, Ritchie remarked that: 'The play is powerful, dramatic, presenting practical and emotional reality. It is confronting, but it emphasises the fact that there is no excuse. Ever.'

The second play entitled In Relation to Inadmissible Evidence was written by Helen Zigmund. Between the ages of four and a half and five and a half, Helen had been sexually abused by her parents' gardener. Helen hoped that the play would: 'open the issue up for debate . . . I want [the audience] to have listened, to have borne witness . . . in theatre the monodrama is a wonderful medium for exploring the random, chaotic thoughts of a person trying to come to terms with something like this'.

DOCUMENTARIES AS PART OF A MASS MEDIA CAMPAIGN

Hoefnagels and Baartmann (1997) have documented a mass media prevention campaign in Western Europe. This campaign, which was directed at children, aimed to increase disclosures of abuse. It began with the screening of a television program entitled Some secrets you have to talk about and this became the campaign's slogan. The initial television program was followed by 20 other programs and documentaries on the subject of child sexual abuse. The campaign also included television commercials, newspaper and magazine articles, stickers, billboards, leaflets and booklets. The campaign ran for nine months. Phone calls to ChildLine services promoted as part of the campaign almost tripled as a result of the campaign.

Mass media clearly influenced the process of disclosure (Hoefnagels and Baartmann 1997). However, as is the case in many social and political climates where child sexual abuse is prevalent and short term media campaigns are run, Hoefnagels and Baartmann (1997) noted that the resources needed to meet the needs of abused children continue to be deficient. Media campaigns that raise awareness of child abuse and neglect may only be effective if supported by at least a corresponding increase in human and material resources to address the problem.

A recent documentary, screened in New Zealand in 2001, graphically depicts the lives and abuse of three children (played by actors). During the documentary, a Detective Inspector informs the audience that the drama is based on the lives of real people, and the audience is told how life turned out for the children and their abusers. 'Only those with ice in their veins could fail to be moved - and there lies the problem. In each case, one adult or more had failed to take responsibility for the safety of a defenceless child'. Reporting in The New Zealand Herald, Herrick asks: 'What can programs like this possibly expect to achieve? Twenty years ago, polite society didn't even acknowledge abuse existed, let alone talk about it. So shows like this, which provoke thought and discussion, must be a sign of progress, even if the statistics say otherwise. Killing tomorrow was punishing if compelling viewing.'

Supported by New Zealand's child protection authority, Child Youth and Family Services (CYFS), consider documentaries like 'Killing Tomorrow' to be a powerful way of educating people about the issues and what can be done to protect children. 'We want to create an environment where child abuse is less able to exist and we're pleased Screentime-Communicado has decided to help raise these serious issues'. After the program was screened there was a panel discussion of the issues presented in the documentary and CYFS booklets that provide tips on parenting were made available to the public. Child protection received 211 phone calls during the documentary and on the night it was screened. Fifty-three child abuse investigations resulted, five of which cases were considered 'very urgent [and were] assigned immediately to social workers for investigation'.

Also quoted in the New Zealand Herald 30/11/01 was Simcock, the National Social Services spokesperson: 'The documentary showed community groups were doing their best on the issue but government measures were sadly lacking . . . the most helpful thing the government could do was to change the law that allowed parents to hit children.' While the documentary appears to have raised awareness of child abuse and prompted some people to act on their suspicions of abuse and neglect, Henare, a Child Abuse Prevention Services spokesperson, noted that 'the objective of the documentary would not be reached without enough money for community providers'.

Planning and Evaluating Mass Media Education and Prevention Campaigns

Child abuse is a community problem and as such it ought to be everybody's business. However, as noted above, as part of the ongoing campaign by Australians Against Child Abuse,

Every child is important, Quantum Market Research found that: 'Child abuse, as a serious social problem, is poorly understood by the public on a number of levels including its true extent and nature . . . only 4 per cent of respondents accurately estimated the size of the problem, 29 per cent of respondents underestimated the problem by at least 90,000 reports'.

These results, a good example of what Freimuth, Cole and Kirby (2001: 476) describe as 'formative research or evaluation', confirmed 'the need for a major community awareness campaign to better inform the public about the problem of child abuse'. Research, such as that carried out by Quantum for Australians Against Child Abuse is integral to a successful campaign. Social marketing principles, which incorporate such research, are increasingly recognised for their relevance to campaign planning and evaluation.

Social Marketing

The social marketing model has much to contribute to planned mass communication campaigns. Successful commercial marketing involves an 'exchange process' that results in the satisfaction of the needs of two or more groups of people. Communication thus plays a significant role, an offer is communicated to the client based on essential information received by the seller about the client's 'needs, wants and resources'. Social marketing uses commercial marketing techniques 'to advance a social cause, idea or behaviour'. Indeed, commercial marketing practices may be applied 'to the analysis, planning, execution and evaluation of programs designed to influence the voluntary behaviour of target audiences in order to improve their personal welfare and that of their society'.

New Zealand's Breaking the Cycle child abuse education and prevention campaign, begun in 1995, was the first to successfully apply 'social marketing as a social work intervention to change abusive parenting behaviours . . .

increasing awareness and self-reported behaviour change, especially with Maori and Pacific Islands people'. These writers (1997: 8-9) summarise the seven key elements of Andreason's (1995) social marketing model (which was used in the Breaking the Cycle campaign) as follows:

- Consumer behaviour is the bottom line: learning new information is only important if it leads to the desired behavioural outcome (raising awareness and changing attitudes may be steps in this direction).
- Programs must be cost-effective: limited resources must always by used wisely in the social services arena.
- All strategies begin with the client: rather than attempting to make an audience accept and carry out the marketer's values and beliefs, practitioners of social marketing recognise clients will only change their behaviour when they believe it is in their interests. It is therefore essential to start with an understanding of the target audience's needs and wants, its values and its perceptions . . .
- Interventions involve marketing theory's classic 'four Ps'.
- Market research is essential to designing, pre-testing and evaluating intervention programs.
- Markets are segmented: initial research inevitably points out how different the client groups are and highlights the limits of mass marketing. (The use of a budget will impact on the ability to segment markets.)
- Competition is always recognised: every choice of action by the client involves giving up some other action. What the client sees as major alternative behaviours must always be kept in mind so the deficiencies of these alternatives can be highlighted and the benefits of the new behaviour promoted.

Windahl et al. (1992) note that unlike commercial marketing, social marketing, often targets less accessible segments of the population; operates in a less competitive environment; promotes products and services that are freely accessible to those who need them; often challenges powerful interest groups, such as the tobacco industry; may promote a product or behaviour that the message's recipient is reluctant to accept, such as a low fat diet; and may produce a demand for a product or service which remains unmet due to an insufficient supply/lack of available resources.

As noted above, the 'classic' marketing approach is to focus on the four Ps - product, price, place, promotion. Windahl et al. (1992), drawing on McCarthy (1975) and Solomon (1989), contended that successful social marketing strategies should focus on five Ps, these are:

Product . . . a thing, an idea, a practice, or a service. In a child abuse prevention campaign, the generic product would be child safety and wellbeing; the specific product might be reporting suspicions to child protection services, seeking help from various sources, or valuing and appreciating children. The target audiences may be likely perpetrators of child abuse, children, mothers, fathers, and/or professionals who come into contact with children.

Price . . . what is paid by the buyer in exchange. For example, various personal costs, such as lost time, income and clients, may deter mandated professionals from making a report of suspected child abuse to child protection authorities. However, the benefits to the child and to the community may counterbalance personal costs, as may the avoidance of a penalty for failing to report suspected abuse.

Place . . . the channel through which the product, service or idea is made available to the target group.

Promotion . . . the communicative/persuasive activities used to create awareness of the product among the target group . . . in Solomon's words, it involves 'activity reaching out to the right people with the right message at the right time in order to obtain the right effects'. Promotion must be adapted to its target public.

Positioning . . . refers to how the receiver perceives a product relative to other products.

A campaign designed to enhance people's attitudes and behaviour towards children and young people, and to increase the availability of supports to children and families, might effectively stress the economic saving and social prosperity to the community resulting from a decrease in child abuse and neglect. Legal sanctions may need to be imposed to ensure a community approach. Campaigns to introduce mandatory reporting of child abuse are one example in the field of child protection.

In addition to the 'rational interplay' of these five 'P' strategies, Windahl et al. (1992: 98) argue the importance of 'goal-setting' in social marketing. Generally, they suggest, the goal is 'social change', and they cite Kotler's (1982) typology of social change, with examples (example in italics related to child protection: Saunders and Goddard):

1. *Cognitive change*
   - Campaigns to increase recognition of high pollution levels in an area
   - Campaigns to inform people of what refugees experience
   - Campaigns to increase people's knowledge of child abuse and neglect, and awareness of its incidence
2. *Action change*
   - Campaigns calling for people to demonstrate against pollution
   - Campaigns asking people to sign petitions on behalf of political refugees
   - Campaigns involving people in consultations about issues affecting children and young people and writing up an agenda for change to be given to relevant government authorities.
3. *Behavioural change*
   - Efforts to make people routinely recycle paper and glass
   - Efforts to prevent prejudiced behaviour against families or political refugees

- Efforts to encourage people to speak respectfully to children and to use non-physical means of disciplining children

4. ***Value change***
    - Efforts to convince people of the value of clean air and water
    - Efforts to create values in favor of the actions of political refugees.
    - Efforts to encourage people to value children and respect their rights to integrity and protection from harm

Windahl et al. (1992: 102) draw on literature reviews conducted by Rice and Atkin (1989) and Rogers and Storey (1987) to highlight the following factors as potential contributors to a campaign's success.

- Mass media may be successful in increasing public knowledge and awareness of issues. However, mass media is unlikely to change behaviour.
- Interpersonal communication, especially among peers and social groups, may instigate and maintain desired behavioural change.
- The characteristics of the source or medium, for example, credibility is important.
- Formative evaluation: 'research carried out before the implementation of a health [or other social issue] communication campaign in the mass media'.
- Campaign appeals that are 'specific rather than general in order to appeal to the values of individuals. For example, appeals in an AIDS campaign should stress the danger to the individual rather than referring to abstract national health standards'.
- Preventive behaviour. As the benefits attributed to prevention may not become apparent in the short term, 'delayed benefits must be related to immediate ones'.
- Timeliness, compatibility, and accessibility. Educative messages will be most effective when they occur at the

right time, are culturally appropriate, and are transmitted through channels that are accessible to those whom they are intended to reach.

Importantly, 'campaign objectives and criteria for success should be reasonable'. Despite inherent difficulties, including resource constraints, 'public communication campaigns . . . typically set higher standards for success than the most successful commercial campaigns'. In answer to the question: 'Can communication campaigns succeed?' Windahl et al. (1992: 113) confidently cite Mendelsohn (1973) who suggests that the success of a campaign will depend on whether: its goals were 'realistic' given that target groups will probably have only minimal, if any, interest in the campaign's message; 'interpersonal communication' was considered along with mass communication; and the target population was segmented and addressed in light of 'their mass media habits, lifestyles, value and belief systems, and demographic and psychological attributes'.

National Media Campaign

Donovan (1992) completed a plan for a national, integrated, comprehensive media campaign aimed at the prevention of child abuse. The recommendations stated that:

'Media campaigns, both through mass and localised media, and through in-home (for example, TV, radio) and ex-home (for example, posters, cinema) media, should be directed to the general community, parents, children, perpetrators, victims and indirect professionals.

A wide range of media approaches should be used, including advertising, community service announcements, publicity (for example, feature articles and documentaries), and 'edutainment' (that is, the deliberate inclusion of educational messages in entertainment vehicles such as TV soap operas).

Media campaigns can serve a number of roles, but primarily:

- Placing the issue on the community's agenda;

- Framing the issue;
- Eliciting reports of abuse;
- Directing individuals to sources of assistance/further information;
- Changing social norms;
- Modelling appropriate and inappropriate behaviours; and
- Increasing the awareness of the target audience with respect to their own behaviour, and hence increasing the likelihood of the individual assessing his or her own behaviour and their self responsibility for such behaviour.'

Using media campaigns focusing on the sexual assault of children as an example, Donovan (1992) draws on Finkelhor to note that child sexual assault is a behaviour that is both premeditated and planned, rather than impulsive. Media campaigns are therefore presented with a 'window of opportunity'. This 'window of opportunity' is the time that lapses between a sexual abuser's thoughts and calculations in relation to the act of assault and the actual abusive episode. Media messages targeted at potential abusers during this lead time may, it is suggested, prevent initial or repeat abuse: 'We need to target perpetrators when they are in the initial stage of planning a sexual assault, and we need to focus on the rationalisations they use to remove the usual inhibitors to child sexual abuse'.

Evaluation

McGuire (1981: 69) argues that: 'Any undertaking as important and expensive as a public communication campaign should have evaluation procedures built into it.' Further, as noted by Bauman (2000), clear guidelines for evaluation are required because mass media education and prevention campaigns 'consume much public resource, but we do not always learn from them'. In order to evaluate the degree to which a mass communication campaign achieves its goals, it will be necessary to first identify the dependent and independent variables impinging on the outcome. Freimuth et al. (2001: 476) maintain that 'a common set of variables is considered in the development of a mass-media campaign and that one can expect a common set of outcomes as a result of the communication experience'. They identify four broad areas under which to organise the campaign's independent variables, the combination of which constitutes the 'campaign strategy'.

These are the psychosocial attributes of the receiver; the source or spokesperson; the settings, channels, activities and materials used to disseminate the messages; and the message itself, including content, tone, type of appeal, audio characteristics and visual attributes. Additionally, Freimuth et al. (2001: 476) contend that 'the outcomes or dependent variables of a mass health [or other] communication effort may be categorised into six broad areas - exposure, attention, comprehension, yielding, attitude change and behaviour'. The evaluation of a mass communication strategy, according to Freimuth et al. (2001), ought to occur in three stages which they term 'formative research or evaluation', 'process evaluation', and 'summative evaluation'. Drawing largely on Freimuth et al. (2001) a brief summary of these stages follows.

Formative Research or Evaluation

As noted above, this is the first stage in the process of planning and evaluating a mass communication strategy. This stage involves research aimed at accurately profiling 'target audiences', and the piloting of 'strategies' and 'tactics' prior to their planned implementation. The four independent variables, listed above, are fully explored at this preliminary stage to determine: 'homogenous sub-groups or audience segments'; 'predictors of behaviour' in these audiences, such as 'self-efficacy, social norms or knowledge'; and communication strategies most likely to be effective for each particular target audience.

Regarding this last point on targeted strategies, possible considerations are confronting messages, perhaps creating reactions in the audience of 'fear' or shock. Alternatively, more comforting approaches may be more effective. Peers of the target group could communicate the message and model positive behaviours such as desirable parenting techniques. Further, the predominant visual images could be of happy, healthy children and families rather than scenes of domestic violence and the misery it produces in victims' demeanours.

According to Freimuth et al. (2001: 478), the next step in stage one is to 'pre-test' strategies to determine which ones will be most likely to achieve the campaign's objectives, and the information needed by the intended audience. Focus groups of individuals fitting the profile of a particular target audience, or one-to-one interviews, are organised at this point to 'ensure the strategy is feasible, produces intended cognitive effects in a sample . . . audience and does no harm'.

A note of caution is found in the research findings of Collins and Zoch (2001) in South Carolina. Formative evaluation may reveal that a mass media campaign is not the most effective direct strategy for reaching some groups of people in the community. These writers stress the need to establish, through formative research, the target audiences' media preferences and habits. In focus groups of predominantly poor adult-education students (aged between 18-65, mainly female, rural white and urban African American) Collins and Zoch (2001: 209-210) found that this group of people were 'media savvy' in a negative way: 'Unlike other groups they zap, zip, flip or change the station when they hear a pro-social message . . . 'I gotta listen when a teacher or minister tells me what to do, I don't have to listen to somebody on TV.' Resistant to media influence, the main source of influence for this group of people are friends, family, government officials and religious or opinion leaders. Clearly, to reach this particular target audience, and audiences like them, campaign messages may need to target 'the opinion leaders in the communities' where the target group live.

Process Evaluation

The next step advocated by Freimuth et al. (2001) is 'process evaluation' which determines the extent to which a campaign unfolds as intended. Process evaluation occurs while the campaign is still running. The results of the evaluation may be used to change, improve or bring the campaign back on track. Through process evaluation campaign organisers can monitor the stages and progress of the campaign. As a result they mày more accurately attribute campaign successes or failures (apparent through summative evaluation) to various aspects of the campaign's strategy. A process evaluation will accurately document how the campaign was actually implemented. As Freimuth et al. (2001: 480) make apparent, process evaluation enables the distinction to made between a 'bad' campaign and a 'poorly implemented' one.

Summative Evaluation

The final step in the evaluation process, 'summative evaluation', determines whether the campaign achieved its goals. Did target groups pay attention to campaign messages, and were their attitudes and/or subsequent behaviour influenced in the manner the campaign intended? 'Even if a program is implemented as planned and desired effects result, these effects cannot be attributed to the intervention without evidence that the campaign reached the intended audience'.

Methods suggested by Freimuth et al. (2001) to determine whether target groups heard and understood campaign messages include:

- Conducting a random survey to discover if people know about the campaign;
- Adding pertinent questions about the campaign to an already existing general survey;
- Adding contact information to campaign messages so that target audiences can contact a helpline or address for assistance: 'a burst of calls just after the airing of a tagged message almost certainly indicates that the audience attended to it'; and
- Requesting that recipients of calls to a helpline, and/or requests for services, endeavour to find out whether the target audience understood the campaign's message(s).

Target group exposure to, and understanding of, print media is harder to determine and may prove to be expensive. Freimuth et al. (2001) identify before and after surveys as the most common means of summative evaluation to assess whether a campaign achieved its intended effect on target audiences. However, they point out that this method is often criticised as 'the lack of a control group prohibits establishing a direct cause-and-effect relationship between the campaign and its outcomes'.

Despite this, campaign evaluators should strive to use the best methods of evaluation available to them: 'Formative research, conducted early in campaign development, is the best way to find the right channels to reach the right audiences with the right messages, delivered by the right sources at the right times'. Problems inherent in summative evaluations of mass media campaigns include the tendency for people to give expected, socially more acceptable rather than honest responses to surveys. Alternatively, people may deny seeing a campaign strategy if they have not accordingly changed their attitude or behaviour. Also, messages absorbed during a campaign may be forgotten soon after the campaign has finished. The greater effectiveness of ongoing campaigns rather than intermittent ones is clearly apparent.

CONFRONTING VS. COMFORTING APPROACHES TO MEDIA CAMPAIGNS

The Victorian Traffic Accident Corporation (TAC) advertisements are continually conveyed to the Victorian community as a means of cutting the road accident and fatalities toll. Their most recent television advertising campaign, begun in November 2001 and part of their 'Wipe off 5' campaign to curb speed, uses a law enforcement approach which warns speeding drivers that they are more likely than ever before to get caught and face hefty penalties. The advertisements are backed by the introduction of new cameras strategically placed and without identifiable flashes. Research undertaken prior to the introduction of the new campaign revealed that, while more than 50 per cent of drivers admitted to speeding, only 38 per cent of drivers expected to be caught.

As reported by Masanauskas (2001:23), Dr Ian Johnston, director of Monash University's Accident and Research Centre, contends that: 'Scare campaigns won't cut the road toll without increased enforcement . . . while mass scare campaigns have been very successful, the road toll in Australia and other similar countries had stabilised . . . We've milked almost all we can milk out of [the campaigns].'

Previous TAC advertisements have presented clear, confronting messages about drunk-driving, speeding, and driving without a seatbelt. Slogans such as If you drink then drive you're a bloody idiot, and Don't fool yourself, speed kills, resound in people's heads. These advertisements are presented in graphic detail. Pictures of mutilated bodies and mangled vehicles, combined with the sounds and expressions of grieving relatives defy ignorance of the reality of road trauma. Tomison (1995) contends that a child sexual assault campaign could adopt a similar approach. He cites McGurk (1995: 11) who envisaged a trial media campaign that would shock audiences with graphic scenes of family violence: 'Confronting perpetrators with the grossness, grotesqueness and total unacceptability of their behaviour. For victims, the campaign would be directed at encouraging them to come out of the cupboard.'

As a secondary or tertiary prevention strategy, confronting campaigns such as this may work. Shaming potential and actual perpetrators through media campaigns may prove to be effective in helping to curb the incidence of premeditated abusive actions. As previously noted, 'social disapproval' is a strategy that may work for some target groups. Most people seek to behave in a manner that they believe to be socially acceptable, in line with current values and norms of behaviour. The prospect of public embarrassment brought on by behaving in a particular manner may act at least as an inhibitor to such behaviour. Again using the example of physical punishment of children, as society increasingly views hitting children as inappropriate parenting behaviour, children are less often hit in public. However, much family violence occurs 'behind closed doors'.

For 'shaming' to be effective in the prevention of family violence, campaigns would need to reach people to the extent that they feel ashamed of themselves for their behaviour, whether or not it is exposed to public recrimination. Constant reminders of public disdain for abusive behaviours, through campaigns highlighting 'social disapproval', may assist in this process. Drawing on DeJong and Atkin's 1995 research on drink-driving campaigns, Yanovitsky and Stryker propose a 'norm reinforcement' approach that attaches 'a social stigma to unhealthy lifestyle behaviours by presenting those who perform them as individuals with poor self-discipline who have callous disregard for others'.

However, many incidents of physical abuse of children result from stressed parents losing control and hitting out. The abuse is not always pre-meditated. Indeed, it may be part of an established pattern of behaviour stemming from one's own harsh childhood upbringing. According to Hawkins et al. (1994: 35), for parents and carers in this target group: 'Prevention of child abuse must . . . make good parenting easier. Assistance must be on tap and its availability promoted as part of the message . . . help rather than condemnation must be a central theme.

If people are caught in a seemingly hopeless spiral of poverty, stress, depression or irritation, particularly if they have a 'difficult' or handicapped child, condemnation is not a positive approach, but an optimistic message can give them hope.' More comforting educative campaigns, portraying happy healthy families, and adults 'doing the right thing' in relation to children and adolescents, may be the most effective mass media prevention campaign strategy. Indeed, comforting campaigns may also be the better strategy when the target is the broad population and the goal is primary prevention of child abuse. 'Much child abuse may be invisible, but many of the children who have been abused know only too well that many of us, including a succession of governments, would rather not see'.

Some people may be turned off when confronted by scenes of explicit family violence or even 'inappropriate or abusive conduct'. Such behaviour may seem too far-removed from what the average person perceives to be 'normal'. While families may increasingly be aware of the problem of child abuse and neglect (though not its incidence), they may distance themselves from stereotypical images of perpetrators of family violence 'pathologising them as mentally ill, abnormal or evil'. As Hall and Stannard learned through the evaluation of the New Zealand Breaking the Cycle campaign: 'People are much more likely to identify themselves as having difficulties with parenting than as child abusers, and they are more likely to seek information or help with their parenting skills.'

Examples of less confronting campaigns presenting more subtle, educative messages are the Use Words That Help Not Hurt NAPCAN 1995 campaign and the Every Child is Important AACA2001 campaign. Continuous portrayal, in mass media, of positive parenting approaches and positive adult relationships with children and young people, may be an effective campaign strategy in the primary prevention of child abuse and neglect. Public awareness of the reality of child abuse and neglect, including its most abhorrent forms, is also important to prevention. Media coverage of horrific acts of child abuse and neglect is inevitable. Such coverage, even when sensationalist, acts as a grim reminder to adults of children's vulnerability and need to be nurtured and protected.

In his article "Emotive Health Advertising and Message Resistance", Brown (2001: 193) observes that: 'Although the use of negative emotion may increase the salience and accessibility of campaign messages, there is also a risk that it may induce resistance toward those messages.' Brown (2001: 197) suggests that, given the likelihood of message resistance to campaigns that arouse negative emotions: 'Emotive components could be used more sparingly, be presented separately from the message, and avoid excessive focus on themes of guilt and remorse.' According to Brown, extensive pre-testing of campaign messages in focus groups will assist in determining whether emotive stimuli have the desired affect on audience cognition, attitudes and behaviour, or whether resistance is encountered.

Society sometimes fails to recognise that children are the most vulnerable group in our community, and are thus in need of the greatest protection. The social and economic costs to societies that have not prioritised children's needs, especially the prevention of child abuse and neglect, are well documented. The media's role in preventing child abuse and neglect is multi-faceted. The early 'discovery' of child abuse is the clearest example. Without intense media exposure, Kempe's (1962) 'battered child syndrome' may have remained largely unseen and unheard of. Children are not only the most vulnerable but their voices are often silenced, especially when the subject is child abuse and neglect.

Examples of the media's ability to confront people with images and messages that they may not want to see and hear have been documented above. Investigative journalism also plays a less direct but nonetheless influential role in community education. And opinion pieces, such as Goddard (2002), are yet another means of educating both the public in general and professionals in particular about best practice. Sustained community education and prevention campaigns, using mass media communication, are integral to the prevention of child abuse and neglect. These campaigns continually confront communities with the reality of child abuse.

They challenge people, institutions, and governments to listen to children and to respond to the needs of all children and families, and particularly the special needs of children who have been abused or neglected. Further, sustained mass media exposure of child abuse and neglect may publicly censure and shame perpetrators, many of whom are relatives and adults well known to the victimised child. However, to be effective, mass media campaigns will need to be part of a broader prevention program that includes the provision of supports and services for all children and families. Abroad prevention program would reflect a society that recognises the value of children, respects children's rights, and optimises children's life chances. As argued by Windahl et al. (1992: 117): 'Information or communication cannot resolve problems that are essentially caused by scarce resources, rather than a lack of knowledge.'

There are limitations to what the media can achieve. Dennis and Merrill purport that the media are 'most powerful in furnishing information and setting agendas for members of a public . . . next powerful in impinging on the thoughts, opinions and attitudes of members of a public . . . [and] least powerful in affecting actions of members of a public.' Mass communication campaigns also have 'a crucial role to play in setting agendas for professional, administrative and political leaders and decision makers'.

The nature of media influence is constantly changing. The power and ever increasing potential of the media, however, remains constant. Positive mass media communication waits to be tapped by those who advocate for children and young people.

Mass communication may be a vehicle that constantly reminds people to value children and to respect children's rights. Moreover, mass media may be 'an advocacy tool to achieve policy change', improving the status of children and addressing the physical and social conditions in which children and young people live.

According to Goddard and Tucci: 'The agenda for our community - and the government which represents us - should be clear. The prevention of child abuse should be a priority. We have education campaigns which respond to problem gambling, speeding drivers, illicit drug use and drink-driving. Yet there has been no equivalent effort, at state or federal level, to prevent child abuse.'

9

Mass Media in the Modern Society

TYPES AND INFLUENCES

Mass media has become an integral part of our lives and can not be separated from our life. Particularly for the urban people, the need for information is more important than ever. Our values and way of life in the society in this information era are strongly influenced by the mass media like newspapers, TV, radio, video, and the internet. Mass media's influence on people's lives is even greater and deeper than many kinds of state indoctrination or priest's sermons from the pulpit in the church. The full range of unfiltered media is now available to most of us by using a parabola and satellite transmission. We can buy many kinds of videos freely. Access to the internet is easy and inexpensive almost everywhere.

We can find many kinds of information using the internet technology. It is worth remembering that there have been three important revolutions in recent history, i.e. agrarian revolution in farming, industry revolution in mass production and information revolution that provides global access. We are now in the midst of the information revolution. Due to continuing developments in media technology, we are flooded by a huge volume of non-stop information. Most of this information comes to us without a filter or censor. The information can be positive and negative. It is important for all, and particularly teenagers, to be able to look critically at the information and the sources and make positive choices. Having a critical attitude means that we can distinguish between positive and negative information and make choices that will give us information that will benefit us and our society, Below are some things we can do to develop our ability to think critically:

- Reading regularly
- Attend a variety of training sessions on media, if any
- Practice to viewing media critically
- Ask and learn from the experts or mature and experienced people
- Read the Bible regularly
- Do daily reflection
- Attend Sunday mass or worship regularly, Etc.

Mass Media's Influences

The research from the US tells us how many teenagers' lives are seriously troubled. The results of the research show us that 43 % of teens in the US have used drugs and alcohol at least once. Around 1 million teens have left their homes and a half of them live as delinquent (naughty) boys and girls and the other half are drug users. About 2,000 teens from the age of 10 to 19 years old commit suicide each year. Most of them come from wealthy families that are not harmonious. There is no love, caring and acceptance in those families.Many teens make all of their own choices about the media they use. No one guides them or restricts them from accessing any type of information that they choose. Everything is allowed. Then the kids grow up and become people who are out of control.

They feel mature enough to make decisions on their own. Many forms of authority, rules, and norms are seen as an obstacle to their freedom and so, should not be followed. Ethics and morality are not really important for them. For many violence, crimes and sex are their daily life and concern. The research from the 1980s in the US shows us that teenagers between 16 and18 years old are wasting up to 16,000 hours of their time per year watching TV. In the same period, the violence and crime in US grew by 293%. *Times* weekly magazine reported that the frequency of crimes committed by students in New York per month was the same as that committed by Japanese teenagers of the same age in a year. Here are some positive and negative influences of mass media on our lives:

Positive Influences

Positive influences of mass media can be seen from several aspects or points of view:

a. From media technology side itself
b. From the side of the owner and sponsor of the media
c. Unintended influences of the media technology and sponsors

a. The influences of media technology

- Media technology reduces the distance between human beings. The world is smaller due to increased communication and access to information. It makes human being closer to each other in terms of space and thinking. We are exposed to a broad range of ideas and thought from all kinds of people from all over the world.
- Media technologies allows us to take part 'virtu-ally' in occasions and activities in other parts of the world. Through the media we know immediately about earthquakes, tsunamis, avian influenza outbreaks, etc that strike any area on earth. We know about the results of champions league which is taking place far away in Europe.
- It allows us to learn more easily and faster by using the internet.
- It help us to get the best results of pictures and sounds.

b. The influences of the owner and sponsor

- Men can use the media to create and invite the people

concerned with certain world issues like AIDS, drug abuse, mass killing, totalitarian government, etc.

- Media can help to create a positive and educated opinion. Media can be used to fight for freedom, truth and justice.
- Media can help us to relax by listening music, dance, etc.

c. ***Unrealized influence of media***

- Media can create a new cultures
- Media can change people's way of thinking about life, culture, existence, etc.

Negative Influence of Media

a. ***Negative influences caused by the media technology itself***

- Information is power and those who control the media empires have great power and a great responsibility to use that power positively. Those who have power over the media have real power in the modern world.
- Media could create new cultures which change the old and original ones from the community. This could be both good and bad

b. ***Negative Influences that caused by the owner and sponsor***

- Media is business. In order to exist media providers must make a profit. The owners and sponsors tend to create a media environment that is driven by materialism, consumerism, and hedonism.
- Media can create the wrong perception of pros-perity. Prosperity is made out to be having an excess of material goods (cars, houses, jewelry, etc). Men are not measured by their character and dedication but by what things they have in life. It is promoted by advertising in most kinds of media.
- Media can create stereotypes of beauty and style which is then imitated by citizens, like fashion and hairstyles, for instance.

- Media can create a sensation of sex, violence, and horror which may be popular with the audience.
- The owner, ruler, and media sponsor can make up any trick for their own business and politics interest.

c. ***Unrealized negative influence of media***

- People's daily schedules and work schedules can be interrupted if most of our time is used by listening to music or watching TV. Communi-cations between family members can also be reduced.
- Sex addiction and violence has a close relationship to TV shows, movies and videos or chatting via internet or HP.
- The trend towards urbanization creates a constant flow of people coming from the villages to the city and is at least partly caused by the unrealistic glamour of urban life as shown on TV.

Much of our view of reality is based on media messages that have been pre-constructed and have attitudes, interpretations and conclusions already built in. The media, to a great extent, give us our sense of reality. Without mass media, openness and accountability are impossible in contemporary democracies. Freedom of the media carries with it certain responsibilities of honesty, fairness, accuracy and accountability. The power of the media to create and destroy human values comes with great responsibility. Such power ought not to be in the hands of a few.

The media are a centre of power in the political system, having great influence on politics and on forming social change. Television can greatly influence the election of a national leader on the basis of image. The power is the power to decide who will communicate what to whom. Today even those who loathe the media must use the media. The Taliban, to take an extreme example, banned television, photographs and computers but now use what they called 'tools of the devil' to refocus world attention on the war in Afghanistan.

The media's main impact is psychological and intellectual. Media and entertainment companies shape public opinion and help frame the terms of public debate. The media is what we read, listen to and watch. In parallel, through its close relationship with advertisers, the media also exerts a powerful influence on the decisions we make, the products we buy, and the sort of questions we ask when we make our everyday choices.

The long view of history proves media's power by showing that the medium itself, in the long run, is more powerful than the messages it carries, because the medium determines what can be communicated and how we think about that communication.

Maintaining that the press plays an important role in the development and stability óf modern society, advocates of Social Responsibility press theory believe it imperative that a commitment of social responsibility be imposed on mass media. In their eyes, the press has a moral obligation to consider the overall needs of society when making journalistic decisions that will produce the greatest good or the greatest number. Moreover, this utilitarian goal can be accomplished only through a concerted effort to further various ethical ideals agreed upon by all concerned with this "improvement" of society. To allow unchanneled and uncontrolled distribution of ideas and information supported by the libertarian press notion was considered neither responsible nor beneficial to society and could not be considered ethical.

Professional journalists do have a code of ethics. Journalists make judgments about what's safe and appropriate to report which often involves difficult choices. Let us consider the journalists' share of responsibility for the consequences of their reporting? German sociologist Max Weber distinguishes between an 'ethics of conviction' and an 'ethics of responsibility.' According to the latter, journalists must take into account the foreseeable consequences of their reporting, the impact on society. The ethics of conviction on the other hand posits that journalists have an absolute duty to tell the truth, regardless of the consequences. War journalism tends to regard this mission to reveal the truth as a sufficient condition for ethical reporting, although according to Weber both ethics are complementary rather than opposites.

The underlying assumption of social responsibility is that moral and ethical commandments diçtate journalistic excellence (even if authoritarian control is needed to uphold such laws) instead of the individual reasoned choices of reporters and editors. For a multi media company, trust is a keyword. It is essential to have mutual trust with readers, viewers and listeners, as well as employees, owners and society at large. One does not gain trust without taking responsibility. For Media companies it is of vital importance to be identified as being ethical and responsible.

The public's right to know of events of public importance and interest is the overriding mission of the mass media. The purpose of distributing news and enlightened opinion is to serve the general welfare. Journalists who use their professional status as representatives of the public for selfish or other unworthy motives violate a high trust. Freedom of the press is to be guarded as an inalienable right of people in a free society. It carries with it the freedom and the responsibility to discuss, question, and challenge actions and utterances of our government and of our public and private institutions. Journalists uphold the right to speak unpopular opinions and the privilege to agree with the majority. Their social responsibilities to the public are paramount. That is the nature of their profession.

No issue is more problematic for those concerned with media freedom and responsibility than the issue of "hate speech". The term is generally used to refer to advocacy of national, racial, religious or other hatred. The issue, in essence, is how far it is proper or acceptable to limit the right to freedom of expression, when the views being expressed support the limitation or infringement of the rights of others. These issues become even more acute in a country with a history of communal or ethnic violence, where the media are known to have played a role in fanning hostilities.

In 1946, the judges at Nuremberg found Julius Streicher, the Nazi publisher of Der Sturmer, guilty of "inciting of the population to abuse, maltreat and slay their fellow citizens, to stir up passion, hate, violence and destruction among the people themselves aims at breaking the moral backbone even of those the invader chooses to spare." The judges sentenced him to death because "his incitement to murder and extermination at the time when Jews in the East were being killed under the most horrible conditions clearly constitutes persecution on political and racial grounds and (therefore) a Crime against Humanity."

Forty- seven years later, in Dec. 2003, in a landmark verdict, the war crimes tribunal for Rwanda convicted three media figures of genocide for inciting people to take part in the wave of killing that swept across Rwanda in 1994. The defendants were found guilty for their use of a popular radio station and a newspaper to inflame hatred against the country's Tutsi minority and to direct and encourage the campaign of slaughter. The lesson in the conviction of the three is that social responsibility is at the root of journalistic practice. In an interview with The New York Times, Stephen Rapp, the senior prosecutor on the case, said "A key question will be what kind of speech is protected and where the limits lie.

It is important to draw that line. We hope the judgment will give the world some guidance. He also noted that in terms of international legal standards there has been no decision since Nuremberg. "Those who control the media are accountable for its consequences," the Arusha, Tanzania, based international court said before handing down the convictions. In my opinion the media should not cooperate with hate-mongers by providing them an uncontrolled platform for disseminating their ideas. This is not to say that the media should fail to report about the conduct of hate mongers. Instead, the media coverage of hate speech should be cautious and sensitive to the interests of the group under attack, and above all be 'responsible.'

Without a doubt information is power, and the big owners of the main medium to get information to the people, the mainstream media, are very powerful people. Therefore we may well ask how can there be credible democratic discourse in any country when the major public information channels, television and newspapers, are owned or controlled by a handful of individuals accountable only to themselves? Interestingly, for Karl Marx, the mass media was simply an instrument of bourgeois control over the proletariat, a part of the overall superstructure of society, along with religion, the family and education.

Whether one agrees with Marx's political dimension or not, what is clear is that Marxism presents to us an extremely useful model in which to study the mass media today. Though Marx was writing at a time when the main organs of mass media would've essentially meant newspapers and books, Marxist analysis can be applied to today's media: the mass media, a privatized means of production, is there to replicate capitalist ideology and to promote a 'false consciousness' amongst the working class. Television and radio stations, newspapers, magazines, and internet sites are, largely, owned and controlled by profit-making businesses. Since it is the bourgeoisie who control the media, it is only natural that it is their ideas get promoted through both things like advertising and the actual media products themselves - movies, soap opera, tabloid newspapers, consumer magazines and so on.

The case for imposing limits on media ownership is based solely on democratic, social and journalistic concerns. The media have a social responsibility that makes them unlike other commercial activities. As such, freedom of the press is not just the proprietary right of owners to do as they see fit. It is a right of the Australian people. The current level of ownership concentration here in Australia continues to be one of the highest in the world. Rupert Murdoch, the world's most powerful media mogul, already decides what's fit to print in Adelaide, Brisbane and many regional cities, where he owns the only newspaper. In Melbourne and Sydney he dominates the newspaper market and he owns the only national daily,

The Australian . Kerry Packer is Australia's richest, most powerful businessman, and owns the dominant Nine TV network as well as a large stable of news, women's and other magazines. Companies run by the two media moguls and their sons, James Packer and Lachlan Murdoch, are also equal shareholders in the pay-TV group Foxtel.

The film *Outfoxed: Rupert Murdoch's War on Journalism*, a recently released documentary about the Fox News channel in the US, exposes the methods and props used by the Fox Network to mold the news. It also displays the influence these methods have had on the major media groups. Fox News claims to be 'Fair and balanced' but in reality is anything but. For the first time ever, this documentary reveals the secrets of former Fox News producers, reporters, bookers and writers who expose what it's like to work for Fox News. These former Fox employees talk about how they were forced to push a 'right-wing' point of view or risk their jobs. Some have even chosen to remain anonymous in order to protect their current livelihoods. As one employee said, 'There's no sense of integrity as far as having a line that can't be crossed.' The film demonstrataes the impact on society when a broad swath of media is controlled by one person.

An Australian media without a strong, independent ABC and an independently-owned Sydney Morning Herald, The Age and The Australian Financial Review would no longer be a free media.

It would be controlled by powerful political and business players, and they will decide what's fit to read, what stories to publish, and what opinions to disseminate. The Australian Broadcasting Corporation, through programmes such as Media Watch, Frontline and the Media Report, has contributed much. The effect has been to raise public awareness of the processes of journalism.

In addition Four Corners has carved a long and proud tradition of investigative journalism, exposing corruption in high places and peering into neglected corners of society. To conclude, the largest transmitter of information today is the mass media. Here a mere fraction of a percent of the western world population decides what the rest of the world is to know and not to know.

Technological advances continue to increase the power of the media to effect cultural change, manipulate public opinion and influence government policy. I don't want to censor the media I just want them to understand their power to influence minds and use it responsibly. The greater the power, the greater the responsibility.

The core problem is that most journalists are employees, not autonomous professionals like, say, a barrister. The main issue for truth in reporting is advertisers or media owners putting pressure on editors and journalists to publish or hold stories. Unfortunately journalists don't always control the end product of their work as published or broadcast. Regrettably the majority of the key decision-makers in media organisations (such as the owners), the people who really wield power and from whom responsibility should be extracted, are not subject to any ethical codes or enforcement system.

Private media ownership; the mass media conglomerate,a concentration of media ownership in too few hands is a danger to society. This can constitute a threat to democracy itself, where major political parties are almost held to ransom by media proprietors, who can wield enormous power through their ability to manipulate the opinion of the electorate, should they choose to do so.

It is my view that such power and responsibility should never be left in the hands of a few. The public need a wide range of contrasting perspectives from the media, not simply the opinions of a handful of conglomerates and their owners. Working journalists in the monopolized television and newspaper media must know that, where there is conflict between the principles of public interest journalism and the direction set by ownership, there is a channel of appeal where professional standards reign.

For this reason there need to be rules which media owners

respect and accept. We need rules to prevent one company from having too much control over the media content. We must have reliable systems developed which ensure a diversity of media ownership, so that competition within the media stimulates a wide range of perspectives on public policy issues and acts as a check on the political power of the media magnates.

Finally, I believe it is our responsibility as concerned citizens to make sure we are not merely passive viewers, readers or listeners, after all we are also voters and consumers. Together we can wield a huge influence on the media by playing an active part in improving the output of all our media services by making our views known where it counts. Each of us has a responsibility to reject any obvious biases and take a stand for what we expect from the media by demanding equal representation of issues and political candidates. Nowadays we have the Internet to assist democracy by giving a voice to every citizen in every library, every office and every home.

Complaints processes exist for anyone wanting to complain about something they have watched, heard or read in a variety of media. This includes complaints in relation to television or radio content; advertising; online content; film, videos and literature; and the print media.

It is important for our society that the media and their owners are accountable. It is up to every one of us to closely follow the critical issues of the day, monitor the performance of the media and, through grassroots activism, use our powers of purchase and persuasion to expose media bias and fraud; bring pressure to bear for media reform; and when faced with cases of continued bias, inaccuracy or unfairness, make our objections heard and direct others toward more reliable and responsible new sources.

Media, the name alone to everyone seems all too familiar, however the meaning and purpose of the word is understood differently amongst people. For ages media has been a key source for knowing what is happening throughout the world. As time evolved the speed in which media information becomes available has increased dramatically, but the quality of media is one to question. In Walter Lippman's "The World Outside and the Pictures in Our Heads," he discusses the changes in media, as well as providing in his terms the role media play's and the role media needs to play in order to function properly. The writer argues that what people think and what the real environment around them is tends to be two different pictures. Thus, the writer provides his conclusion to solving this problem. In this essay I will argue that even through Lippman's conclusion, a solid solution to the problem media plays will still obtainable.

Lippman begins his article by referencing to earlier times in history when information wasn't shared at a rapid pace. At this point he notes the importance the mind played in creating the events that happened in the world. Without information being rapidly supplied to someone, it was up to one to in turn "believe" what they want to be the true picture. From this Lippman turns to another key in media, the symbolism of public opinion, in which he notes is easily manipulated during insecure times in the world, such as war. During such times as war, the symbols become subject to "check, comparison, and argument." With this come his three key factors analyzing public opinion, the scene of action, the human reaction to the scene, and the response to the scene imagined. Through providing an example of a misinterpreted scenario of a wartime event, we are able to understand the consequences and large effects that can come with wrong information.

JUVENILE CRIME AND THE INFLUENCE OF MEDIA

With several arguments for both sides can we truly determine if there is only one main role in juvenile crime? There are many statistics that show there is a higher aggression level formed in people who watched a great deal of violent television or played violent video games as a child. People must begin to consider that there are several contributors to youth crime and violence. Youth crime is often fueled by media violence and can depend on how a person is raised and the adult influence that, while growing up, surrounds them.

Youth crime is far to present in the current generation. There are children harming each other at school and harming their families at home and unfortunately it is far too difficult to pin point only one cause for this violence that we can get under control. In a report for parents and policy makers (Children.. 1999) there are statistics stating the influence of media violence and the barring that it has on juveniles. There are statistics showing that in 1997 alone there were approximately 2.8 million juveniles arrested (Children 1999). Of the 2.8 million, 2,500 were arrested for murder, 121,000 were arrested for other violent crimes, and the remainders of that number were arrested for lesser crimes that are unknown (Children 1999). In 1997 youth arrests accounted for 19% of all arrests, 14% of murder arrests, and 17% of all violent crime arrests (Children 1999). According to statistic reports from the Department of Justice youth arrests increased by 49% between the years of 1988 and 1997 (Children 1999).

In 1999 there was a survey done by the Centers for Disease Control and Prevention that showed with in the 30 days before the survey was done 5.9% of students had carried a hand gun to school, 18% of high school students admitted to currently carrying a knife, razor, firearm, or other weapon on a regular basis, and 9% of them take a weapon to school. The Mass Media is a unique feature of modern society; its development has accompanied an increase in the magnitude and complexity of societal actions and engagements, rapid social change, technological innovation, rising personal income and standard of life and the decline of some traditional forms of control and authority.

There is an association between the development of mass media and social change, although the degree and direction of this association is still debated upon even after years of study into media influence. Many of the consequences, either detrimental or beneficial, which have been attributed to the mass media, are almost undoubtedly due to other tendencies within society.

Few sociologists would refute the importance of the mass media, and mass communications as a whole, as being a major factor in the construction and circulation of social understanding and social imagery in modern societies. Therefore it is argued that the mass media is used as "an instrument", both more powerful and more flexible than anything in previous existence, for influencing people into certain modes of belief and understanding within society.

The question of medias influence on society and its cultural framework has often been debated upon from leading theorists to anyone with any form of media connections, but to contemplate that a character in Coronation Street or Eastenders can have an influence on an audience members attitude, beliefs or interpretations of society is a very simplistic and debatable version of the truth. The media does influence, but using more diverse and subtle roles of impact. Some theorists suggest that it is even a case of society influencing the media and not the more widespread and presumed version.

IMPACT ON YOUNG GENERATION

How do the media influence young people in today's society? Our society still seems confused about what to think about children and young people. It seems to be gripped with a fear of children, blaming them for much of society's ills: crime, vandalism, drugs, drink, sex, teenage pregnancy. The list goes on.

But if these theories are true, where do these rebellious attitudes stem from? The obvious answer would be from the upbringing of children, but in my opinion the media also plays a substantial role in the attitudes, behaviour and physical aspects of youth today, in particularly that of young women. We are constantly being bombarded with advertising, opinions, images and stories which appear to be forcing us to conform to a specific image of how we are supposed to be, whether it be slim, more intelligent or prettier.

Media strongly affects youth culture. The media executives are quick to defend their role in youth violence and bullying while selling millions of dollars in ads focused on youth. TV producers, network executives, motion picture companies and others in the media deny any impact of their programs on the attitudes and actions of youth. Meanwhile they continue to spend millions on special effects and marketing geared to increase appeal to youth markets. While corporations spend millions on market research and advertising to create products and campaigns targeted at a youth demographic, they still deny their ability to influence youth. If this were true to fact, would NIKE continue spending millions every year on product development, marketing and advertising? Would McDonalds still be using cartoon like characters to sell hamburgers? Would music labels be increasing the level of violence and sexual content in the music geared towards the youth audience? Would liquor companies be using youth oriented activities in their advertising? Of course it works on influencing youth and its ideals advertising would not be a multi-billion dollar a year business. If it had no influence, MTV would not have consultant on staff spending huge amounts of money to ensure them keeping up with youth culture.

We've all heard it before. Blame it on TV or other means of media. If a child bludgeons another child to death with a wrench or shoots a classmate, it is the violent TV programs that they watch which are to blame, not the parents or the supervisors who are supposed to be there to make sure their kids do the right thing. How far is it true that the media is responsible for trivializing death and violence, thus causing the children of America to go out on shooting rampages, or kids in Britain to murder innocent toddlers? First let us look at the way the media portrays death. Death has always been a taboo subject. People do not usually sit around talking about death, especially to children. It may be for that reason that children do not really understand the concept of dying. We constantly see instances in cartoons where a character is killed, but in the next scene, that same character is alive and well again. The fact is that they do not actually die. Characters like Warner Bros. Wild E Coyote never die.

As clichéd as it may sound, it has been rightly said all things have their good as well as bad effects. In the similar conduct media also has its good as well as bad influence on youth. Well these were the negative influence of media on youth. Now we focus on the affirmative aspects of media. Media plays a very important role in creating awareness. There are certain issues which remain untouched among youngsters as they feel guarded concerning it. Media helps in providing information regarding such topics. There are many such topics that are highlighted by the media. The current one that can be talked about is the quota system in colleges. Media created awareness that how injustice was being done with deserving candidates due to reservations in colleges. There was procession taken out by students in order to object regarding this bias discrimination.

One other such issue is the debate carried on regarding sex education. Media was trying to highlight both the aspects of the matter that whether sex education must be allowed in schools or not. There were a group of people who were all for it and there were people who considered it a taboo. Even though we are heading towards westernization, our roots still remain Indian. And that is the reason why we fell anxious discussing such issues with young ones. But if we think practically then there are so many instances where children head the wrong way just in the anxiety of knowing certain issues. So, the only acceptable approach in which we can guard our child from choosing the wrong path is by talking to them and educating them about the issues that need to be learnt at the right instance. Media being one of the important means to reach out to the masses and influence their thinking and decision making, only to the positive media cannot attract attention of the masses, and to gain viewer ship, negative media has to be incorporated to balance out and attract the masses, but a line has to be drawn between the positive and the negative media in the interest of the younger generation.

Information is essential input for decision-making while media is an important source of such information. Media are of many forms of communication, which comprised of print media, electronic media and information technology. Print media includes newspapers, magazines, billboards, pamphlets, leaflets etc. and electronic media includes radio, television, cable network, audio cassettes, video cassettes, video games and the like whereas information technology includes computers, internet and various other magnetic data storage devices. All media have a common ability to provide information and make communication possible over larger distance. The media saturate, drench and overflow our lives: an endless torrent of words, images, sounds. It is the media which connect people with machines and in turn create awareness in the society. Radio and television played a vital role in creating awareness.

Media has the greatest impact on the young generation more that the family or the school has. The means of media which influence the young generation are television, radio, internet, newspapers, magazines, books, broadcasting and text publishers. All these manipulate teenagers in what concerns culture, politics, social life, religion, fashion, education and other interests. Almost each teenager has a TV in his room and he may stay stuck for hours in front of it to watch a show, a movie or to find out some interesting information on a discovery channel. Then, the internet has become much more important than the TV because it offers a range of facts on different areas of interest. Now teenagers prefer to download a movie from the internet and watch it at home instead.

Moreover, through e-mails they can communicate with teenagers in other countries and find other ways of thinking and behaving in society. Girls, buy all types of magazines so find out some spicy facts about famous people and stars, while boys prefer magazines about cars or technology. Anyway, in what concerns newspapers young people almost don't buy them, as they prefer to read them on the internet and the same happens with books, too. Teenagers find out about fashion from the internet and they like to navigate on the internet to see which trends have appeared lately.

They can also read about sports, music, politics and culture. On the other hand, advertisements and propaganda play a special role as they can influence young people to buy different things or to follow certain behaviours. Apart from this, mass-media represents an essential source of enrichment and education for the young generation as they receive informal education from a variety of sources, from books to internet. Mass-media also means entertainment, through music, sports, acting, video and computer games activities that help young people to escape routine and enjoy themselves. Still, media does not always inform and manipulate teenagers on a positive way, because it also represents a source of violence through movies or news. And there seems to be no radical ways of how to diminish this state, for the moment.

Mass media have pervasive influence and regarded as powerful agent of social change in the society. In the present digital age, societies are highly dependent on mass communication. Urbanization, industrialization and modernization have created the societal conditions for the development of mass communication. It performs the essential functions of society and reflects social structure, functions and social values of a society. Media act as both causes and effects or in the language of social theory are both dependent and independent variables. The personality of an individual makes up of his genetic and social inheritance and mass media have greater influence on the latter component of human personality. Both media and social scientists deal with human beings whose thinking, feeling and behaviour keep on changing according to changing political, social, economic and physical environment and off course depends on the mood, which is eternal to mankind. It is the media through which thoughts of human minds are transferred to other human beings.

The importance of media and communication can be judged from the fact that human relations can not be promoted without these. Humans are more concerned about their feelings and emotions and how these feelings and emotions can be altered or changed. Now media is being used as tool and technique to do all these. Mass media activate and reinforce latent attitude and contribute significantly in the formation of new attitude. It brings the world into our homes and ultimately into our minds. In every day of life we are dependent upon mass media to know what is happening or going to happen in our physical, social, economic and political environment. The commutative impact of both material and non-material cultures on human minds is shaped by mass media. Media today are occasions, for and conduits of a way of life identified with rationality, technological achievements and the quest for wealth but also for something else entirely, something we call "fun," "convenience," or "pleasure".

It is the instrument of social control and social change and mostly target young generation. The element of fiction, crime and yellow journalism in print media create environment for a particular style of writing and aim to leave a particular impact on young arid adults or to safeguard the interest of particular personality, political or ethnic group. The element of bias reporting develops wrong traditions and promotes many social ills. Media reporting of facts revealed that some facts are selected and interpreted for a particular purpose perhaps to protect particular interest, to sensationalize scandalous aspects or to promote a particular thinking in favour or against a particular group, sect or society. Reporting of sectarian clashes in Pakistani media leaves adverse and harmful impact on the community. Action movies have been shown on television and viewed on computer or access through Internet develop the element of domination and gradually promote aggressiveness. Young people watch violence on media that left unpunished casting adverse impact on their cognition.

The excessive view of violence on television program promotes the aggressiveness among children and may appears in the form of hitting other children, screaming at them, threatening them or intentionally destroying their toys. Such kind of people become less sensitive to violence around them and pays no heed to the pain and sufferings of others in society. This micro-level study was conducted to ascertain what impact the media is leaving on our society. The data was collected through audience response on pre- designed structured and unstructured questionnaire during field survey.

The information on the socio- economic characteristics of the respondents is of vital importance, which help to categorize the sample on the basis of educational attainments, income, profession etc. and also aid in the understanding of emerging trends. The study reported that majority of the respondents were young and fell in the age category of 15-25 years while 28% were in the last stage of their working ages and only one fifth of the total respondents were from middle age group of 26-45 years. The mean age of the respondents was calculated as 31.8 years. The sex distribution revealed that 52% were males and 48% females. The data on the residential background and family type show that 67% were from rural background and 61% belonged to nuclear families.

This indicates that most of the people living in the industrial city of Faisalabad shifted from rural areas and started living as nuclear families in the city area. They identified themselves with rural areas, as their roots are still there where their parents and other relatives are living. The majority (39%) of the respondents was graduate and little less than this i.e. 35% were post-graduates. The presence of University of Agriculture and network of public and private educational institutions are the major reason for this high literacy in the study sample. As regards occupation, 50% of the respondents were students 11% were government servants and 17 % identified themselves as professionals which Includes doctors, engineers, professors and 22% were running business.

During survey, respondents were asked to indicate their opinion about the impact of mass media on the young generation. Different opinion statements were used to get the responses and measured on Likert scale with categories of strongly agree, disagree and strongly disagree. All the respondents were educated and the researcher comfortably obtained the responses in the appropriate category. When asked about the impact of mass media on the religiosity of the respondents, 17% strongly agreed and 57% agreed that media is making young generation irreligious while just 16% disagreed to this. As regards the impact on attitude and behaviour, 61% strongly agreed that violence in programs and shows promote the element of aggressiveness among young generation while just 2% showed their disagreement. Forty seven percent were of the opinion that media is increasing fashion phobia, 47% said people are becoming materialistic, 43% agreed that mass media contributed in increasing crimes and almost same percentage agreed that media contributed in prevailing vulgarity among the young generation.

These were some of the adverse impacts that mass media cast on young generation. The study findings also revealed that 21% and 57% respondents strongly agreed and agreed to the opinion statement that media is responsible for improving living standard respectively. Similarly 47% showed strong agreement while 37% simply agreed that media is turning this world into global village. The respondents were asked to indicate up to what extent mass media serve as a source of increasing political awareness, 39% and 48% respondents agreed to great extent and some extent respectively while 13% said that media is not doing this at all. One another statement regarding awareness about social problems, 45% of the respondents agreed to great extent 45% to some extent that media is increasing awareness about social problems.

The media contribution in increasing awareness about international affairs in the community has also been explored where majority (43%) showed their agreement to great extent and 44% to some extent in this regard. Similarly 52% respondent in the second category of response that media is increasing awareness about environmental issues. It is strange that media role in promoting awareness about health issues could not be proved. About 85% acknowledged that media promote business with split of 40 and 45% in the first and second category of response while just 8% showed their complete disagreement. Another important response recorded by the study was that 58% identified media responsible for spreading religious education up to some extent while about half (30%) responded in the category of not at all.

Majority of the respondents were young belonged to the age category of 15-25 years with mean age as 31.8 years. In case of educational attainments, 39% and 35% were graduates and post-graduates respectively. The mean years of schooling were 14.17. Sixty one percent of the respondents were from nuclear families. One half of the total respondents belonged to student category while from the other half 11% and 17% were Government servant and professions such as doctors, engineers and professors. From the total sample 37% of the respondents reported household monthly income as Rs. 10,000- 20,000, 26% as less than Rs. 10,000 while 21% had monthly income of Rs. 20,001 to 30,000. The role of mass media in globalization has been confirmed by 77% of the respondents.

The media role in increasing awareness about different social issues has been greatly acknowledged during the survey. In this regard, a significant majority of 87%, 90% reported that media is responsible in increasing awareness about political issues and environmental issues. An absolute majority of 92% and 97% confirmed that mass media is increasing awareness about international affairs and aid in the promotion of business respectively. Forty one percent of the respondents maintained cable connection at their homes. Majority of the respondent i.e. 61% and 47% strongly agreed that mass media is increasing fashion phobia and turning this world into global village. The majority of the respondents i.e. 76%, 74% and 83% agreed with the view that mass media is making young generation irreligious, aggressiveness and materialistic. Similarly an absolute majority of 94% agreed that media promote fashion phobia in young generation and 77% agreed to the view that it is responsible in prevailing vulgarity in the society.

Majority of the respondent reported their household income as Rs. 10,001 to 20,000 per month while little more than half of this had monthly income of Rs.20,001 to 30,000. The income level indicates that respondents were from well to do families and can afford all sorts of mass media i.e. newspapers, television, cable computer, Internet etc. This supports that selection of sample was appropriate because the impact of media can be measured from those who afford variety, of media. Forty one percent maintained Internet connection at their homes. Majority of the respondents (25%) confirmed computer as their favorite media and 24% identified themselves with television whereas 21% liked all media. Eighty one percent of the respondents viewed movies, out of which 39% watched movies sometimes and 33% occasionally. Majority of the respondents (39%) liked movies with suspense, romance, action and fiction. In the individual category 15.3% and 16% liked to entertain with movies based on action and romance respectively while just 9% liked to see documentaries. Being an Islamic country, Pakistan allows media to work within the specified boundaries of social norms.

Religious parties keep an eye on the media to keep it on the right track and prevent vulgarity and nudity. But the revolution of information technology and its high rate of diffusion restricted the authority of both Government and religious leaders. The Internet and magnetic data storage devices allow easy and safe access to all sort of social ills through Internet café and home connections. Cable connections are available with small payment of Rs. 150/- to 300/- per month depending on the circumstances. Various TV channels ranging from *Star-Plus, ARY Digital, Star Movies, Movie Magic, V-channel, MTV, HBO, LBC, Star World* and dozens other are working day and night to promote special type of culture. Television promotes consumerism, migration and desire for urban goods and entirely changes the social landscape of village life. Further the element of arrogance and lack of respect for elders are the other negative impact of this electronic media. No doubt media provide an easy access to different sources of knowledge and aid to research and development but low level of literacy limits the users' abilities to acquire knowledge oriented benefits.

The means of outdoor entertainment are almost scarce and

electronic media and internet technology were the only available means of entertainment. A significant majority turned towards these and yields negative utility from mass media especially from information technology and ignores long term beneficial aspect of positive utility. In the modern information age, societies are in a continuous process of social change, which is a central concern of social scientists and especially the sociologists. The traditional societies are under the severe threat of media war. Nations can not deploy any sort of army to keep the enemy media out of their frontiers. Media is travelling at a very fast speed from west to east or from developed to developing countries or from non- Muslim to Muslim societies. The impact can be easily observed in Pakistani society where the cable network and Internet cafés and number of users are multiplying arithmetically.

Children lack the abilities to make accurate judgement of the benefits and harms of the information being fed to them and hence consciously or unconsciously accept it as a truth of life. They gradually develop a particular attitude and behaviour. This not only influences the social aspect of individual personality but also influence other members of peer group. Mass media influence human behaviour and attitude in childhood and adulthood and also play crucial role at the policy as well as decision making level. There is a need to take immediate steps to minimize adverse impact of mass media on young generation, especially from Internet.

Parents are required to keep an eye on their children while working on internet through home connections and Government is required to morally bound internet café owners to restrict users access to those websites which promote vulgarity in the society. A further study may be conducted to explore the effect of Internet café on young generation. Media simply means 'that through which something is conveyed'. In utilising the news media we seek to convey information from point A; the group, to point B; the public. Most of what we know about the world is constructed from brief snippets of information, which we accept and take for granted. As we cannot be scholars and experts on everything, the news serves to provide us with access to information in a very succinct and summarised manner. The mass media is our society's information superhighway and is now taken for granted by so many people that for the most part we do not even think to question the truth of what we are told or to realise that we have only been shown a tiny snippet of the real event.

By using the media, we as social change activists can offer the public summarised snippets about important social issues in which we are involved. This is not sufficient in itself to educate people, but effective news story can provoke further thought on our issues. When a subject is given good media focus it is deemed socially important. This is essential for bringing an issue into the public eye and encouraging people to take it more seriously. The audience is then able to seek further information if suitably engaged. Ideally, this can mean more keen supporters for your campaign.

When the media bring an event into the public arena it is harder for the target of the story to write off community activism against them. We seek to bring social injustice out from behind closed doors and let society witness it. This means that effective media can put major pressure on governments, companies or individuals of which it seeks to inform. Sometimes NVDA can incite aggression and violence from other parties. The presence of journalists can help reduce unprofessional behaviour by police and security personel. What are the downsides?

Journalism is alas no longer a valiant mission to bring truth to the public eye. The media is primarily a business. Mass media aims to sell advertising to companies. This means that they must focus upon what, in their perception the public wishes to engage. Mass media rely upon business ties to survive that inevitably create a bias in favour of what their shareholders and clients wish the news to be. To use the media we have to commit the necessary evil of supporting this most undemocratic and elitist system. Running effective campaign media is time consuming and energy draining. If a group is too few in numbers, time or resources then it can seriously cut into the more important tasks for the group.

Media have their own perceptions about what interests the public. This means that involving media risks negative exposure of your efforts. A news story about how uneducated, disorganized and radical your group is certainly worse than no media exposure for that event. Dealing with media effectively means thinking like the media. Those of a not so cynical outlook who wish to avoid this irrevocable tarnishing of the soul need not apply. To begin to think about effective media representation, we need to view the event we wish to promote as a journalist and as an audience member. This limits the ability of the medium to distort our message. It also helps to ensure that the final package contains positive and useful content to impact society.

Journalists are people too and must be treated with politeness, friendliness and respect. This means they are less likely to dismiss your campaign out of hand based upon a personal whim. For an event to appeal to a journalist and their employer as a story, it must meet certain criteria. As a media liaison, you must remember news values and endeavour to portray your event as encompassing as many as possible.

Journalists are anxious to sell their story in the light that best fits these values. Crazy, fruity stereotypes are rarely helpful for swinging widespread public support. You need to remain aware that if your journo is not convinced of the legitimacy of your claims or of their relevance to the programme's audience then the news will not be positive. Having a news story about the radical and misguided activities of your friends is never a positive experience.

If you are friends with a journalist, then talk to them often about your campaign and encourage them to give you some coverage. When you deal with a channel, station or paper for the first time you need to think about building a professional relationship with them and the journo they dispatch. Keep the media updated on your group's activities. This allows you to benefit from having more reliable and respectful coverage and they benefit from gaining a regular scoop in your interesting activities. Endeavour not to go behind your journo's back and give coverage to a rival from their workplace.

Media Audiences

Audiences are sometimes actively engaged in what you have to say. Other times they are passive 'sponges' who soak up our message. We have to assume that most people are a blend of these two extremes. Our worldview is shaped in a large part from what we are told. Most people continue to view the mass media as a credible authority. Accordingly, the news story you create defines what actually happened. While a news story may only include ten seconds of your dialogue, the public will mostly not question this. If the news only played you saying one thing then this was obviously the only important point you had to say. Amazingly, the audience will feel informed about your campaign. They will feel qualified to pass judgement, on both that event and your group as a whole!

Stereotypes are very important and what you say is equally weighted by how you say it. If the audience identify with you and see you as 'one of us' then you have succeeded. If they marginalise you as 'one of them' you may have damaged your message. Being 'one of them' is good if 'they' happen to be the educated, moral, rational and informed people 'we' look up to. Being 'one of them' is terrible if 'they' are unruly, uneducated, unemployed, druggy misfits! Think about the way you present yourself to general society. Mainstream and normal is the best because then the focus is not on you as a person but the message you are conveying. Keep the following in mind always; Body language - arms at sides of body, avoid excessive gestures and strange expressions.

Comfortable and confidant posture: You are an authority on your issue and you need to convey that. Presentation - Formal is good because it makes you look professional. Smart casual can work well too to help your audience see you as one of them (but always consider which audience you are attempting to communicate to... what is suitable in one instance may be totally inappropriate in another) Speech- confidant and clear speaking. Stick to the point. Try and use catchy and concise phrases.

Language- Avoid jargon and acronyms: Keep your word choice formal; generally avoid slang and colloquialisms if you don't want to be stereotyped. Emotiveness- be relaxed and comfortable but not smug or arrogant. Do not let anger come through into your presentation. It is sometimes appropriate to adopt a light-hearted or solemn tone depending upon the event but still keep this to a bare minimum.

Your media appearance is effectively an advert for your campaign. What is successful or unsuccessful in advertisements? How to act as a media liaison? The media liaison in social change activism sits at a focal point between social change activists and wider society. Like a journalist, a media liaison operates within a restrictive structure of communications, allowing certain behaviours and discouraging others.

Working with other activists:

Your job is to be informed, educated about the issue and able to communicate it clearly and succinctly. Contemporaries of yours may have totally different views and opinions on media and its relevance to the campaign. This is fine, because as social change activists we seek to tackle societal problems using a raft of different and hopefully complimentary techniques. You can help each other best by keeping those around you informed about your own ideas and focus, and listening to theirs.

It is however your responsibility to ensure that media representation is professional and effective. Make sure anyone else present is briefed on how to behave around the mass media. Other people's rude, aggressive and frivolous behaviour has potential to completely compromise your work. Some people have a natural talent for speaking to journalists. Although such people may have little interest in media strategy they are an asset whenever you meet a journalist who seeks to run a more human interest-based story. Inevitably the journalist will wish to glean views on your campaign from a grassroots perspective. Such people can be very good at casting the basic image of your movement's 'typical campaigner' in a positive light.

A media event often involves important visual activist roles. These central figures in the action are generally the focus of the media. Inevitably the media are interested in hearing from them directly. Make sure that the activists are briefed with appropriate media soundbites that they agree with, and positively promote your campaign message. It is up to you to arrange interviews between these people and journalists. Allow as many of your fellow campaigners as possible to be part of constructing your soundbites and media angle. You will learn more from fellow activists than any other source. Always remember that your job is to reflect the opinions of the group. The more internal networking and communication you do, the better you can perform.

The Media Event

Because social change movements are rarely in and of themselves newsworthy, it becomes necessary to orchestrate events that are, in order to promote your message to society. If a campaign event cannot be done professionally and appropriately without sending out a bad public message then do not involve the media. Many of the more militant and controversial illegal actions that a social change group might undertake in the name of their cause fall beneath this category. They are simply better left as covert actions. Sometimes an action undertaken to achieve a campaign goal will be newsworthy of itself, and attract media attention whether this is wanted or not. In this instance, you have little to lose and much more to gain by dealing critically with the media.

A media event needs to frame your campaign in the context of as many news values as possible. They work best on days of slow news like Sunday and Monday. Use visual displays and evocative demonstration to highlight your issue. If you can get a banner with your website on TV then you have given the movement a very epic plug indeed. Because media are fickle, you need to be prepared to create your own media. Have people about on the day taking stills and video of key points in the event.

Before the event:

- Collaboratively develop your media interview angle and practice all the possible journalist questions you can conceive of.
- Ring any outstanding media contacts you already have and strike up a conversation about the issue and whether there might be interest in running a story on it. Be vague, but try and capture their attention. Never say any names, dates or places. Never trust a journalist not to inform the authorities of a pending illegal event. Never give a specific description of what will happen, because if you fail to capture their interest in this conversation you may not be able to regain it when it matters.
- Write a press release. A wealth of literature is available on how to do this. In brief though, stick to one or two paragraphs. You need to be concise and capture a journalist's attention in the title and first sentence. Provide accompanying notes where appropriate. Include several quotes from within your campaign. Include your name, contact cell-phone number, the date and the time of release. Do not email this out until the action is about to begin if it is illegal. Send it a few hours in advance otherwise. Generally you will need someone absent from the action itself to do this emailing.
- Arrange people who will not be present at the event itself to take charge of press releasing and emailing of further footage to absent reporters.
- Charge your cell-phone and ensure it has lots of money on it. Ideally have two cell-phones, one for incoming calls and one for your own use. Being caught without a phone is something to avoid. Also memorise the number of your contact phone.

Get a good night's sleep On the Day:

- Find out exactly the timeline of events for the day. Make

sure you know who the designated police liaison is, and have an idea of who will be where and how to get hold of them.

- When it is time, immediately begin ringing your media contacts. Start with TV, then move to newspapers and radio. You must be prepared for these conversations as you now need to convince each journalist of the importance of the event, and why they need to come and report on it. Give them a very specific location to meet you, and leave your contact number.
- Police officers at this stage will probably begin to take an interest in you if something illegal has happened.

Politely tell them that you are simply the media liaison of the event and direct them to the police liaison. Legally you must provide them with your name, address, and occupation if asked. If you are feeling extra helpful, then why not also provide them with the media cell-phone number which is all over the internet with the press releases and they can get anyway? As journalists arrive, immediately take charge, introduce yourself and show them around the demonstration site. Help them find good angles for camera shots (especially if you have really impressive visual displays with slogans and your campaign website).

Treat all of your interviews as professional job interviews. In the event of being asked a subversive question that attempts to trivialise the event or comes from an unwanted tangent then you must be on the ball. My favourite tactics include answering in a long rambling fashion that is inappropriate for broadcast on TV and turning every answer back around into one of the key soundbites. Wherever possible, say only your pre-planned soundbites. Journalists may also ask you questions about the organization of the protest demonstration. Never, ever say anything that might implicate you or your fellow campaigners.

TV, never look into the eye of the lens. Radio, always make full use of questions like 'Anything else we should know?' your soundbites are the lifeline of the event. Many journalists simply wish to repeat the quotes listed on your press release. If you can get away with this, instead of winging it on the spot, then so much the better. Media has a particularly vital role to play in a democracy. In a democracy the rule is by the people. But his control comes once in five years - when he votes. How does he remain in control the rest of the time? Through public debates for which the media is a platform. Media in acts as a watchdog. An eye has to be kept on people in power who often tend to misuse it in the absence of checks. The performance of this watchdog role was most dramatically seen in what has now come to be known as 'yellow journalism'. This genre of journalism came into vogue in early 20th century United States and owes its name to a cartoon strip drawn by an artist called Occault.

Yellow journalism represented two things at the same time. The first was that it aimed to expose corruption by people in power at a time when business was expanding and government role too was spreading. This naturally led to abuse of power for personal gain. By exposing corruption in high two American journals - New York World and New York Journal - hoped to increase their readership by projecting an image of being crusading journalism. Yellow journalism also symbolised crass commercialism in the form of a competition between the two papers run by Joseph Pulitzer and Randolph Hearst. In efforts to outdo each other the two papers not only tomtomed their achievements but also tried to pass outlandish but fictitious stories as facts.

But the difficulty is that often instead of performing its watchdog role the press itself comes under the influence of dominant groups in society and acts in a way calculated to perpetuate their dominance. A more modern example of the watchdog role of the press was seen in what came to be called the Watergate Scandal in the United States of America which nearly resulted in the impeachment of the president. "Watergate" is a general term used to describe a complex web of political scandals between 1972 and 1974. The word specifically refers to the Watergate Hotel in Washington D.C.

The Burglary

Watergate has entered the political lexicon as a term synonymous with corruption and scandal, yet the Watergate Hotel is one of Washington's plushest hotels. Even today, it is home to former Senator Bob Dole and was once the place where Monica Lewinsky laid low. It was here that the Watergate Burglars broke into the Democratic Party's National Committee offices on June 17, 1972. If it had not been for the alert actions of Frank Wills, a security guard, the scandal may never have erupted.

The story of Watergate has an intriguing historical and political background, arising out of political events of the 1960s such as Vietnam, and the publication of the Pentagon Papers in 1970. But the chronology of the scandal really begins during 1972, when the burglars were arrested. By 1973, Nixon had been re-elected, but the storm clouds were building. By early 1974, the nation was consumed by Watergate.

Richard Milhous Nixon is one of the most fascinating political figures of the 20th Century. His long political career began in 1947 when he was elected to the House of Representatives. By 1952, Nixon had been chosen as Dwight Eisenhower's vice- presidential running mate, but nor before he was embroiled in a scandal that led to the infamous Checkers Speech. Nixon served as Vice-President for eight years, then lost the 1960 election to John F. Kennedy. He recovered from political defeat to be chosen again as the Republican Party's candidate at the 1968 election. Following a year of turmoil, including two political assassinations, Nixon became the nation's 37th President on January 20, 1969. Later that year, he delivered his 'Silent Majority' speech on the Vietnam War, articulating his belief that the bulk of the American people supported his policies and programs. He was vindicated by winning a landslide re-election. He was sworn in for a second term in January 1973.

Nixon made three major speeches on the Watergate scandal during 1973 and 1974. The first was on April 30, 1973, in which he announced the departure of Dean, Haldeman and

Ehrlichman. A more defiant speech was delivered on August 15, 1973. Perhaps the politically most difficult speech was the one on April 29, 1974, in which Nixon released partial transcripts of the White House tapes. The initial investigations of Watergate were heavily influenced by the media, particularly the work of two reporters from the Washington Post, Bob Woodward and Carl Bernstein, along with their mysterious informant, Deep Throat. Political investigations began in February 1973 when the Senate established a Committee to investigate the Watergate scandal.

The public hearings of the Committee were sensational, including the evidence of John Dean, Nixon's former White House Counsel. The Committee also uncovered the existence of the secret White House tape recordings, sparking a major political and legal battle between the Congress and the President. In 1974, the House of Representatives authorised the Judiciary Committee to consider impeachment proceedings against Nixon. The work of this Committee was again the spotlight a quarter of a century later when Bill Clinton was impeached. Nixon's last days in office came in late July and early August, 1974.

The House Judiciary Committee voted to accept three of four proposed Articles of Impeachment, with some Republicans voting with Democrats to recommend impeachment of the President. The final blow came with the decision by the Supreme Court to order Nixon to release more White House tapes.

One of these became known as the 'smoking gun' tape when it revealed that Nixon had participated in the Watergate cover-up as far back as June 23, 1972. Around the country, there were calls for Nixon to resign. At 9pm on the evening of August 8, 1974, Nixon delivered a nationally televised resignation speech. The next morning, he made his final remarks to the White House staff before sending his resignation letter to the Secretary of State, Dr. Henry Kissinger.

Gerald Ford became the 38th President of the United States when Nixon resigned on August 9, 1974. He was the first Vice-President and the first President to ascend to both positions without being elected. Regarded on all sides of politics as a decent man, Ford will be remembered for his controversial pardon of Richard Nixon. Watergate had profound consequences in the United States. There was a long list of convictions and other casualties. For example, the aftermath of Watergate ushered in changes in campaign finance reform and a more aggressive attitude by the media.

By the time the 25th anniversary of Watergate occurred in 1997, a vast library of books and films existed. Watergate's influence was felt in the Clinton Impeachment of 1998-99. Nixon died in 1994 and was eulogised by the political establishment, although he was still a figure of controversy. The investigations into Watergate that led to the resignation of Richard Nixon are a case study in the operation of the American Constitution and political values. The Aftermath of Watergate In November 1976, Jimmy Carter defeats Ford to become the 39th president. Read Carter's Inaugural Address. Some commentators attribute the increased level of cynicism about politics to the Watergate affair.

The media becomes more confident and aggressive. Watergate was unravelled by the Washington Post reporters, Bob Woodward and Carl Bernstein. Their work led to the development of teams of "investigative" reporters on newspapers around the world. "Deep Throat" became an everyday term, referring to the anonymous official who leaked information to Woodward and Bernstein. An excellent article on the possible identity of "Deep Throat" appears in the Washington Post. A new wave of Democratic congressmen is elected in 1976 and there are dramatic changes in the composition of committee chairmanships. Many of Nixon's subordinates are jailed, some discover religion, and others write books. Political scandals are termed " –gate". Nixon sets about rehabilitating his reputation, writing books and travelling the world. He dies on April 22nd 1994 at the age of 81.

In 1991, Len Colodny and Robert Gettlin produce a book

called "Silent Coup - The Removal of a President". In 1995, Oliver Stone produces a film called "Nixon", starring Anthony Hopkins as Nixon. The film is condemned by the Nixon family. Former Vice-President Spiro Agnew dies on September 17, 1996, in Berlin, Maryland, aged 77. More of the White House tapes were released in 1996 and 1997. Read a backgrounder about these tapes and a discussion from The News Hour with Jim Lehrer.

The Washington Post also discusses the tapes. John Ehrlichman, Nixon's Domestic Policy Adviser, dies on February 14, 1999, aged 73. Elliot Richardson, Nixon's Attorney-General, who defied Nixon's instruction to dismiss Arcibald Cox, dies on December 31, 1999, aged 79. The role of the media in a democracy becomes clear if one takes a look at how it functions during elections - a time when behind-the-scenes activities are open for viewing to the public. This is the time when factions and faction-fights, jockeying for party tickets and moves and counter moves by parties for alliances and understandings is open for public viewing.

BIBLIOGRAPHY

Abu-Lughod, L. 2005. *Dramas of nationhood: the politics of television in Egypt*. Chicago and London: The University of Chicago Press.

Allen, S. (ed.). 1994. *Media anthropology. Informing global citizens*. Westport, Bergin: Garvey.

Andreassen, R. 2005. *The Mass Media's Construction of Gender, Race, Sexuality and Nationality. An Analysis of the Danish News Media's Communication about Visible Minorities from 1970 to 2004*. Unpublished PhD thesis: Department of History, University of Toronto.

Ang, I. 1991. *Desperately seeking the audience*. London: Routledge.

Ang, I. 1996. *Living room wars*. London: Routledge.

Asad, T. 1990. 'Ethnography, literature and politics: Some readings and uses of Salman Rushdie's The Satanic Verses', *Cultural Anthropology* 5(3): 239-269.

Askew, K. and R.R. Wilk (eds.). 2002. *The anthropology of media*. London: Blackwell.

Aspers, P. 2001. *Markets in fashion. A phenomenological approach*. Stockholm: City University Press.

Bakker, F.L. 2005. 'The image of Muhammad in The Message, the first and only feature film about the Prophet of Islam', *Islam and Christian-Muslim Relations* 7(1): 77-93.

Barber, K. 2000. *The Generation of Plays. Yoruba Popular Life in Theater*. Indiana University Press.

Bausinger, H. 1984. 'Media, technology and daily life', *Media, Culture and Society* 6: 343-351.

Becker, H. 1982. *Art worlds*. Berkeley: University of California Press.

Benson, R. and E. Neveu (eds.). 2005. *Bourdieu and the Journalistic Field*. Cambridge and Malden, MA: Polity Press.

Bird, S. E. 2003. *The audience in everyday life: Living in a media world*. New York: Routledge.

Bird, S.E. 1992. *For enquiring minds: A cultural study of supermarket tabloids*. Knoxville: University of Tennessee Press.

Carey, J. (ed.). 1988. *Media, myth and narratives*. London: Sage Publications.

Couldry, N. 2003. *Media rituals. A critical approach*. London: Routledge.

Davila, A. 2001. *Latinos, Inc.: The Marketing and Making of a People*. Berkeley, CA: University of California Press.

Debray, R. 1996. *Media manifestos*. London and New York: Verso.

Deger, J. 2006. *Shimmering Screens: Making Media in an Aboriginal Community*. Minneapolis: University of Minnesota Press.

Dickey, S. 1997. 'Anthropology and its contributions to studies of mass media', *International Social Science Journal* XLIX (3): 413-427.

Doostdar, A. 2004. 'The Vulgar Spirit of Blogging: On Language, Culture, and Power in Persian Weblogestan', *American Anthropologist* 106 (4): 651-663.

Fishman, M. 1980. *Manufacturing the News*. London: University of Texas Press.

Fiske, J. 1989. *Television culture*. London: Routledge.

Goody, J. 1997. *Representations and contradictions. Ambivalence towards images, theatre, fiction, relics and sexuality*. Oxford: Blackwell.

Gupta, A. 1995. 'Blurred boundaries: the discourse of corruption, the culture of politics and the imagined state', *American Ethnologist*. 22: 375-402.

Jarvie, I.C. 1970. *Towards a sociology of the cinema*. London: Routledge and Kegan Paul.

Jensen, C.B. 2003. 'Communicating models: The relevance of models for research on the worlds of the Internet', in S. Hjarvard (ed.), *Media in a globalized society*. Cop-enhagen: Museum Tusculanum Press.

Johnson, K. 2001. *Television and the Social Change in Rural India*. New Delhi: Sage Publication.

Kemper, S. 2001. *Buying and believing. Sri Lankan advertising and consumers in a transnational world*. Chicago: University of Chicago Press.

Kinsella, Sh. 2000. *Adult Manga*. ConsumAsiaN Series. London: Curzon.

Kumar, S. 2006. *Gandhi Meets Primetime: Globalization ad Nationalism in Indian Television*. Urbana and Chicago: University of Illinois Press.

Liebes, T. and J. Curran (eds.). 1998. *Media, ritual and identity*. London: Routledge.

Lule, J. 2001. *Daily news, eternal stories. The mythological role of journalism*. New York: The Guilford Press.

Machado-Borges, T. 2003. *Only for You! Brazilians and the telenovela flow*. Stockholm Studies in Social Anthropology. Stockholm: Almqvist & Wiksell International.

Marshall, J. 2002. 'The Sexual Life of Cyber-Savants', *The Australian Journal of Anthropology* 14(2): 229-248.

Mazzarella, W. 2003. *Shoveling smoke. Advertising and globalization in contemporary India*. Durham: Duke University Press

Mazzarella, W. 2004. 'Culture, globalization, mediation', *Annual Review of Anthropology* 33: 345-367.

Mithen, S. 1996. *The Prehistory of the Mind: The Cognitive Origins of Art, Religion and Science*. London and New York: Thames & Hudson.

Moeran, B. 1996. *A Japanese advertising agency. An anthropology of media and markets*. ConsumAsiaN Series. London: Curzon.

Morley, D. 2000. *Home Territories. Media, Mobility and Identity*. London and New York: Routledge.

Nyamnjoh, F.B. 2005. *Africa's Media. Democracy & the Politics of Belonging*. London: Zed Books.

Peterson, M.A. 2003. *Anthropology and mass communication. Media and myth in the new millennium*. New York and Oxford: Berghahn Books.

Rothenbuhler, E. and M. Coman (eds). 2005. *Media Anthropology*. London: Sage.

Rotherbuhler, E.W. 1998. *Ritual communication: from everyday conversation to mediated ceremony*. London: Sage.

Scollon, R. and S. Wong Scollon. 2004. *Nexus analysis. Discourse and the emerging Internet*. London and New York: Routledge.

Street, B. (ed.). 1993. *Cross-Cultural approaches to literacy*. Cambridge: Cambridge University Press.

Taghioff, D. 2005. 'Another Subject is Possible: Reporting in the Indian Press on the World Social Forum (WSF)', *SOAS Literary Review*, Spring 2005.

Winegar, J. 2006. *Creative Reckonings: The Politics of Art and Culture in Contemporary Egypt*. Stanford University Press.

Zeitlyn, D. and M.D. Fischer. 2003. *Visual anthropology in the digital mirror. Computer-assisted visual anthropology*.

Index

R

S

T

V

Y